THE INVINCIBLE

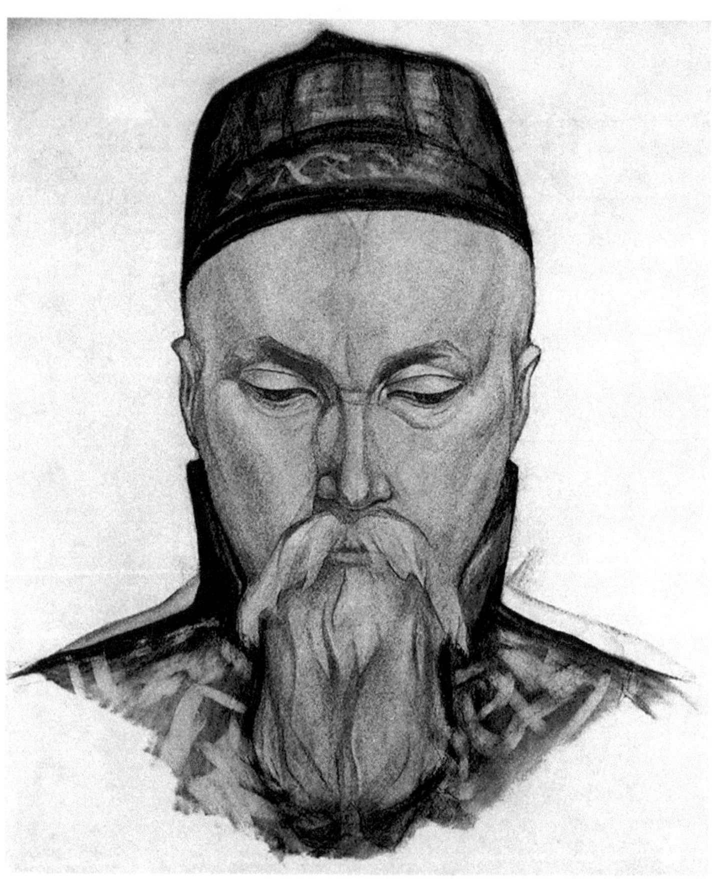

Portrait of Nicholas Roerich by Svetoslav Roerich

THE INVINCIBLE

NICHOLAS ROERICH

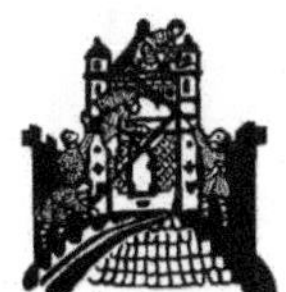

NICHOLAS ROERICH MUSEUM

NEW YORK MMXVII

Nicholas Roerich Museum
319 West 107th Street
New York NY 10025
www.roerich.org

© 1974 by Nicholas Roerich Museum.
First published in 1974.
Reprinted 2017.

Cover illustration: Nicholas Roerich. *Three Glaives.* 1932.

PREFACE

*T*HE *Invincible (Nerushimoye)*, the book by Prof. Nicholas Roerich, was published in Russian in 1936 in Riga by the publishing house Uguns. The preface to that book is significant enough to repeat it in this English edition:

"In the present eleventh volume of his works, called by the author *The Invincible*, Nicholas Roerich, indefatigable and widely recognized as a cultural leader of humanity, remains faithful to his task and to the goal that he sets before himself. He stands invincibly on watch over culture; invincibly and yet steadfastly he molds the steps of the consciousness of the new man; invincibly and strongly he lays the stones into a beneficent, true, spiritual culture as the basis of the structure of new life; invincibly and fearlessly he battles with ignorance, superstition, and prejudices and, in spite of the attacks of numerous adversaries, he continues to carry out unalterably the ideas of a peaceful, cultural structure of life.

"Vigilantly watching all that happens in life upon our planet, the author in this work also reacts constantly, like a sensitive barometer, to all events and manifestations of life, positive as well as negative. Any and all, the great and also the smallest manifestations of life find a living response in his many faceted heart, and a just, impartial evaluation by his all-embracing mind. There is no realm of knowledge or sides and issues of life that would be unattainable to his understanding and are not widely examined in his numerous letters and articles.

"Standing on guard over culture, Roerich dedicated his entire life to the battle with ignorance, for culture is to him the hearth of Light, a constant saturation and transmutation of consciousness by the light of higher knowledge and active love.

"In this incessant drive for the annihilation of darkness is disclosed the astonishing quality of his spirit, which ever delighted his friends—to approach everything without negation and intolerance, to observe in each cultural endeavor something positive, and to incorporate this actuality into the common evolutionary treasury of the world. This is precisely that high ideal of cultural constructiveness which Nicholas Roerich brought into being in the many organizations and societies in which he realized a League of Culture—precisely that affirmatively synthesized undertaking in which is revealed that all-creative spirit of unity, cooperation, and service, and where are put together the bases of the best future for humanity."

There is little we can add in 1974 to this just evaluation. Let *The Invincible* summon forth and exalt the best qualities of the human spirit.

CONTENTS

THE INVINCIBLE

FEARLESSNESS

SCIENCE, if it is to be redintegrated should primarily not be limited, and thus be fearless. Any conditional limitation will be an evidence of mediocrity, and thus will become an unconquerable obstacle on the path of achievement.

I recall a conversation with a scientist who so insistently wanted to be the defender of modern science that he even attempted to diminish the significance of all ancient accumulations. Whereas, precisely, each young representative of modern science must first be open to everything useful and more so to all that bears the testimony of ages. All negation is contrary to creativeness. In his enlightened, constantly progressive movement, a true creator, first of all, is not negative. A creator has no time for condemnation and negation. The process of creativeness proceeds in an unrestrained progression. Therefore it is painful to see how a man, because of certain prejudices and superstitions, entangles himself with phantoms. In order that no one might suspect a scientist of being old-fashioned, in his fear he is ready to inflict anathema and oblivion upon the most instructive accumulations of the experiences of antiquity.

Verily, a free, unlimited science reveals again to humanity many long forgotten useful discoveries. Folklore again marches hand in hand with the disclosures of archaeology. Song and legend strengthen the pathways of history. The pharmacopoeia of ancient peoples revives again in the hands of an investigating young scientist. No one will say that all this ancient pharmacopoeia should be applied literally, for many of the hieroglyphs and inscriptions are deliberately symbolical. The very meaning of many expressions has been lost and changed through the centuries. But the experience of thousands of years nevertheless offers an unlimited field for useful research. Thus, much of that which is forgotten must be rediscovered and benevolently explained in contemporary language.

Turning to archaeology, we see that many excavations of recent years have astonished us by the refinement of meaning and forms of numerous, often fragmentary remnants. This refinement, this subtle elegance of antiquity, once again points to the cautious, reverent attentiveness with which we should touch these ancient testaments. We dream of forgotten lacquers, of the lost technique of jewel-mounting, of means of preserving materials unfamiliar to us. Finally, we are compelled to recognize many ancient methods of healing those scourges of mankind which are equally frightening at present. When we hear, and become convinced, of ancient methods successfully applied in the cure of certain forms of cancer, or tuberculosis, or asthma, or heart disease, is it not our duty to give most benevolent attention to these echoes of accumulated wisdom from ancient times?

Negation, which is limiting, must not have any place on the horizon of young scientists. Only mediocre thinking can cut off and impede progress. Absolutely everything that can help evolution should be welcomed and heartily accepted. All that can serve for the development of human thinking—all must be listened to and accepted. It is unimportant in which garment or hieroglyphics the fragment of knowledge is brought. The benefits of knowledge will have a revered place in all parts of the world. Knowledge is neither old nor young, ancient nor new. Through it there is accomplished a great, unlimited evolution. Everyone who obstructs it will be the progeny of darkness. Everyone who according to his strength will assist it will be a true warrior, a co-worker of Light.

Peking, December 22, 1934.

AESOP'S FABLE

TELL me thy company, and I'll tell thee what thou art."
Some dogs once barked at a caravan. First let it be said, and justly, that not one of the dogs could have been of use to the caravan. Is it not remarkable that in the entire dark pack, although it was obviously a natural assortment of fitting companions, not one animal was fit to be acquired? There were small ones with crooked legs; red, and piebald ones, and black, slobbering mongrels; some limping, some without tails. This seeming variety was but one of purely outer appearance; the inner distinction throughout this entire batch of hounds was quite uniform—the same baseness, the same cruelty and bloodthirstiness, the same cunning and two-facedness.

Is it not astonishing that the pack came running from many different points—the well-fed, the hungry, greyhounds, and awkward cripples—all following an animal instinct to come running and bark at the passers-by as if so commanded. The traveler wonders by whom and by what means this vermin-ridden pack has been gathered, and why just this ugly brood, stained by their own bloodshed and by all kinds of beatings, must gather into a pack and, with tails flying high, rush through the village. Besides, this is not springtime. The cats have not yet begun their roof-top serenades, but the pack is already on the loose and runs about, growling and yapping. And how did it come to pass that not one thoroughbred joined this rackety pack?

There are, after all, certain laws of nature through which, in the human and likewise in the animal kingdom, "a fisherman sees another fisherman from afar." Old treatises about the natural selection of species are not far removed from truth. Indeed, sometimes "there is no family without a black sheep," but, also perhaps more often, "an apple does not fall far from the tree." And if the trunk of the tree is worm-eaten, the fruit from such a tree is bad.

Some coachmen like to flick barking dogs with a wicked whip, and others smile, "Let him howl at the top of his voice." But if a mastiff gets under a side horse the coachman may remark only, "The beast got its due."

Bestia is a Latin word. It means a beast, an animal. It spread over the face of Earth, because this definition was needed in the most diverse circumstances. Bestiality and brutality have frequently struck human thinking. Mankind has tried by all possible means to get rid of beastly instincts. The worst of human conditions have been rightly termed *bestiality* and *brutality*.

It is said that want and suffering purify human consciousness. One may ask, What kinds of suffering are still needed? What other deprivations must humanity go through in order to remove itself from low bestiality? Someone warns that many more catastrophes must sweep over our beclouded Earth. Someone affirms that certain islands will sink, that new seas will rise; but how vast must the areas of these new aquatic expanses be before people will think seriously about this! It is deplorable to think that people become so easily accustomed to even the most terrible state of affairs. It is as if there were some sort of demand for a hastened progression of reactions for the purpose of perplexing the contemporary mind in order to compel it to think about the paths of the near future.

It is said that most of today's young people look first of all for the sports and film pages in the newspaper. It is said that many of them have difficulty in enumerating the greatest philosophers, but at the same time will name without one mistake the prize fighters, sports celebrities, and moving picture stars. Maybe it is not quite so, but the stories told by professors and schoolteachers make one ponder about the contemporary trend of thought. Likewise, all this makes one reflect about what has pushed the present generation to such extremes. Whoever reads about the last years of the Roman Empire or about Byzantium finds perhaps to his amazement many parallels with today. Among these the most striking will be the gravitation toward the circus, prize fights, races, and all kinds of lotteries.

Very soon every village, and perhaps every street, will have its beauty queen, or its remarkable arm or leg, or its own special kind of hair! It is as if human imagination cannot be inspired by anything else, while at the same time the unsolved purely mechanical problems impede the flow of progress.

Countries, institutions, private persons, are living beyond their budgets, multiplying the grand total of earthly indebtedness. This material insolvency is not limited to earthly, mechanical conditions only. It will pass into another, far more dangerous, indebtedness; and if the planet becomes a spiritual debtor, this frightful debt can become an overwhelming impediment to all success.

"Dogs are barking—the caravan goes on," says optimism; and pessimism recalls how packs of wild dogs once devoured the watchman of a powder magazine. All that was left of him was his rifle, his cutlass, and a few buttons. And after this incident any passer-by could without interference set fire to the powder magazine and cause irreparable harm. But let us follow the ways of optimism, and let us accept each dog's bark as a sign of some new movement, useful and undeferrably needed.

At times, even the worst pessimistic signs will be only that natural selection which, for the good of the constructive process, has to take place in any event.

Monsters are especially terrible when they are hidden in darkness. But when they sooner or later crawl to light, then even their ugliest grimaces cease to be terrifying. To know will already be to advance.

Peking, December 23, 1934.

THE FAR-SEEING EYE

AN endless snowy plain. A distant traveler moves on it like a little black dot. Maybe, and most likely, his goal is quite ordinary. Probably he walks in deep snow from one habitation to another, or maybe he is returning home, complaining at the difficulty in walking. But from afar he seems somehow unusual on this snowy plain. The imagination is ready to adorn him with most extraordinary qualities and, mentally, to give him quite a special mission. The imagination is even ready to envy him, walking free in the fresh air, far beyond the limits of a city full of poison.

Somehow this distant figure seen from a train window remained especially clearly impressed in the memory of a bygone day when, after the winter holidays, the time had come to go back to school in the city. Many years later, in the vistas of Asia, a similar sensation arose more than once when glimpsing some distant travelers ascending the ridge of a hill or fading into the enfoldment of a valley. Each such wayfarer, who looked like a giant dwarfed by the distance, invited all kinds of conjectures within the caravan. It was discussed: Was he a man of peace? Why is his path off the road? Why is he hurrying, and why does he travel alone?

The long ear of Asia, that one which at times acts faster than the telegraph, listens carefully. The eye accustomed to the distant horizon, searchingly watches each moving point. Let us not think that this happens only because of cautiousness, fearfulness, or mistrust. The traveler in Asia is provident and armed, and ready for any rencontre. Watchfulness is generated not only because of dangers. An attentive eye will certainly be an experienced eye. It will also be accustomed to a great deal that is unusual. The eye of an experienced traveler knows that unusual things happen not only at midnight. They may take place at midday, in the bright sun, precisely when they are least expected. Inexperience, or rather heedlessness, is ready to let even something remarkable slip by, "like a goat looking at a new gate," not noticing anything special or making any deductions.

An experienced traveler in Asia is always ready for something special. He has experience in watching the weather. He will prudently consider an unexpected horse's trail which crosses the road. He will distinguish the trail of the horsemen from that of a load. The appearance of various animals or birds also will be prudently noted. An experienced traveler appreciates it when his companions understand why he turns around, or becomes thoughtful, or senses the wind on a wet hand, or anxiously looks at the horse's ears, or observes a peculiarity of gait.

Truly, when this experience in the school of life is recorded and evaluated, it is evident that it is more sensible, as well as jollier, not to travel alone. And instead of absurd superstitions there arise before you pages of original and often very refined knowledge. It is deplorable to observe how at times this knowledge is rashly and carelessly effaced. Often one had to notice how an experienced, authoritative traveler who had begun, or was about ready, to narrate something truly significant, upon looking into the eyes of those present became silent, shaking his head or hand. "No use to scatter pearls—anyhow, they will not want to understand and may even put a wrong construction on one's words." Thus, the experienced traveler will always prefer to remain silent rather than scatter knowledge to the unworthy.

How many songs and unrepeatable tales one listens to on the desert byways! Secrets are revealed that are tightly shut in the turmoil of the cities. Often I had occasion to meet former desert traveling companions in city surroundings, and it was always amazing to observe that they appeared different, less important. Their keen ears and vigilant, searching eyes were dulled, as it were, by the dust of the city. They seemed quite ordinary people. Their remarkable knowledge and breadth of horizon seemed chained by something. This is why special details of the travels are indelibly imprinted in our memories.

There are many stories about the unusual speed of transmission of news in most remote parts of Asia and Africa. I recall a story of our friend Louis Marin. In Paris on one occasion a telegram was received about the successful arrival on a certain day of a French expedition to one of the most remote parts of Africa. When friends began to calculate how much time was needed to send this news in the usual way, to their dismay, they felt convinced that this information was obviously wrong, because it could never have been transmitted in such a short time. But later it became clear that the news was correct, and the fact that it had taken such a short time was due only to the peculiar local customs. Over great distances news was transmitted by the natives, in the nightime, by means of prearranged drumbeats on drums or on dry wood. Such transmission has existed since ancient times among the tribes, and certain European settlers have also used it.

What romance is contained in these mysterious night sounds, which send urgent messages from some unknown source! Just as speedily did the "Flowers of Tamerlane," the watchtowers, transmit by prearranged fires the most urgent communications.

The heart resounds to all that is unusual, and sharply stamps these most valued impressions upon the consciousness. When we see a distant traveler upon an endless snowy plain, we think that he makes his difficult journey not by chance and not without purpose. Probably he carries important news and is expected by those who will understand the signs of the future.

Peking, December 25, 1934.

CULTURE, THE VICTORIOUS

A ND so you like my definition of culture and civilization. One should note with justice that in India and
China such a definition of the concepts of culture and
civilization was understood quite readily and welcomed as
something entirely natural.

But it was not thus everywhere. Sometimes it was proposed that I exclude altogether the word *culture*, because
civilization fully expressed both concepts, as it were. I had
to take down from the bookshelves various dictionaries in
order to prove, at least formally, the difference between
these two words. Of course my opponents did not convince
me, and I am not certain that I convinced them. Maybe
because of certain prejudices they still consider civilization
as something tangible and culture as something abstract,
ephemeral. Maybe, in spite of all proofs, some still think
that the presence of a starched collar or a stylish dress is
a guarantee not only of a sound civilization but also of
culture. So often purely external, conventional signs are
light-mindedly taken for an unquestionable achievement.

But in culture there is no place for light-mindedness.
Culture is verily conscious cognition, spiritual refinement
and convincingness, whereas the conventional forms of
civilization depend entirely upon the passing fashion. Culture, when it arises and is affirmed, becomes indestructible. There may be various degrees and methods of its manifestation, but in its essence it is invincible, and it lives
primarily in the human heart. The mind from which hap-
hazard phrases spring up can be satisfied with mechanical civilization, whereas an enlightened consciousness can
breathe only through culture. It seems, as was said long

ago, that culture is that refuge in which the human spirit finds ways for religion and for everything uplifting and beautiful.

Culture is a guarantee of the impossibility of retreat. If you hear somewhere about some kinds of festivals and holidays dedicated to culture, and later learn that on the very next day something anti-cultural took place there, then do not attach much importance to these festivals. They consisted only of vain talk and falsehoods. They only defiled the luminous concept of culture. At present official days of culture are frequently observed on which people swear to each other that they will not permit any more acultural manifestations. Devotion to everything cultural is solemnly avowed, and everything coarse, negative, corrupt is denied. How good it would be if all these oaths were sincere and immutable! But shortly afterward look at the pages of the very same newspapers and you will be shocked to see that the usage of expressions and strivings not only is not purified but became somewhat more false and abominable. Does it not mean that many of those who but recently proclaimed publicly their participation in culture did not even understand the true meaning of this lofty concept? After all, taking an oath to culture imposes an obligation. One should not utter big words in vain or with evil intent. Advisedly did the apostle remind the Ephesians: "Neither filthiness, nor foolish talking, nor jesting, which are not convenient, but rather giving of thanks." "Let all bitterness, and wrath, and anger, and clamour, and evil speaking, be put away from you, with all malice: . . ." And he also warned: "Redeeming the time, because the days are evil."

How ugly it is to utter obscenity near the concept of culture. There cannot be any vindication for this. No matter how one may try to forget the very word *culture* and limit it with the concept of civilization, nevertheless, even upon the lowest steps of civilized society, all coarseness is definitely excluded. Someone sorrowfully remarks about the existence of civilized savages. Of course, different forms of savagery are possible. On the one hand, one can see that at times people who were compelled to remain in the most complete solitude not only did not lose but, on the contrary, uplifted their own humaneness. On the other hand, quite often, even among the so-called civilized forms of life, people have fallen into unsocial customs, into an animal-like state. Let us not cite examples, although there are plenty of them.

All this only proves the extent of the frailty of the signs of civilization, and how necessary it is to be reminded of the principles of culture. And not for pseudo-days of culture, but for the establishment of its foundations in daily life. One should not delay any longer the establishment of real days of culture. Otherwise the pseudo-festivals may become sufficient for some people. The repetition alone of the word *culture* does not mean that the basis of this concept is being applied.

There exist many anecdotes about the ridiculous application of various scientific terms. It is also unfitting to profane that great concept which should improve and illuminate the twilight of contemporary existence. If the lights of the cinema signs are glaring, if newspaper reports are blaring the appraisal of the blows of a prize fight, this does not mean that the days of culture are nearer.

Young people often have every right to ask their elders about the extent to which culture enters into their free time. This is not to be regarded as some impermissible rebellion of youth. This will be simply a question about a beautiful well-ordered structure of life. Often it merely shows a young mind striving keenly beyond the limitations of conventional civilization. Children often have an insatiable desire to learn that about which they usually receive such meager formal answers from their elders. And at times there may be added *ergo bibamus*—let us have a drink. And thus is underscored a complete bankruptcy of thinking.

Life, in all its new aspects, is outgrowing the concept of conventional civilization. The problems of life, growing daily, insistently propel people toward higher decisions, in the making of which it is impossible to shift the blame in conventional outworn ways. Either all the newly found possibilities are to be blended into a beautiful, truly cultural decision, or the survivals of civilization will drag the weak-willed into a savage state. And then no pseudo-festivals of culture will inspire, nor will they hold back falsehood and destruction.

But, even if in the minority, even if persecuted as in the days of old, let a few gather; and in true festivals of culture, without sophistry, without pompous twaddle, they will firmly swear to each other to follow only the paths of culture, the paths of spiritual perfectment. It should be thus in all the various countries, in all corners of the world where the human heart is beating.

Peking, December 27, 1934.

SELF-DESTRUCTION

IN the middle of the seventeenth century Stepanov reported to the Yakut chieftains ". . . and because of the uprisings of these people, life on the great river Amur has become hard and unbearable." Such reports and the local chronicles related in detail the difficulties with which the building up of this frontier country proceeded, not so much because of the foreigners and members of other tribes, but precisely because of various strange internal rebellions. The breaking out of these rebellions usually is not described, but there are recounted most distressing irreparable consequences. And the result was that because of the internal disorders blows were dealt to values of external significance.

Was it because of a lack of vision and imagination that these aimless, self-destructive flare-ups took place? And now, are we not witnessing the same kind of logically un-explainable clashes, which are taking place with the very same impermissible coarseness, just as in remote ages? Does not middle-of-the-road thinking, as one of the reasons, lie at the very core? There are inexpressible words in the beats of the human heart as it strives toward something better; but the mind deprived of wings limits itself by the conditions of today only. It is indignant in the face of these chance happenings; but precisely through them, and not in any other way, does it wish to find a solution.

The most complicated controversies, the piling up of newly invented complicated terminology as a seeming token of erudition—all this does not lead to, but draws away from, the needs of existence. And yet now the simple, hearty word is so needed. Not a three-storied cumbersome term, but a particle of an illumined life of fulfillment is awaited. People, ordinary folk, wish to live. They wish to adorn life as much as possible. We see how ancient tribes under even the most meager circumstances aspired and found original ways for such adornment. The masses wish to learn. The people understand very well that knowledge is not by any means an arbitrarily piled up incomprehension, but something that can be imparted in very simple, clear, not snarling, not malice-bearing words.

Everyone who has had occasion to talk to people, even in very remote localities, of course knows of this quite sensible striving toward the simplest expression. We ourselves in recalling our school and university years turn with especial warmth to those teachers who taught clearly and simply. It matters not what the subject was, whether higher mathematics, or philosophy, or history, or geography—absolutely everything could be, and was, presented in clear terms by the gifted instructors. Only the limited and the untalented became entangled in their own verbal accumulations, and often, to the secret amusement of the students, tried painfully to get out of the difficulties which they themselves had created. Frequently such ill-fated pedagogues ended their meandering explanations with a tragic, "Well, you understand." And precisely because of this lack of clarity offensive nicknames were created, uncontrollable jeering spouted forth, and an internal split resulted.

Precisely now many fields are overloaded with newly invented complications. And yet at present people are passing through a particularly responsible period. No one is now satisfied with the middle-of-the-road thinking of recent years. On the one hand, nets are cast into the future, at times hurled ungovernably. And on the other hand, consciousness is directing thought to those primary sources whence the keen ear catches a great deal that unexpectedly corresponds to the latest theories. A period wherein this combination of the newest with the most ancient occurs is a responsible one. Strange as it may seem, the nineteenth century, with its many researches, appears to be one of the least convincing. The very primitive structures of nihilism in this century render it unconvincing. Each negation, every insistence on the void and non-existence are already rejected. They are rejected not only by philosophy and studies of antiquity, but also by the latest discoveries in the physical sciences. Leading scientists quite calmly speak about their religious and philosophical views, of which their fathers often would not have dared to speak openly, even for the sake of preserving their "scientific integrity." In this way, the moves that easily turn into achievement become indisputable. Truly, an achievement, in its essence, cannot be limited. Precisely in an achievement the most ancient wisdom as well as the answer to the most modern problem are easily accessible. And besides, we will be evaluating something not only in regard to its antiquity. We shall study it fully, conscientiously, and with good will. And only these honestly unlimited investigations will en able us to retrieve that which can he most concretely applied to the problems of the future. Again, if someone insists that he will take only just a bit from ancient wisdom, he will reveal himself as a hypocrite; because this "bit" can be applied only after an all embracing true study. And he who wants to put any negation into the foundation of a structure will thus mix into his cement a poisonous, corroding substance.

Many new discoveries have been given to people in recent years. And many times because of them one becomes convinced of the indescribable link of ancient times with our problems. If clear words can be found about the possibility of life and progress, the dark rebellions will recede into the realm of legends. People reading about them will only regret the lost opportunities and rejoice that the new boundaries of knowledge will help them restrain themselves from self-destruction. Clarity and simplicity—these are what the heart is waiting for.

Peking, December 28, 1934.

BENEVOLENCE

HOW odd that things which are both benevolent and significant so often remain unrecorded anywhere! Just today we heard that the Russian Ecclesiastical Mission in Peking was saved only by the personal intercession of the Tashi Lama. In the history of religions such a sign of benevolence should be carefully preserved. It is regrettable that around religions too much evidence of coldness and negativity has accumulated. And so when one hears, in old Peking, a beautiful story of how a body of priests and religious societies once went to the Tashi Lama to beg him to help preserve the most worthy Russian Orthodox Mission in Peking, which had guarded many fine traditions for so long, and how benevolently he responded to this plea, one is sincerely glad. And not only was this plea accepted benevolently, but desirable results followed, and this significant act of high benevolence has entered into the history of the Russian Mission in Peking.

When humanity is possessed by the devils of malice and mutual destruction, every token of affirmativeness and mutual help is especially valuable. True, a great deal is known about the good acts and magnanimity of the Tashi Lama. But it is one thing when his countrymen relate it and quite another when strangers also bear good testimony about it.

People often do not realize and reflect about how valuable is the inculcation of good signs. There are certain kinds of persons who warn against all enthusiasm and even against speaking a good word out loud. Naturally, with such a way of thinking all submerges if not into total darkness then at best into greyish twilight. Antagonists of any kind of enthusiasm would like to have people respond to nothing, react to nothing, and remain shamefully indifferent to both good and evil.

In our anxious days there are quite many such grey dwellers. In great measure the responsibility for the confusion deeply imbedded in the social structure lies with them. This shocking and, at the same time, vacillating confusion is nothing but formlessness and ugliness. The very words *confusion* and *perplexity* are not far from distortion, doubt, and fear. In confusion vague insinuations are engendered. It also gives birth to all manner of anonymous calumnies. When the heart loses the tremor of exaltation, it can become prey to the tremor of confusion. And just as the tremor of exaltation impels upward and toward the beautiful, so will the tremor of confusion be limiting, depressing, frightening. What could be uglier than the spectacle of fear? The very highest concepts—honor, dignity, devotion, love, achievement—can, after all, be violated and mutilated precisely through fear. Because of fear people keep silent, renounce, and betray. And what a mass of silent disavowals and cowardly silences are revealed in daily life!

For disavowals no high words or beautiful surroundings are needed. Usually, disavowals, silence, belittlement are more suitable to the dusk. They live in a grey atmosphere wherein clear-cut forms are blurred by twilight and every thing becomes indefinite. Vagueness of thoughts, indecisive-ness are in reality confusion. Confusion does not sing, or mold beautiful forms, but distorts everything in trembling reflections. Thus, a bird flying over the water lightly touches the calm surface, and long afterward the forms which before had been beautifully reflected will be atremble.

One should cure oneself of confusion and fear. As one should undergo lengthy restoration of one's strength after many illnesses, so also a recovery from confusion is needed. One should not allow the confusion to become corrupt in boils and abcesses. New strong thoughts and powerful actions will be salutary and can carry the spirit out of confusion into a renewed condition. Naturally, by a change of location alone or of the living conditions, confusion will not be conquered. The potentiality of the spirit, the consciousness, must be struck by something, and still better, should become enraptured by something.

It is impermissible to say that rapture, or to use another word, enthusiasm, cannot be accessible even to confused souls. For there are such actions, such conditions in the world as will transport the heart and thus enable it to conquer disturbing tremors. Beautiful creativeness, lofty knowledge, and finally the pure heart's striving to the Heavenly World—all these miracles, of which there are so many in earthly life, can easily lead even a drooping spirit into the gardens of rapture.

If people were to attempt to erase from their existence the words *enthusiasm* and *rapture*, at times ridiculed by them, how would they fill up this frightful void in their consciousness? In such desolate hearts anguish and lack of faith begin to dwell, and there appears that deadly mustiness which is found in abandoned, empty places. Entering an abandoned house, people say, "It will take a long time to make it livable." And truly such neglect even threatens with physical ailments.

To make a dwelling place livable does not mean simply to light a fire. Precisely the human presence is needed, in other words, the beat of the human heart, in order to enliven and spiritualize the arrested life.

One of the simplest examples of spiritualization will be each news about some good, unusual, and benevolent action. Thus, let us rejoice at each benevolence; for it dispels someone's confusion and replaces ugliness with beauty.

Peking, December 29, 1934.

THE UNREPEATABLE

"RASMO —kropo—go—dilos!"
"No, colleague, not right!
"Rasmo—kropo—godilos!
"But this is only Vanka; he simply wrote,
"Rasmokrop-ogodilos!"

There was such a joke long ago about the Radlov Expedition for research and study of inscriptions upon the rocks and stones of Siberia. It was a joke not only because the inscriptions were undecipherable for quite some time but because people in general smirked, not understanding the significance of archaeology. The destiny of antiquities, particularly Russian antiquities, describes a tortuous path.

When there was opportunity to sketch the cross-sections of the tumuli, then it was especially painful to notice the trenches left by marauders. And often these marauders were practically the contemporaries of that very same tumulus or grave. Often the trench was dug with evident knowledge of the details of the burial, showing understanding of the value of all the objects placed there. In Egypt, in Asia, in the southern steppes of Russia the marauders frequently followed on the heels of the burial. And how many professional treasure hunters, mound diggers, tumuli seekers irreparably hindered scientific deductions!

In the chronicles of Siberian history, for example, we read: "In spite of all the dangers connected with the pursuit of this trade, some tumuli diggers turned it into a means of livelihood; they acquired such skill that from the exterior view alone of the tumuli they could determine their relative antiquity and the contents of precious metals in them. Since many of the tumuli were of considerable size, and some were also covered with heavy stones weighing from 400 to 800 pounds, the tumuli diggers organized companies of from 200 to 300 people and made a business of 'mounding.' "

In the eighteenth century one such company of 150 men found a tumulus along the midstream of the Irtysh and dug from it upwards of 50 pounds of gold in various forms. True, not all Siberian tumuli were so rich, yet there was so much "grave" gold and silver in circulation that in Krasnoyarsk, in the chief market of tumuli jewels, in the eighteenth century the "grave" gold was sold at 50 to 90 kopecks per zolotnik (96th part of a Russian pound). These valuables in their time formed an important part of trading in the Irbit Fair, where they were readily bought by Russians and strangers, and were widely spread beyond the Urals.

The same destiny also overtook those monuments of Siberian antiquity from which some usefulness could have been derived. The remnants of the ancient structures—"stone babas"[1] and tombstones—often covered with the most curious inscriptions and images, were used up to recent times as grindstones or simply as material for new structures, of course without any consideration for the scientific significance of the monuments of antiquity which had thus been destroyed.

Hand in hand with marauding and greediness were encountered the most insufferable evidences of vandalism. Many beautiful cave frescos and carvings were destroyed by fanatics. And yet—seek closer. Do not lull yourself with the thought that such destruction took place only long ago. Do not blame only those long since moldered vandals.

Fanaticism still flourishes, and in what ingenious garments! Either it is directed by religious delusions or, in contrast, it is inspired by godlessness. The plundering of the tumuli marauders pales before the savage sweep of fanaticism.

Sometimes out of the pilferer's hands an object would come into good hands. But the rage of fanaticism knows

---

[1]   Stone sculptures of women.

only destruction and mutilation. Is it not terrible to think that fanaticism exists even today? Often during the hours of lectures about monuments of art and ways of life these very monuments are actually being destroyed. Say after this that the destiny of creativeness is safeguarded! Dare to insist that all is well!

Only ignorance will lull a just watchfulness. Conventional behavior will say, "Let us not disturb the orderliness of the gathering with unpleasant news." But the real danger is great. One cannot become reconciled to the knowledge that fanaticism exists in a very extensive, ugly variety.

Whether the marauder breaks an amphora, or a jeweller melts down a Cellini goblet into mere metal, whether a priceless statue be destroyed by a fanatic, or a monument by an ignoramus—in all this there is an abysmal savagery. Next to this destruction there stands also the mutilation of the beautiful creations of antiquity! Crude structural additions, patchwork, and quasi-restorations kill the soul of a monument.

After the hand of the fanatic comes the hand of the hypocrite, the haughty, and the ignoramus, each of whom in his own way changes the finest creations. As a rule, senselessly, without feeling, these often irreparable sacrileges take place. The lost beauty becomes forever frozen in a grimace of distortion. A pitiful, repulsive aspect replaces the original enchantment.

Leaving a valuable monument in the desert, we often asked the guide, "Will it be safe?" And, wise in experience, he would shake his head, "Maybe from beasts, but hardly from people."

Sorrowful is such a remark from a person of experience. Yet many problems are solved through opposition. Let precisely this contrariety help the benevolently minded co-workers to gather in courageous defense of all that is sacredly beautiful.

Chiefly, know more. Harken, love to read, and discuss reality. There is too much ignorance.

Peking, January 1, 1935.

ANCIENT SOURCES

WHEREIN lies the truth of ages? In laws and commands or in proverbs and fairy tales?" In the first the will is intensified and in the second is the imprint of wisdom.

The shortest proverb is permeated with reverberations of place and age. And in the fairy tale, as in a buried treasure, is hidden faith and the strivings of people. The proverb may be sad, but it will not be destructive, and likewise one will not find distasteful fairy tales or repulsive folk songs. The proverb, and the fairy tale as well, are for the good. But the sources of the commands are different. How many commands become obsolete and quickly evaporate! Yet try to eradicate a proverb or legend. They may go underground, but they will persistently emerge again.

"Know how to catch the smallest devil by the tail and he will show you where his superior hides." This old Chinese proverb points out the significance of the smallest details for revealing the most important. Truly, the minute detail will be the best key to a great achievement. It is wrong to think that details are unimportant for the path of ascent. Even some most excellent heroic acts have rested upon details that were foreseen in time. How carefully he who follows the Teacher notices all the stones! He will miss nothing extraneous. Only a poor disciple will say, "Guru, in my exaltation I broke my nose." Such incommensurate-ness will only show how far the disciple is from being observant. This Chinese proverb means, furthermore, that the greatest criminal is more easily detected by the smallest details of his conduct.

It is wonderful to observe the subtlety and correctness of all details in proverbs, legends, and fairy tales. Of course, sometimes in an inaccurate translation something may appear superfluous and clumsy, but one need only turn to the original to find that the old proverb "One cannot omit a word in a song" has a deep meaning. And not only can a word not be omitted, it even cannot be transposed. And from this point of view it is instructive to observe the chiseled conciseness of folk language. As the best seeds are separated by repeated winnowing, so in the furnace of the ages the tongue of folk wisdom is forged.

In all ages and nations there will always be short periods during which all these accumulations will be haughtily rejected. Like buried treasure they will go underground for the time being. As in forbidden catacombs there will remain only the whisper of prayers. Thus somewhere, and yet in full care, will be safeguarded the signs of people's observations, and later on they will be unearthed from their hiding places. Again, with renewed fervor they will be studied. And again, precisely from these inexhaustible sources will the founts of culture be renewed.

Some thoughtful explorers will again go deep into the unravelling of the sense as well as the forms of ancient heritages. Again they will admire the refined details of these forms, so well forged, so well chiseled, born of long patience in bygone rhythms of life.

Precisely, one wishes to emphasize that in these ancient heritages the meaning and the structural form can give equal joy to the explorer. Perhaps superficial people will speak of an "old-fashioned" language; but a true revealer of the runes, an inquisitive scientist, will recognize how remarkable, how simple and fitting are the definitions and in what combinations the greatest emphasis is brought out, correctly drawing the attention, just where it is needed.

Take any ancient proverb and try to change the sequence of words in it. You will see as a result that much of the sense will be lost. We have seen many distortions of sense due to poor translation. Only recently have languages be gun to be studied without prejudice, and therefore in certain well-known monuments of the past, modern translations reveal new and significant details. The historical names themselves have undergone in the various translations such a multitude of changes that at times it is difficult to realize that one and the same person or place was meant. Especially guilty of this have been the textbooks of the secondary schools. A great number of children in a hurried course of study, at times learn terms which later, in mature years, are met again, but with an entirely different connota tion, giving rise to unnecessary complications. But now, in many branches of science, we turn inquiringly to the origi nal sources, with an open mind. Thoughtful study will help again to appreciate the most characteristic, the most minute details and definitions.

And what could be more profound and all-embracing than the observation of thought itself and its structure? People speak, not without reason, about the art of thinking. Precisely in the structure of thought is expressed the same general concept of creativeness. Lovers of art for art's sake always will emphasize especially not only that which is said but also how it is said. The way things are said, the way they are done, the way they are thought—all this is a source of delight for every true observer; and now, when so much must be spoken about the loss of quality in all of life, precisely the quality of all that is created is especially significant.

All problems requiring a quick solution are in need of a high quality of expression. The famous "somehow or other" is more than out of place. Everyone must realize his responsibility for his way of thinking and acting. Let us not imagine that the mode of thinking is unimportant; as in all creativeness, the manner of expression, of technique, have an enormous significance. A painting is convincing only when it has been executed in such a way that it cannot be changed, when the observer feels that it could never have been otherwise and that what is presented to him has been composed as was necessary. What great observation of all details is necessary for this convincingness!

What a wonderful school of convincingness is contained in the true creativeness of peoples—anonymous, full of character, and ever living.

Peking, January 3, 1935.

WORTH

EVEN in grammar school the pupils hear about dynasties being replaced by the score in various countries. These radical changes are spoken of with dispassionate calmness as if they were a new, quiet nest-building. No one says that scores of dynastic changes and scores of tragedies can be spoken of with equal detachment.

Can one recall any absolutely peaceful changes of government? Almost every one of them is accompanied by shocking violence, killings, and all kinds of terror. Actually, a real tragedy was at the basis of each such change. It not only had to do with the head of the government, together with the whole regime, but usually the entire class system changed, the psychology of the people changed, and the goal of aspirations changed.

New rhythms were painfully stratified. They were accompanied by outcries and terror; but now, after the passage of centuries, one talks calmly in schools about the change of dynasties. Often, not only the students but the professors themselves forget what is hidden in such an epic. When one talks about wars, pestilences, and all manner of catastrophes, then naturally the tragic side impregnates the very expressions and words. But a "change of dynasties" Bounds very remote, very undisturbing. "Change of conditions of life" also sounds peaceful in the minds of people, whereas in these clear passionless words there is hidden a veritable tempest, often of many years, with many horrors of destruction.

Hence, even in primary schools a more detailed and expressive nomenclature should be adopted. A vivid recounting of ancient historic events will strengthen the consciousness of youth. On one hand it will sow the seeds of enthusiasm and heroism, and on the other it will safeguard from despair.

"All despair is finite—the heart is infinite." "Beauty is contained in each participation in construction . . . This is the true realm of the heart. This desired purification of life gives solemnity, which is like an inextinguishable Light."

"Where is that sentiment, that substance, with which we can fill the Chalice of Great Service? We shall gather this feeling from the best treasures. We shall find its components in religious ecstasy, when the heart quivers at the Highest Light; in the feeling of heartfelt love, when the tear of self-renunciation glistens; in the hero's achievement, when power is multiplied in the name of humanity. We shall find it in the patience of the gardener who ponders over the mystery hidden in a seed. We shall find it in the courage that pierces the darkness. We shall find it in the smile of the child who stretches out its hand to a sunbeam. We shall find it amidst all flights that carry us into the Infinite. The feeling of Great Service is unlimited; it must fill the heart, which is forever inexhaustible. The sacred tremor should not become the daily gruel. The best Teachings turned into soulless husks when the tremor left them. Thus, in the midst of battle, think of the Chalice of Service, and take an oath that the sacred tremor shall not leave you."

"Ancient decrees about the sacred tremor should be understood with broad consciousness. Precisely, the warmth and heat of this tremor safeguard the heart from cold—that terrible, deadly cold which cuts off all communion."

"One can observe the dead two-legged ones, wandering corpses, who by their very approach defile and even desecrate places where the precious and the beautiful have already been uttered. Indeed, not an abstract command but a patiently instilled new understanding may warn those who are becoming ill with the terrible epidemic of decomposition. Indeed, horrible is the spectacle of a decomposing body. But such decomposition even happens during life. If purely physical measures can ward off such a condition, then to what an obvious extent will spiritual reactions act us a better prophylaxis."

"Spiritual healings will help not only to prevent bodily complications, they will not only stop the decomposition of the spirit, but actually they will give a healthy, progressive motion to the desiccated spirit. The spirit, as the subtlest substance, is close to the spatial vibrations, so affined with this motion."

If one could prompt in time the young active doer in life about what complexities, beautiful as well as terrible, are contained in the short formulas in epics, this transmutation of thought would forever strengthen the direction of such a traveler. If he understands the entire tragedy, the pain and sorrow caused, he may then find in his own actions more worthy, one may say, even more cultural paths for evolution can thus be built with a greater preservation of human dignity. In his heart man will sense the bitterness of tragedies and the lofty exaltation of service and heroism.

Peking, January 10, 1935.

MADNESS

PROFESSOR Harry M. Johnson, of the University of Virginia, speaking about the consequences of fatigue said, "If you are tired, you are insane." Dr. Johnson, giving the results of his seven years of research at the Mellon Institute, explained: "A tired man reveals characteristic symptoms of one form or another of insanity, and not always in a small degree.

"Sluggishness, inattentiveness, defective speech, lapse of memory, stubbornness, painful obstinancy, hallucinations, loss of consciousness, vacuity, fits of anger—all these are the usual symptoms of fatigue, even if they begin gradually.

"After a good sleep a tired man becomes liberated from these symptoms and usually regains his strength. But it may happen that sleep will not establish the normal balance. It may happen that as a result there will appear new types of abnormalcy, and the man will become prey to inactivity, depression, insensitiveness, and will remain apathetic to everything, showing not the slightest interest or attention, and unable even to undertake any work in his own profession. Such a condition may continue for several hours, and even for several weeks."

In another field of research, physicians at Columbia University have announced a new theory about colds. According to this theory, it is not the man who catches the cold, but the bacteria and microbes; and the illness of the man himself becomes a secondary factor. Comparatively recently bacteriologists have established that one and the same microorganism may be either pathogenic or saprophytic, depending upon conditions in which it is placed.

The most harmless microbe, after a change of surroundings and conditions of existence, may become pathogenic. Harmless microbes and bacteria, which are found in the nose and mouth, under the influence of dampness or a sharp change of temperature become generators of illness.

One should not forget that in reality the inner conditions of a man are subject to change, not only due to external circumstances but also under the influence of the condition of the nervous system. In other words, we again approach the identical conclusion that depression and imbalance of the nervous system create numerous cases of disorders that but recently were regarded as resulting from exterior causes.

The assertion of the investigator that fatigue creates the conditions of madness is not paradoxical. Indeed, the inner nervous energy may fall into such an unnatural state that its being defined as madness may be not far from truth.

That identical very strong poison that is created by fits of anger and irritation, even if it undergoes a change afterward, nevertheless is precipitated into the nerve channels during various unnatural elations and depressions.

One may congratulate the investigator who dares to call the condition of depression madness. Usually people hesitate to define so drastically such commonly accepted conditions. Madness is understood as a state demanding isolation; but if many people even legally insane are walking free, then how many of them are to be found in various temporary stages of madness!

Recalling various former legislative measures, teachings, philosophic theories, one notices that they were actually concerned primarily with the establishment of equilibrium. Not some special psychiatrists but practical psychologists have called upon people to adopt conditions in which the least self-poisoning could take place. The awakening of bacteria and microbes to action, in the majority of instances, will be a case of self-poisoning, because it will occur owing to a consciously directed pseudo-activity.

So-called fatigue, with all its burdens, is primarily a result of incorrect distribution of labor.

Many times have the most ancient as well as the newest doctrines suggested a wise change of labor to avoid burdensome fatigue. During a sufficiently varied change of labor fatigue as such is impossible. Besides, deadening inactivity may engender a most harmful kind of fatigue. Especially now when so many seemingly hitherto unnoticed ailments are revealed, each investigator will first look for means to establish balance. After all, we live not only in a time of excessive labors but also in a period of most unnatural and, at times, murderous interrelations. Take practically any page of a newspaper to prove to yourself that the most unheard-of symptoms of madness are now broadly spread. For instance, take the following account from a newspaper of 1934:

"As has happened usually in past years, in the course of 1934 several singular records were established:

"A German woman, Edna Asselin, received first prize in an international contest for housewives for sweeping a corridor two meters wide and seven meters long in thirty-eight seconds.

"An American, James Aagord, was proclaimed victor in a shouting contest, which took place in the state of Nebraska. He yelled so loudly that he was heard at a distance of a mile and a half.

"In Cincinnati a bridge tournament which started in 1924 has just ended. Each player scored over a million points.

"Eighteen-year-old Rose Rooney from Rhode Island ate at one sitting eighteen quarts of shellfish.

"A tailor, Einduber, from Denver, threaded into the eye of a needle twelve extremely fine threads, one after another."

It may be concluded that such records of that year should be sufficient to remind us about the dangerous stages of madness creeping and hiding amidst the present day masses of humanity. There is really a vast field of research here for psychologists. Thus it would seem that many otherwise unsolvable state and social problems could be solved by striving for equilibrium. The same Golden Path, ordained long ago, is again sought by humanity amidst an unusual and probably unrepeatable twilight of madness. The daily news speaks of extraordinary crimes, perpetrated with unusual, cold cruelty.

Of course all cruelty is madness. Possibly, one could trace the manner in which the progressive madness of cruelty and malediction was stratified. These paths, being the most negative, will undoubtedly remain forever within the limits of madness. Investigations as to why a man falls into cursing and all sorts of disgusting cruelties very probably would have saved many from these dark paths. If, in accordance with the justified assertion of the investigator, fatigue is but a step of madness, then how much the more should cruelty be recognized as an acute degree of madness. And one should not be lulled by the thought that in our enlightened age cruelty is being outlived. It is not so, regrettably. There are appearing even new kinds of cruelty, subtle, penetrating into all forms of daily life. Let us hope that madness, in all its forms and degrees, will be thoroughly investigated.

Peking, January 24, 1935.

STARS OF DEATH

ABBÉ MORÉ, the French astronomer, calls to the attention of all diplomats the years 1936 and 1937. During these years, he says that a great increase and activity of sunspots will be observed. This astronomer reminds us that periods of increased activity of sunspots have often coincided with wars and all kinds of social disturbances.

"During the periods of least activity of sunspots, peaceful times usually have been observed on Earth; and a maximum activity of these spots apparently causes nervous upheavals, which impel nations toward evil and savage battle," so says the abbé.

"If solar activity increases various magnetic deviations, then in the consequences which follow there is likewise developed a strange, feverish condition which takes an epidemic possession of mankind. At times, such a feverish condition begins somewhat earlier than the recorded sun-spot maximum, as happened during the World War of 1914.

"Whether another war in approaching is unknown, but I wish to point out that according to statistics of many centuries the years 1936 and 1937 should be considered especially dangerous."

Thus, to all the various calculations regarding 1936, one more is added. In many countries, due to the most diverse causes, people focus their attention on the year 1936. Of course, it is hard to say whether this year will be significant in a crude earthly sense, or will lay a foundation for results in the near future. Very often a decisive event had already taken place somewhere, while at the same time, in other places people were already growing desperate because it had not yet happened. Something akin to this was noticeable in the hours of waiting for the armistice of the Great War. The awaited moment passed as if nothing had taken place. People were still sorrowing, but at the same time the armistice, although not yet announced openly, was already agreed upon.

Thus, the French astronomer has added his experienced word to the various statements about the significance of 1936. Concurrently, across the ocean, some very significant discussions about so-called "stars of death" were taking place.

At a recent meeting of the Smithsonian Institution in Washington, its secretary, the well-known astronomer, Charles Abbot, read a report about "stars of death," whose rays could destroy all life on Earth, if they were ever to reach it.

Dr. Abbot had been working at the Mt. Wilson Observatory in California with a group of assistants. With the aid of new astronomical instruments they took most exact measurements of the power of the light of different stellar rays and of their spectrums. They succeeded in taking measurements of the minutest reflections from the stars seen on Earth, despite the fact that these stars are separated from the Earth by trillions and quadrillions of kilometers. The study of the rays from the star Regel belonging to the constellation of Orion presented special interest. These ultraviolet rays are extraordinarily short. "The majority of the rays of the star Regel do not sustain life but kill organisms. The rays of Regel do not impart the sensation of light to the organism upon which they fall. They are veritable rays of death. In a small measure similar rays issue from the sun. Luckily for us, they hardly ever reach Earth, since it is difficult for them to pierce the strata of ozone that are in the atmosphere high above Earth.

"We have discovered," relates Dr. Abbot, "that all stars of blue color belong to the death-dealing category. Their temperature is three times higher than that of the surface of the sun."

It is well that in the cosmic flux such powerful rays are transmuted in space. Apparently, instead of direct destruction they bring great benefit. Altogether, many remarkable observations are currently being accumulated in various fields, which, in the end, draw attention to the very same high energies; and the details of these observations, at times consciously, but more often unconsciously, fall into the hands of humanity.

Often, we also encounter another factor worthy of special attention. In some professional domain there may be raised even from a narrow utilitarian point of view, questions which have truly universal significance. For instance, the "American Weekly" gives some curious data about various unexplainable manifestations which sometimes cause all kinds of accidents, including automobile accidents. The following are of interest: "Recently a chauffeur who had wrecked his car insisted that while driving at full speed he had seen a large dog approaching and so swerved to one side. He had driven into the ditch and wrecked the car, but afterward became convinced that there had been absolutely no dog and that all this had been a strange hallucination.

"Often he who had been sitting calmly at the wheel of a car and suddenly finds himself in an accident cannot explain logically what caused him to lose control.

"Here is another recorded case which happened in Great Britain: A bus that made regular trips between Portsmouth and London was proceeding on its way, with a very experienced driver. Suddenly, passing near a precipice, the bus began zigzagging and plunged over. As a result one passenger was killed and five injured. The driver insisted that he had seen a little girl run across the road, right under the bus, and that he had tried to avoid hitting her.

"In the United States, in Arkansas, there was recorded a case of collective hallucination. Four students were speeding along in a car when the driver saw a carriage crossing the road and applied the brakes. Two of the other students also saw the carriage, but the fourth one did not see anything and was quite astonished at the sudden stop. It was said that the driver had mistaken a shadow, which fell on the road, for a carriage.

"In general, one can observe that collective hallucinations are not so rare. An American student once, during a quarrel with a fellow student, took a flashlight out of his pocket shouting, 'I will shoot you!' And all those present claimed they saw a real revolver.

"Another interesting case of hallucination was reported from Chicago. A woman was cleaning a room. Suddenly a revolver shot rang out. She fell and began screaming that she was wounded in the chest. When taken into the hospital it was revealed that she had no wound whatsoever. But there had been an unloaded revolver in the room, which had fallen to the floor upon being dislodged. The woman imagined that she heard a shot and that she had been wounded.

"After the terrible catastrophe of 1912 in which the Titanic struck an iceberg, many passengers on other ships traveling in the same latitudes visited the captain's bridge and told him that they saw dangerous icebergs. These were nothing but hallucinations.

"An interesting and well-known case of mass hallucination took place in England during World War I. The battle of Mons took place on the same location where in the fifteenth century English archers fought the French.

"And so when at one time the Germans attacked particularly strongly and the Tommies were about to retreat, the regiment beheld its ancestors in cuirasses, with crossbows and halberds, who, together with them rushed in to attack the Germans. The enemy was repulsed.

"How could science explain these hallucinations? Simply as imagination, as caused by fatigue, by alcohol? An interesting explanation is given by Dr. Raoul Mourg, a Frenchman, who says that a hallucination is a sudden appearance in the consciousness of an idea which jumps out of the subconscious, and precisely because of this suddenness acquires a great vividness.

"In any case, the process of 'visions' is by no means a 'seeming so' if it can become the cause of catastrophes, crimes, accidents, etc. Responsible workers should have full control of nerves and not admit any illusions."

At the same time that an American magazine in its own way is approaching the question of hallucination, most interesting experiments are being performed in Europe with the transmission of thought over a distance. Let us also quote these data and considerations.

"Between Vienna and Berlin, under the control of a scientific commission of physicians, physiologists, and psychiatrists, experiments were held in the transmitting of visual images over a distance with the help of only intensity of thought. These experiments were organized by the Metapsychical Society in Vienna, whose president is a professor of the University of Vienna, Christofer Schroeder. The 'dispatching station' was Professor Schroeder himself, the 'receiver' was a German physician, a member of the Berlin Institute of Psychic Sciences.

"Prof. Schroeder and his two assistants sat at a desk, on which a powerful electric lamp cast a vivid circle of light. Into this circle were placed various objects and drawings on which the three 'dispatchers' concentrated their entire attention to such a degree that after a few minutes they fell into a sort of hypnotic trance.

"The 'receivers'—the Berlin physician and his two assistants—at the same moment (previously arranged for an exact time) began to think with increasing intensity about the study of the Viennese professor, about the table and the circle of light on it; in short, about the surroundings which they had seen previously, during their visit in Vienna. Gradually, before their closed eyes there began to appear indefinite outlines of objects. At times they became diffused, not reaching completion, but at other times they became so clear that the 'receiver,' sketching with a pencil on a white sheet of paper, achieved a coherent drawing.

"Out of forty tests performed in November, six were fully successful, twenty tests were doubtful, the rest did not completely succeed. Some of the successful tests were as follows:

"The Viennese 'dispatcher' had before him a drawing of a snake with a twofold bend of the body. The Berlin 'receiver' drew the snake but with only one bend.

"The 'dispatcher' concentrated upon an arrow placed horizontally. The 'receiver' drew an arrow in a slanting position.

"The 'dispatcher' transmitted the figure 9. The 'receiver' drew an 8, but it was afterward noticed that in the drawing placed before the 'dispatcher' the lower tail of the 9 was so curled that it could have been easily taken for an 8.

"Especially curious was the sixth test. From Vienna the figure 5 was transmitted. The Berlin 'receiver' drew a 5, but placed a triangle under it. This circumstance was of great interest to the members of the commission, who concluded that Prof. Schroeder, at the time of transmission had momentarily become abstracted and thought about a triangle. Some members suggested that the mysterious triangle was the result of 'parasites,' which undoubtedly exist in telepathic transmission as in radio; i.e., in the transmission some alien thought became entangled which carried upon the invisible waves the image of a triangle."

Let us rejoice at these tests, although, in the final analysis, they are not new and rather meager. One could quote a number of others, far more instructive in this regard, but we note only these, since according to accompanying information they were conducted under the control of a scientific commission. Maybe precisely the influence of other people, present by chance, reduces the possibility of obtaining results.

Wherever people come close to the subtlest energies, they must be greatly harmonized in spirit and, in general, consciously refined in highest perceptivity.

But, comparing the above-mentioned considerations

about so-called hallucinations with the images transmitted over a distance, it may be said that one person's
thought-sendings will be at the same time hallucinations for another. It is presupposed that a thought sent
from a definite place will be received also in the definite
place where it is expected; but, like radio waves, these
thought-images will be absorbed by suitable receivers in
many other places. This simple consideration once again
reminds us of the great responsibility of man for his
thought and what connection this mental nerve energy
may be found to have with cosmic manifestations of the
greatest scope.

I repeat that I am writing down the news in today's press
not only because it is especially new and striking but also
to show precisely the manifestations that are emphasized
in the daily press. Although in many regions fanaticism
and ignorant narrowness still dominate, yet through all
these obstacles human consciousness continues undoubtedly to conquer new steps of the most urgent knowledge.

It often happens that people, from some professional
point of view, without even noticing it touch upon problems of vast significance. Therefore all the latest deductions must proceed with complete broad-mindedness by
the observer. Today some "stars of death" are discovered,
and tomorrow rays of salvation will descend. And thus
one should gather knowledge with full magnanimity and
should await a messenger, not because of our limited control, but with understanding of all the breadth of true
possibilities.

Peking, January 26, 1935.

ATTENTIVENESS

IN a large German sanitarium a special meteorological observatory was founded for the study of the effects of changes in weather upon sick organisms. This influence, extremely unfavorable, is at present regarded as definitely established, and the question remains only one of details. The University clinic in Freiburg notes that sharp deviations in the atmospheric pressure, connected with a special kind of wind—*föhn*—bring about an increased death rate among recently operated patients by causing a weakening of the heart action and embolism.

"Dr. Otterman, who is the head of the meteorological station, recommends that surgeons, when preparing for an operation, take into account the weather charts, and in any case place the patients to be operated in rooms having constant pressure, humidity, and temperature, so as to safeguard them from any harmful effects of weather."

It is strange to read about these "new deductions," which it would seem have been known for many, many centuries. Even without mentioning the fact that the physicians of old and the folk healers long ago took into consideration all sorts of atmospheric conditions, we must note that in ancient medical books and manuscripts there are to be found many indications about the very same thing. Ancient medical science often not only puts conditions for successful cure upon definite locations but also mentions climatic and atmospheric conditions, good and bad.

Local physicians and folk healers often indicated in precisely what locality the medicines prescribed by them would be especially effective. They also suggested the best time of day and other quite carefully observed details about the taking of medicine.

An experienced physician, not only an Eastern one but also one of the West, will advise not to worry about anything at the time of taking medicine and even not to think about extraneous matters, but to try to accompany the taking of medicine with a good thought about it.

Talk with an experienced gardener and he will point out to you a multitude of curious details about different atmospheric and also psychic effects on plants. The well-known experiment of the effect of human thought upon a plant has been indicated many times in literature. Even people greatly removed from science observe at times that flowers and plants in contact with certain people may wither quickly, whereas when close to others they may even blossom and get stronger.

One can rejoice that even in contemporary observations, often made quite difficult owing to conventionalities, definite relations between man and nature become apparent. These observations lead to fine uplifting conclusions.

The French writer Maurois was unjustly ridiculed when he pointed out that a dead body showed a difference in weight. The weight of higher energy, the weight and evidence of the effect of thoughts, is also not a subject to ridicule but should be studied very carefully.

It is very easy to laugh, and it is also not hard to deride, but each application of tolerance will be one of the avenues of possibility of discovery. True, the laws of subtlest conditions, while immutable, are quite elusive in the earthly strata. We observe that sometimes even a simple film gives an unexpectedly refined and sharp photograph. But this "sometime" is almost impossible to define with a meager earthly dictionary. Many times there have been mentioned unusually successful photographs of the usually invisible world. Attempts have been made to establish the most fitting conditions for the improvement of these processes. And, as a rule, instead of an improvement, certain subtlest possibilities were disturbed. Attempts were made to make experiments with utmost cleanliness in seemingly least polluted places, and they were accompanied by best thoughts and wishes. Yet, instead of a successful improvement, the results disappeared altogether. One had a strange feeling that the more primitive conditions had apparently brought better results. It means that these conditions contained some details still eluding the investigator, which could not be maintained even during formal better conditions. True, a very anti-infection vaccine, it seems, can hold a deadly infection; and water poured over one's hands to wash them may be poisonous. There are not a few absolutely counteractive conditions which arise even during proper observation. And yet how many still unfathomable, most subtle, conditions exist and govern processes of extreme importance.

It is necessary not only to perform observations, not only to cultivate within oneself the greatest measure of tolerance, not only to acquire magnanimity, but also from the very beginning to learn attentiveness. One should acknowledge with justice that in modern education too little time is given to attentiveness. And yet, in any field of endeavor, could an inattentive man be successful? The inattentive man first of all sinks into selfhood and egoism and gradually loses sensitiveness of receptivity toward his surroundings.

But if from an early age attentiveness is nurtured in most attractive forms, then an unlimited beautiful power of observation will develop under any conditions of life.

With every new experiment observation will mount a new turn of the spiral—still more subtle, still more elevating, still more penetrating. And the power of observation is a threshold of possibilities. A man who has attained perception of possibilities will never become prey to disappointment, because the fascination of new searches is the most captivating and high joy.

Peking, January 20, 1935.

KITÄB-UL-AGHĀNI

L ET us proclaim:
"This is the day of completion of the Testimony,
revelation of the Word, and coming of the Affirmation!

The Lord ordains that which bears good for you, and
wills that which will bring you closer to Him.

In the name of the Lord.

All glorious.

All high!"

"The purpose of these lines is to show that people cannot find the Sea of Knowledge if they do not renounce all
else.

"O earthly peoples, cast off all bonds if you wish to
reach the encampments prepared for you by the Lord and
to enter the kingdom erected by Him.

"Those who walk the Path of Faith and desire to drink
from the Chalice of Certainty must sanctify their soul and
purify it of all that is casual; that is, dismiss from the ears
human words; from the heart doubt born by the great
veils; from the mind worldly cares; from the eyes the sight
of passing things; and, relying upon the Lord and calling
to him constantly, they must follow the Path until they
become worthy to receive the Light of Divine Knowledge
and become holders of unlimited Blessings.

"For if a man takes it into his head to question the
Teachings of God and his Chosen Ones, with a partiality
toward words or actions of others like himself, be it the
learned or the ignorant, never will he enter the Garden
of Knowledge; never will he draw near to the Source of
Wisdom and the cognition of the one and only King; and

never will he attain the eternal encampment, nor will he partake of the Chalice of Approach and Weariness.

"Let us glance back at the past. Many people, from all walks of life, have awaited the appearance of God in a pure image, have prayed and hoped continuously for the waft of divine grace and for the Bridegroom to descend upon Earth from a mysterious cloud! And when the door of Bliss opened, and the clouds of Compassion rose, and the sun of Truth ascended to the Heaven of Power, no one believed in Him, and all averted their faces from His glance. Yet this was God's glance! This is revealed to us by sacred books. Can one explain now why those who were asking for and awaiting Him began to contradict Him so much that it could not even be expressed by pen or word? Not one of the pure manifestations, not one of the dawns of the Lord's Unity, could reveal itself without inciting controversies and hatred everywhere.

"It was said by the Lord: 'Oh, how miserable are these men! A prophet comes to them and they only ridicule him. Every one of those tribes plotted against the envoy sent to them so as to gain the upper hand over him. They entered into dispute with him in order to overthrow the truth through lies.'

"And the words, as if descending from clouds of Power and Heaven's Majesty, were so numerous that they all cannot be cognized. Read this chapter with attention, and ponder until you understand the missions of the Prophets and the resistance to which they were subjected by the evil one. Maybe then one could succeed in compelling people to shun the state of carelessness in which their soul is immersed and to direct it to the Nest of Unity and Knowledge, and could persuade them to drink the waters of Eternal Guidance and to acquire the fruits of knowledge of the Lord's greatness. That is the holy and eternal lot destined for pure souls, the Divine Bread descended from Heaven."

We have witnessed prayers in the desert. Among many touching images we cannot forget the solitary figure of a traveler who had spread his rug upon the pink sands and was bowed in prayer. Precisely this aloneness amidst endless reddening sands may be better remembered than Tamerlane's leaden seal itself.

In the desert it is not easy to picture numberless hordes, but a solitary figure is most evocative. "Flight into Egypt," "Hagar and Ishmael." These images, beyond the boundaries of centuries and peoples, are always convincing.

A white bone in the desert gleams from afar, a desert eagle, a wild horse—perhaps not wild but loose. The entire desert, precisely because of its barrenness, draws attention even to the smallest bush of tamarisk. And if you see in the desert a pigeon, what unusual pictures will be linked with this unexpected appearance! Certain words must ring out in the mountains, others demand the silky feather grass of the plains, a third kind are in need of the green forest's voice. So also are words which are born only in the desert. Toward the same God, toward the same central point, the words are calling out of the sands. If the heart knows how to welcome the words of caves and mountains, if it cherishes calls from beneath the sea and above the clouds, it will smile tenderly at the words of deserts. The heart will smile at that solitary traveler who, not in a snowstorm, whirlwind or cyclone, but in the sunset glow of hillocks has broken his journey, abandoned his earthly affairs, and invokes the highest.

Numerous are the designs of the sandy hillocks. Where is the old "silk highway"? Where is the path of the armed host? Where is the path of the envoys of peace? In the hieroglyphics of the desert, ways and footpaths are erased. Jalaluddin Rumi sang: "My place is placeless, my trace is traceless." Somewhere, also in the desert, stand the palaces of the Queen of Sheba. The Arabs guard them, but iron birds already trace the air above them. Then are the treasures no longer safe?

* * *

Vabissa ben Mabad narrates: "Once I stood before the Prophet. He divined that I had come to ask him what virtue is. He said: "Ask thy heart—virtue is that upon which rests the soul, upon which rests the heart. Sin is that which incites anxiety in the soul and raises storm in the breast, whatever people think about it. Place your hand upon your heart and ask it what gives it anxiety—and that you should not do."

Peking, January 25, 1935.

FAIRLY TALES

A NEW book of fairy tales, edited by V. N. Ivanov, including Vassilissa the Beautiful, the Grey Wolf and Ivan Czarevich, and The Pike's Command, has just been published in Harbin. It is a small book, costing only ten fen and hence very accessible. Long ago V. N. Ivanov had this excellent idea to publish in the most accessible form fine examples of Russian literature. In the fairy tales, in epic works, in the great creations of our poets and writers are truly to be found those pearls which should be brought to the folk consciousness without delay.

Take for example quotations from Gogol, Pushkin, Dostoevski, and from the half-forgotten, half-understood, profoundly thinking Slavophiles. You find here so much that is so urgently needed for the healing of people's hearts. Fragments from Gogol, or diary leaves from Dostoevski's writings, or thoughts of Leontiev, Khomyakov, and all those well-wishers of Russia—how ever-fresh are these thoughts, since they were born of great, self-sacrificing love and striving to help a people upon its difficult paths. And the thought about making these books popular is also good, because at present they have to penetrate into the most obscure and remote places, where the hearts of the scattered, oppressed, and homeless are atremble in expectation and still aglow with great love for construction.

In one month recently, besides the above-mentioned fairy tales there were published also eight popular Russian fairy tales: The Wolf, The Bear, Little Sister-Fox, She-Goat and Kids, The Crane and the Heron, The Tomcat and the Rooster, The Fly, The Turnip; and on the 20th of January there came out *The Greatcoat*, by Gogol—one of the most unusually penetrating, although not always understood, works of the great master.

If only the Russian people could make an effort to throw off all accumulated husks and shagginess and come together again in labor! This one thought alone about popular editions of the pearls of folk consciousness would help much toward mutual understanding.

And not only in Russian is there a need and demand for these little books. They should be published in different languages in similar popular editions. In other languages also they should penetrate into the masses. They should reach there where a thick, expensive book will not. Let these pearls become completely attainable and reach even the most remote farms, the farthest islands, huts, where most of the time every printed word is so eagerly awaited. At a time when we may think that a great deal has already become accessible and understood, reality often tells us quite a different story.

We personally have seen little children picking the colored pictures off matchboxes. We know that for any crumpled illustrated page of a newspaper people are ready to exchange provisions, just so they can adorn a wall in their hut with it, and, if possible, also read it. I say "if possible" not as a reproach about someone's illiteracy, but I refer to literacy in many languages, and in all these languages one should speak about the beautiful.

Thoughts ancient and new should be given to a majority among all the different peoples, because they all speak about the very same—that which is not ancient and not new, but eternal. Translate our fairy tales and epics into many different Western and Eastern tongues, and how many hearts will rejoice, sensing that which is close to them!

Take the story about Vassilissa the Beautiful, which is based upon the tales about teraphim; and the Grey Wolf, who changes his image by throwing himself upon the ground; and the Pike, whose thought and will cause objects to move and act. All this will be understood by a Hindu, an Arab, a Chinese, and one more bridge of cordial mutual understanding, hearty, ethereal, yet firm will be woven. Tell about the City of Kitej, and a Breton shepherd will nod his head in understanding. Read the *Song of Igor* in the Scandinavian countries, or tell about werewolves in distant Assam, or about Antaeus in Greece, and everywhere one's own understanding will be augmented. And how many hearts among different peoples will be atremble in understanding the images of Gogol; and how startling may be the understanding evoked by the pages of Dostoevski's *Diary*. But, indeed, one should not rely upon expensive editions of many volumes, but should issue most popular ones. For this popularity one should adopt the best means; hence, fairy tales can become narratives, and narratives will delineate the eternal epic.

Likewise, let us not overlook the fact that popular fragments of the treasures of Eastern and Western wisdom must be issued also in Russian. And they must be given in an attractive, ringing translation akin to the Russian language. I recall how beautifully Baltrushaitis translated a song of Tagore; how inimitably Balmont gave us the resounding forms and images of the best foreign poets; and, last but not least, the *Bhagavad Gita* sounds beautiful, precisely in Russian—perhaps even better than in some other Western languages. And the *Edda* and the *Kalevala*, and *Hiawatha*, and the *Panchatantra* yield excellently to the sonorous and elastic Russian language.

But all that was hitherto published was either in a large expensive edition of many thousands or in luxurious books. Yet all this beauty must be given broadly to all peoples, and sound and color must be united in the resounding work. Also icon images must be given broadly to the people, and in really artistic, even if in popular, reproductions. Their true beauty is known to but a few. And because of ignorance and lack of knowledge things of real value may be censured. Chiefly, accessibility is now needed everywhere for everyone.

Humanity has become impoverished and has grown

spiritually poor. Therefore, we so rejoice in seeing each beautiful publication made accessible. Thus, a short legend will become a story, and out of a story will again grow a fairy tale.

Life is a beautiful fairy tale.

Peking, January 30, 1935.

SEROV

A QUARTER of a century has passed since Valentin Alexandrovich left us. So much has happened, so many things have come and gone during this time, but the image of Serov stands out, fresh and important, not only in the history of art but in the minds of all who knew him in life.

Precisely in the importance of that image is contained that convincingness which accompanied his creativeness and his life. It was Serov who used to say, "No matter what a man is, at least once in his life he will have to show his true passport." And Serov's real passport was known to all his friends. His sincerity and honesty became proverbial; he truly followed firmly the dictates of his heart. If he did not like something, it was shown even in his glance. But if he was convinced of something and sensed devotion, he was not afraid to express his conviction in word and deed.

The same sincerity and thoroughness was revealed in all his work. Even in his sketches, seemingly carelessly drawn, one could observe the complete inner attentiveness, refinement, and depth with which his entire being lived and breathed. His taciturnity was the result of his watchfulness. Many a time, after a long silence, he performed some action that indicated how attentively he had followed all that had been taking place.

He rarely participated in any gatherings. For the most part he was silent, but his inner conviction greatly influenced a decision. It took him an extraordinarily long time to paint a portrait. Not infrequently he demanded many sittings even for a drawing. The same stern penetration which guided him through life demanded his utmost attention, in order that he might bring out all that was most characteristic.

Let us recall some of his portraits, beginning with the unforgettable girl in the Tretyakov Gallery. Remember Mr. and Mrs. Hirschman, Morosov, Rimski-Korsakov, the portrait of the Czar in a military tunic, with remarkably painted eyes. I was told that after the revolution this very portrait, mutilated, with the eyes cut out, was brought to our school of the Society for the Encouragement of Arts, having been picked up by somebody on the square of the Winter Palace. Were the eyes cut out because they were painted so well? Such cruelty! Were some other portraits by Serov spared? Often the destiny of the treasures in private collections was so unspeakable. One may also justifiably worry about the destiny of a huge mural curtain which Serov painted for Diaghilev. He painted this mural not in the simple way such decor is usually done, but with the greatest care, as if it were a fresco. Could it happen that amidst outworn theatrical canvases this mural, unusual for Serov, will also be found among the discards? I recall how my "Battle of Kerjenetz" and "Polovetzky Camp," suffered indescribable vicissitudes because of constant transportation. I do not know where this mural by Serov could be at present. I only know that if it has not been mutilated during cruel wanderings, its place should be in one of the best museums.

It is instructive to observe that in his early portraits (for example that characteristic one of the girl in the Tretyakov Gallery), Serov, without changing his ideals, forged ahead as if upon the crest of a wave—in all his quests as well as in his technique. I remember his later works, "The Rape of Europa" and "Pavlova," and his penetrating works of the epoch of Peter the Great. He always remained himself, yet he spoke the language of contemporary life. These were not passing imitations, because there could not be any imitative quality in his nature. He always remained original and true to his heart. He did not imitate, but used a language understandable to all. Quite naturally, at times he searched for new materials. I remember his coming for advice about a new priming for canvas, and about the so-called Wurms and Munich colors, which I liked greatly at that time.

Now, with passing years, the figure of Serov becomes more and more important in the history of Russian art. In the "Mir Iskusstva" group the presence of Serov gave unusual prestige to the entire structure. If there were arbiters of elegance, then Serov was always an arbiter of artistic honesty.

In recalling his participation on the Board of the Tretyakov Gallery, one may definitely say that he was most impartial, a just and stern member of that Board. The period of his participation in the affairs of the Gallery remains especially valuable, and his insistence upon impartiality and thoroughness in its selections influenced the subsequent conduct of its affairs.

There was no casualness in the actions of Serov. This man, self-contained, silent, with occasional piercing side glances, knew what he was doing. And he accomplished creative, honest, beautiful work in the history of Russian art. Unchanging in his heart, Serov also changed little outwardly. I have a sketch by Repin of Serov in his youth. It is one of Repin's character drawings, made lovingly and, as it were, seeing through the essence of the impressive face. The same introspection, the same penetrative eye, the very same realization of creativeness as was always present throughout the entire life of Serov.

How fine it is that alongside Surikov, Repin, Vasnetzov, Nesterov, Kuinji, we had Serov, glowing like a beautiful precious stone in the necklace of invaluable Russian art.

Peking, January 31, 1935.

THE WINGED PLAGUE

IN San Gimignano we were present when a chamber in a church was opened which had been sealed after one of the plague outbreaks during the Middle Ages. In this beautiful city of towers nothing now reminded one about the Black Plague. It was known, according to calculations, that the danger of plague infection had disappeared and that it was safe to open the chamber. But, naturally, people were still afraid, and only a few dared to enter this high hall, decorated with Gozzoli frescoes. Indeed, the sealing of that chamber primarily had beneficially affected the preservation of the frescoes themselves. No one had thought of cleaning, washing, or restoring them.

Stories about the plague were revived with especial agitation when news of this sealed chamber became known. Among other appellations given to the plague long ago, it was for some reason called "winged." Apparently in this manner the suddenness of the appearance of this epidemic was stressed. Actually, the terrible Black Death usually flared up suddenly, without any apparent cause. Then, after exhausting its wrath, it flew further and again alighted unexpectedly in a new place, amidst unlooked-for conditions. In the final analysis, all the so-called epidemics always flared up without any previous local symptoms.

For some reason, they usually flared up especially strongly where they were not supposed to be. And their very disappearance, although conditioned by special measures was, as it were, dependent upon some other invisible factors.

Tales and beliefs of the remote past aside for the moment, the following relates something which took place in present times. "An American biologist, Bernard E. Proctor, undertook a series of experiments to establish the height above Earth at which all life ceases to exist. Proctor engaged an American army flier who specialized in flying at high altitudes. To one wing of the aeroplane there was fastened a pipe divided in the middle by a sheet of greased paper. At the speed of the aeroplane—250 kilometers an hour—the air rushed with great force into the pipe, whereupon the greased paper played the role of a filter, capturing all microorganisms.

"After each flight the paper filter was delivered to the laboratory of Prof. Proctor where it was subjected to a careful bacteriological analysis. As a result of forty flights at an altitude of 5,000 meters it was established that in these strata of air there exist not less than twenty-nine species of various kinds of microorganisms, bacteria, bairm fungi, etc., and also the spores and seeds of plants.

"Above 5,000 meters the number of species diminishes, but bacteria and fungi are found in great quantities up to 7,000 meters. Higher, between seven and ten kilometers, the filter retains only a few kinds of bacteria, which, nevertheless, endure excellently the rarefaction of air and likewise the low temperature of the region just below the stratosphere. The experiments were not performed at a height above ten kilometers, but the graph drawn by Prof. Proctor on the basis of the material obtained permits the conjecture that life continues also in the stratosphere itself.

"As a result of these experiments Prof. Proctor came to a curious and unexpected conclusion: he pointed out the role which could be played by storms and cyclones in spreading infectious diseases. A whirlwind which circulates over a locality stricken by an epidemic is capable of catching up and carrying away myriads of microbes. And they, in turn, following the aerial currents of the upper strata of the atmosphere, could travel hundreds and thousands of kilometers. (In this way the volcanic dust cast out during the eruption of Krakatoa was carried to Europe.)

Thus the medieval concept about the 'winged plague' acquires, as it were, the character of a scientific theory.

"Prof. Proctor believes that many epidemics which flare up suddenly over vast territory have precisely this origin."

Here once again we learn to what an extent cosmic conditions are linked with the way of human life. Once again we are shown how from unexpected (according to human understanding) regions there may come sinister as well as healing messages. The ancient peoples, while not knowing how to employ more detailed formulas, characterized, according to their essence, such cosmo-human manifestations rather expressively. The winged flight of the epidemic remains also at present, as we see, a rather apt description. Upon unknown wings dangerous particles are being carried. Upon some other wings salvation comes flying. It would seem fitting to hope that the scientists also will seize upon the possibility of healing epidemics.

One has occasionally heard about whole islands and parts of continents seemingly doomed to inevitable sinking. With exact figures in their possession the scientists prove that either some vast submarine gorges must be filled up or whole verdant islands will sink into these abysses. If the Black Plague and its sinister allies are winged, then similarly the subterranean and submarine processes threaten incalculable catastrophes. True, it will be explained that all such dangers may manifest only after many millions of years. We will be reminded about the listener who, in the course of such a lecture, once asked the scientist whether the end of the world was to come in one or in two billions of years. And upon being told that it might be two billions, he breathed more easily. Such hypotheses are naturally soothing for humanity. But if we examine certain accounts of earthquakes, the same scientists will tell us that dates calculated in billions of years may have to undergo considerable revisions. Thus, if even the plague was called winged, then what appellations could be applied to other, no less vigorous, natural processes?

In any event, if the term *winged flight* was applicable to

such dark messengers, then a still greater mobility and salubrity must be demanded for the restoration of health. The same records of antiquity enumerate many islands which undoubtedly at one time existed and then disappeared, and they also tell us in foreboding language about the causes of these disappearances. Usually these disappearances are ascribed to an upsurge of human impiety or pride, or excessive presumption. In these legends people sought to express in their own way the link between the human spirit and cosmic manifestations. Verily, this link is strong, and, significantly, among the forthcoming tasks of science lies the investigation of thought.

Peking, February 2, 1935.

INEXHAUSTIBILITY

CAN it be exhausted? Can it be drained? On the physical plane everything can be exhausted, but on the spiritual plane at the base of everything lies inexhaustibility. And it is by this measure that the two planes are primarily divided. When we are told that something has become exhausted, we know that this pertains to purely exterior physical conditions.

A creator may imagine that his creativeness is at an end, but of course this will be untrue. Simply, there are, or there have arisen, some factors which have impeded creativeness. Perhaps something has taken place that harms the free flow of creativeness. But in itself, creativeness when once called into action is inexhaustible, just as psychic energy, as such, is ever-flowing and invincible.

In the confused life of today this simple fact at times must be remembered. People insist that they have become tired, and they suggest to themselves that their creativeness has become exhausted. Repeating in various terms about difficulties, they actually enwrap themselves in a veritable cobweb. Space is actually filled with a multitude of harmful cross-currents. They can influence the physical side of a manifestation. But to people who are accustomed to build everything within physical bounds it seems that these outer intrusions kill the very essence of their psychic energy. Yet this very expression will often seem to be something indefinable, because people up to now seldom have pondered over this fundamental blessed energy, which when realized is inexhaustible and ever-present.

In general, the question of tangibility is very unclear when discussed in human society. One repeatedly hears how at times a person gives quite definite data, but his listeners, having a lax, untrained faculty of attention, are unable to grasp them, and afterward insist that they have been given something abstract that could not be applied. I have often been a witness when someone gave precise information founded on facts, which evoked the response, "Can't we have something to the point, more definite?" Such questions only show that the interlocutor had no intention of accepting what was said to him; he wanted to hear only that which for some reason he expected. And under such autosuggestion he often was unable to appreciate all the precise facts told to him. How often people want to hear not that which is, but that which they will be pleased to hear. "Verily, he is deaf who does not want to hear!"

The desire not to listen and not to see not only gives rise to great injustice but often almost amounts to spiritual suicide. A person may assure himself to such an extent that he is unable to do something, and to such an extent he may suppress his basic energy that he really falls under the sway of all outer physical and psychic intrusions.

Everyone has heard that persons with so-called nervous diseases often cannot cross a street, or approach a window, and finally become prey to the horrors of suspicion. If one could trace how these fatal symptoms began, one would always find an insignificant, often hardly perceptible, suppression of psychic energy. At times it may be caused indirectly and may begin with something quite accidental.

Precisely such accidents could have been easily avoided if attentiveness to everything around one had been developed. This attentiveness would have helped one to notice that the basic energy is inexhaustible. This simple and clear realization would have saved many from the abyss of discouragement and despair. Thus, a person who suffers from insomnia may often find the cause of it in the most real, external condition. Likewise, a man must understand why there is an old saying that if it is difficult to make oneself think, it is still more difficult to abstain from thinking.

When man extinguishes his enthusiasm, he does so because of some purely external conditions. If, with all attentiveness, he would realize how accidental and ephemeral are these circumstances, he would chase them away, like an annoying fly. But children are not taught attentiveness—either at school, or in the family—and yet, later on, one is surprised at why "one cannot see the forest for the trees." But, then, does one often speak in the family circle about the fire of the heart, about inspiration, about enthusiasm? Too often the family gathering is confined only to condemnation and mutual malicious criticism. Nevertheless, from ancient times, from everywhere, calls and commands reach us to preserve in purity the wells of inspiration and creativeness—as in thought, so in action.

"Raj-Agni—thus was called that Fire which you call enthusiasm. Truly this is a beautiful and powerful fire, which purifies all the surrounding space. Constructive thought is nurtured by this fire. Magnanimous thought grows in the silvery light of the Fire of Raj-Agni. Help to the near ones flows from the same source. There are no bounds, no limitations, for the wings radiant with Raj-Agni. Do not think that this fire can be kindled in an evil heart. One must develop in oneself the ability to call forth the source of such transport. First you must develop in yourself the assurance that you offer your heart to the Great Service. Then you should reflect that the glory of the works is not your own, but belongs to the Hierarchy of Light. Then it is possible to be uplifted by the infinitude of Hierarchy and to affirm oneself in the heroic achievement needed for all worlds. Thus, not for oneself, but in the Great Service is Raj-Agni kindled. Understand that the Fiery World cannot stand without this Fire."

Peking, February 3, 1935.

STEADFASTNESS

I RECALL unforgettable episode from my first exhibition in America. In one of the large cities a wealthy patron of art arranged a festive dinner in my honor. Everything was luxurious and on a large scale, and the best people of the city were present. As usual, many speeches were delivered. The host and hostess, both already grey-haired, heartily and cordially entertained the guests. Everything was magnificently arranged, and the hostess drew my attention to the rooms, which were decorated in blue and purple flowers, and said, "It is precisely these shades that I love so much in your paintings."

After dinner one of the lady guests present said to me, "This is indeed a remarkable reception," and added confidentially, "probably this is the last dinner in this house."

I looked at my companion in amazement and she, lowering her voice, explained, "Don't you know that our host is absolutely ruined and only yesterday he lost his last three millions?"

Naturally I was shocked. But the lady added, "Of course, it is not easy for him, especially considering his age. He is already seventy-four."

The incongruity of this revelation with the calmness of the host and hostess was amazing. After this conversation I began to take especial interest in their fate. Three months after this dinner they moved to their former garage. It seemed that everything was lost, but after three years this businessman was again a millionaire and again lived in his former palatial home.

When I spoke to his friends about my surprise as to why his numerous friends and, after all, the city itself to which he had given so much had not offered to help him, I was told, "First of all, he would not have accepted any help, and secondly, he is used to such storms in life."

This last conversation took place in a large club where, near tall windows, in easy chairs, many distinguished members were sitting, reading newspapers and talking. My companion, pointing to them, said, "These are all millionaires. Ask how often every one of them ceased to be a millionaire and then became one again."

And the club members continued to read quietly and to chat cheerfully, as if no troubles ever disturbed them. I asked my friend how he explained this. He shrugged his shoulders and replied with one word, "Steadfastness."

Verily, the concept of steadfastness should be greatly stressed, among other basic principles of life. Courage is one, a second is goodwill and magnanimity. A third is desire to work. A fourth is perseverance and inexhaustibility. A fifth is enthusiasm and optimism. But among all these foundations, and also many other luminous affirmations so greatly needed, steadfastness always remains as something apart, irreplaceable, providing a firm basis for progress.

Steadfastness issues from true equilibrium. Such equilibrium is not a heartless calculation, neither is it a despising of the surroundings, or conceit, or selfishness. Steadfastness always stands in relation to responsibility and a sense of duty. Steadfastness will not be allured, or slip or waver. Those who advance firmly to the very end are truly steadfast.

In our days of confusion, of many disillusions, of narrow distrust, the basic quality of steadfastness is especially blessed. When people so easily become unworthily panic-stricken, only a steadfast person can provide healthy understanding and can thus save many from the horror of falling into chaos. When people try to convince themselves of all sorts of antiquated mirages, only a firm person can decide in his heart where there is a safe way out. When people fall into such madness that even a short squall appears to them like an endless storm, then only steadfastness will remind them about true co-measurement.

Perhaps someone will say that steadfastness is nothing other than common sense. But it will be more correct to say that from common sense steadfastness is born. The quality of steadfastness is already an expression of reality. Steadfastness is required precisely here on the earthly plane where there are so many circumstances against which one has to hold out. Therefore, it is so useful, amidst many concepts of good will, cooperation, and progress to perceive the meaning and value of steadfastness. Not without reason people always emphasize with especial respect how a person steadfastly withstood various attacks, strain, and unexpected blows. In such cases vigilance and presence of mind are stressed, but steadfastness will also be acclaimed as something positive, based upon firm realization.

As an example of steadfastness and firmness, I recall a story I heard in San Francisco. A foreigner had arrived. Apparently he was wealthy. He was received everywhere in society. He acquired many friends. He won the reputation of being a good, kindhearted, and rich friend. Once he asked his self-proclaimed new friends to lend him ten thousand dollars for a new business. Something curious, though quite usual, happened. All these friends found sufficient reasons to refuse or evade his request. More than that, everywhere people showed alienation and coldness toward him. Then this foreigner went to visit another person who from the very beginning had been rather cool toward him. He explained his project and asked for a loan of ten thousand dollars. This time the checkbook appeared on the table at once and the required amount was handed over to him. The next day the foreigner again came to see the same person. The latter asked, "What has happened, did you miscalculate the amount? Perhaps you need more?"

But the foreigner took the check from his pocket and, returning it to the giver, said, "No, I need no money. What I need is a partner, and I invite you to join me."

And to all the other so-called friends, who began again to return most amiably, the foreigner said, "You have fed me with your dinners. Remember, my table is always ready to serve you." (Mr. L. in San Francisco remembered this story.)

How many instructive experiences are presented by life itself! Imagination is nothing but recollection.

Peking, February 6, 1935

EPIDEMICS

IN the history of mankind, epidemics of madness present a particularly curious page. In addition to many other kinds of contagions, epidemics of madness frequently appeared upon various continents. Whole countries suffered from the intrusion of malicious ideas into various domains of life. Naturally, these epidemics broke out especially frequently in the spheres of religion, superstition, and within the bounds of official suspiciousness.

If we now glance back over the pages of all the religious martyrdoms, bringing sinister recollections of the Inquisition and various mass-madnesses, a not exaggerated picture of a true epidemic will emerge quite clearly. Just as any epidemic, this malady of madness flared up suddenly, seemingly from a small beginning, and grew with extraordinary speed into most violent forms. We are reminded of the various persecutions of "witches," which are even hard to believe. In the recent writings of Dr. Lévi-Valency several curious details are related which remind one again of the possibility of an epidemic of madness.

The doctor tells us: "In ancient times the madmen complained that the devil was anxious to harm their soul and body; they prophesied, and blasphemed.

"The insane people today," says Dr. Lévi-Valency, "rave about the Stavisky affair, or that of Prence, propose to reform the state, etc. A few years ago, at the height of the housing crisis, many sick people complained that they were being put out of their apartments. Now the housing crisis is passed, but mass unemployment has begun. And the insane repeatedly insist that they are being deprived of their work, their livelihood, their unemployment compensation. In the ravings of fevered brains plots of the Masons and of the Sûreté are constantly mentioned." Dr. Lévi-Valency tells about a bank clerk forty-four years old, who complained that he was "being persecuted by the Jews and the powerful foreign syndicates who conspired to treat him like Prence. . . . He was always followed by two individuals—a one-armed man and a police agent with the 'face of a murderer.' His wife was also in danger. . . .

"A thirteen-year-old boy is in the grip of a mania of persecution. He is convinced that he was involved in the Stavisky affair and that the 'Mafia' is going to put him out of the way."

True, all these data of the doctor are fragmentary and extrinsic. Of course, his colleagues, the psychiatrists, could add to those he has cited a multitude of other examples. The investigators must continue with observations not only within the walls of the hospitals. They must observe broadly throughout the life of today. After all, the majority of madmen do not get into hospitals. They remain at large, often occupying very responsible posts. In order to evoke medical supervision, repeated and quite striking manifestations are needed. And how many mad actions take place while the madman is regarded as fully responsible for his actions and enjoys complete freedom to commit many crimes!

From the historical point of view this problem is quite complicated. Even statesmen in high positions and heads of governments, while still occupying their posts, have been known to become subject to acute madness. In spite of all attempts to hide the fact, some such attacks became so apparent that the madmen by one means or another were removed from their official activities; and then it could no longer be kept secret that they had been ill for some time before.

One may ask what is to be done with all the decrees, dispositions, and resolutions which were made during the period of madness. It means that the state and public life of whole countries, perhaps even for a lengthy period, was invaded by madness. The hand of a madman continued to perform actions while he was in an obviously sick state of mind. Should such actions be accepted as authoritative? This is a very weighty question which is avoided in every way by jurists.

In the final analysis it cannot be answered. Let us recall even those cases of madness of public officials which have been revealed in our time. Who could accurately determine precisely when this madness, which was so obvious at the end, began? How many times, because of a so-called acute nervous breakdown were these officials hastily offered a vacation, and later appeared in some special hospital? Yet, prior to the moment of this leave-taking or resignation a great deal had taken place.

Is there always an examination of that which was enacted during the time of the sick condition? Cases are known wherein the heads of governments acted when already in a state of complete insanity. What, then, should be done with those official governmental acts sanctioned by madmen? Many such deplorable actions are known through the records of history.

At present, Dr. Lévi-Valency's raising the question of epidemics of madness is quite timely. People poisoned by all kinds of unhealthy conditions of life become subject especially easily to various insane manias.

We do not know at all how the many new energies currently being evoked into action react upon psychic excitement. Such fields of tension cannot be neutral; they must react somehow, but this "somehow" is seen at present as an especially large "unknown."

In any case, one should welcome the voices of scientists, physicians, and, in this case, psychiatrists, whose help is urgently needed for examination of the confusion of minds now rampant in the world.

If attentive observers would not be reluctant to relate to physicians all sorts of unusual manifestations noted by them, the results might be useful. Such extraneous information could impel the thought of an investigator toward possibilities of great benefit.

At present many new forms of epidemics occur. Especially exasperating is influenza, which sometimes becomes a form of pulmonary plague. Also many psychoses are developing—to an unprecedented degree.

Here is a broad field for undeferrable action by all investigators. Even the brief and specific annotations of history could also lead to many useful deliberations.

Peking, February 12, 1935.

ARTISTS

THE artist Constantin Korovin now lives in Paris. How many thoughts pertaining to Russian national painting are linked with this name! It is remembered by many as the name of a magnificent designer, the executer of most diverse theatrical productions. But this is only a part of the essence of Korovin's art. Most important was his original gift of imbuing his art with national feeling. He is verily a Russian artist, a Muscovite, not one having a "Moscow quality" but one encompassing the span of all Russia. Observing the rich range of his paintings, we see in them that true Russian value which delights us all in the works of Surikov, Ryabushkin, Nesterov, and Appolinary Vasnetzov.

And a chronicler of the history of Russian culture will never discard the names of these great artists. It is of no importance that they varied in temperament. But it is important that they thought about and glorified the concepts of great Russia, each in his own way. It is an invaluable fact that they have created in the history of Russian painting a beautiful necklace which will be remembered by every foreigner who wishes to learn about true Russia.

There are many Russian artists. Many of the best of them were drawn to Paris. Malyavin, Alexander Benois, Yakovlev, Somov, and Grigoriev who came there from time to time—a whole family, covering one of the best pages in the history of Russian art. Now, a very meaningful date is approaching—the 35th anniversary of the International Exposition in Paris, which was of such significance for Russian art.

Everyone remembers a wonderful mural by Korovin at

this exhibition and the exultation evoked by the creative power of Malyavin. Thirty years later many a seed sprouted that had been sown by this group of Russian artists.

There have always been many Russians in Paris, and they passed through both good and bad times. At times they had easy periods, but then again there would be nothing but crisis after crisis. Through all these fluctuations, through the storm of diversified opinions, many times did the statesmen of France definitely mention Russian art as one of the indisputable magnets which forged the former Franco-Russian understanding. Diaghilev—his ballet, his opera! And Chaliapin! Not just theatrical undertakings, these were the most wonderful envoys, Russian messengers, who forever strengthened a deep, welcoming respect for unforgettable Russia.

And now, will foreigners ever think of Russian music without recalling the names of Moussorgsky, Rimski-Korsakov, and without our renowned Stravinsky and Prokofiev who are living now in Paris?

And all those writers, philosophers, scientists! They rose like luminous milestones, leading out of the past into the enlightened future! In Europe who does not know at present the names of Merezhkovski, Remisov, Bunin, Aldanov, Grebenstshikoff? They are known, translated and valued. One is aware not only of the great names of the past—Pushkin, Tolstoy, Dostoevski, Gogol, Turgenev— but also of the presently living and creating renowned Russian writers. Who does not know Berdyaev or Lossky? Could international conventions take place without Taube or Nolde?

Each time, upon entering the path of enumeration of Russian names, one feels all the weight of the impossibility of mentioning the many who have made a valuable contribution to Russian culture.

I mention these names not only for the sake of enumeration, but to point again to the unusual envoys of Russian culture, through whom, even amidst upheavals, world appreciation and understanding of Russia became strongly affirmed.

Russian artists as banner-bearers in all domains of creation are recognized and accepted in foreign opinion.

It was sad to read recently that life again has become hard for the Russians in France. We believe that this is only a passing wave. There are so many unforgettable testimonies to the fact that everything Russian always has been understood precisely in France.

All the proclamations of rapture before Russian art were not casual. And what could enter the consciousness more strongly and firmly than the understanding of creativeness! If the importance of a certain creativity has been evaluated, this does not mean a passing infatuation; recorded appreciations of culture do not glide along dubiously, they become strong cornerstones. Similarly, international ties of friendship are forged through creativeness. Since long ago Russians have heartily evaluated and revered the treasures of great French culture. In Russia the French language could almost have been called the state language. French writers were translated into Russian, and were read and repeatedly quoted. In Russia, French painting and sculpture were collected and preserved with solicitude. Until recently, French works in painting and the theater have especially attracted the Russian heart. And since thirty-five years ago, at which time France became more intimately acquainted with Russian art, many heartfelt tokens of mutual understanding have been manifested.

I recall with what hearty feeling French exhibitions were organized in Petersburg. And I will also not forget the brilliant evaluations of Russian art events in Paris by the French critics. All this is unforgettable and unalterable.

No matter what different paths the travelers take, if they start out under one blessing they will meet joyously at the crossroads.

It was sad to read about the difficult life of the Russians in France. In the final analysis it is difficult now for all, and everywhere. Humanity, entering a great crisis, has become crowded and is jostling on the crossroads, but the crossroads is not the road. And the wayfarers who follow one path cannot remain in ignorance.

I know that between great France and great Russia bonds of unity have been woven through great creativeness. And, as bearers of banners of light of both nations, the artists in all fields of creativeness will proclaim the guarantee of hearty understanding, invincible values, and the path to the future.

Great faith is laid into creativeness. Since ancient times the paths of art have been sanctified. On these paths mutual understanding and friendship remain steadfast.

Peking, February 18, 1935.

TACTICA ADVERSA

GENGHIS Khan often resorted to a feigned retreat in order to lure the enemy into pursuit, and then he would use his own reserves to attack the enemy much more easily in the rear, so it is related. Also it is told that the tireless conqueror sometimes set fire to the steppe in order to speed up the movement of his troops. It is quite probable that the tales about the varied military tactics of the great conqueror are true. At any rate, in his long marches Genghis Khan apparently used the most diversified strategy, continually surprising his enemies.

A desire to preserve a healthy austerity in daily life was also attributed to him, it being said that he ordered his ministers to tear their expensive silken garments on brambles so as to demonstrate the impracticality of such attire. Similarly, he was said to have simulated a sickness contracted from imported beverages, in order to attract the population to local milk products.

In ancient history one can find many examples of the most unusual *tactica adversa* which produced very convincing results.

* * *

In a battle a soldier cannot discern just when he is being subjected to the greatest danger. At the time of a collision it is impossible to perceive just what situation was precisely the most dangerous or the most beneficial. Some kind of blow may have saved one from a still stronger blow. A fallen horse by its fall may have warded off sudden death. A casual shout perhaps caused one to turn around and thus avoid a deadly missile. Therefore, the ancient wisdom was so correct which directed attention to the final result as the effect of all that had happened before.

Though it may be impossible to establish the end by premeditation, the end may reveal the reason for the molding of that which preceded. For these observations a tested keenness is needed. But also needed is knowledge of just what *tactica adversa* is. This factor, which worked so salutarily in many historic events, often remains unnoticed. True, people like to repeat, "There would not be good fortune if misfortune did not help," but in this saying there is presupposed some kind of accidental misfortune. Yet tactica adversa knows no misfortunes. It knows only coordinated actions which are difficult to examine when in close proximity.

Every traveler knows how clear and beautiful is a snowy peak seen at a distance, and how in the steep dangerous approaches to it this aspect is lost. Similarly, in judging events it is difficult to survey something at close range. But *tactica adversa* proclaims with reassurance that wherever there is a pure fiery striving, there, also, all accompanying manifestations will become well coordinated. But much refined consciousness must be applied in order to evaluate the unusual actions of *tactica adversa*. True invincibility will always be concomitant with utmost resourcefulness. People cannot discern the paths leading upward and therefore must apply all sensitivity in resourcefulness and mobility.

Every active worker knows the value of mobility. How far removed is this true mobility from the petty bustle which only impedes proper movement. When an active worker is asked what his direction will be, he will answer that he may not know all the turns in advance, but he has firmly known the goal from the hour he set forth. Thus, no "surprises" on the path can perturb a true worker. He has already understood that there will be an element of usefulness in all that happens.

He also knows that certain counteractions that are met

on the way must be brought to an extremity of opposition, for only then will their meaning become clear and a panacea can be found. Every absurd sally reveals a greater evidence of absurdity when one allows it to roll to the very end. Then all the abominable *Infusoria* unfold, and even very uninformed spectators will understand the degree of ugliness.

How many times an experienced leader, when able to arrest a flow of absurdity, has restrained his co-workers, saying, "Let it roll on to the end." An experienced leader calls up his reserves only after the necessary measures have been carried out. What kind of leader would he be if he were to call for maximum help prematurely? The enemy would not yet be fully manifested. The enemy forces would not have reached their utmost tension, and the reserve troops would thus be uselessly spent. Therefore, *tactica adversa* knows, first of all, the value of prudence.

An inexperienced onlooker may exclaim, "Stop! This is absurd!" But an experienced worker will correct him, "This is not only absurd but also ugly. Wait a minute and you yourself will perceive an intolerable degree of ugliness and ignorance which will devour itself."

The history of many nations constantly, and with reason, reiterates a variety of manifestations of *tactica adversa*. These reiterations permit us to remember examples of the means of conquest available in adverse action. People say: "Give a thief enough rope and he will hang himself," or "Do not wave, do not wave, he will enter of his own accord." And it is the very same folk wisdom which prescribes that the rope should be given and predicts that the voluntary entrance will take place—not carelessly but, on the contrary, with full alertness and care.

How often the most benevolent counsels speak about the defeat of darkness. This means that a defeat must take place; therefore, *tactica adversa* should be a means employed in battle, but in no way a permissible inactivity. When people say, "Give a thief rope and he'll hang himself," in this saying there is foreseen a whole chain of actions. The thief must be detected, the rope must be at hand, it must be long enough, and it must be given. And the thief himself must also perform an action, for he must eventually hang himself with that rope.

History does not tell how Judas found his rope. It may be surmised that he found it in some special way, because his unparalleled crime brought him to self-destruction. Observe and you will see how crime defeats itself. There are many opportunities to write about diverse ways of defeating crime. Indeed, in this multiformity of self-retaliation there is contained an unusual subtlety of the law.

We speak here about justice; but *tactica adversa* abides near this concept, and, through its often unfettered reactions, helps to reveal the full extent of evil. For construction a purified place is needed. Every builder is, first of all, engrossed with thought about the ground on which the foundation rests. He will make sure that there are no cracks and dangerous crevices. By the best measures he will divert eroding waters and, first of all, fill up all cracks.

When a structure is being erected, one rarely pictures the extent of the underground work done for the support of the walls and towers. Before considering the upper structure the builder will take into account any unforeseen developments. If water appears, he will not begin to cover it at once with clay soil, but will carefully observe what are the ultimate quantities of the moisture in the area affected and determine the source. We know how even urgent structures were often held up until the causes of underground surprises were rectified.

"Blessed be the obstacles, through them we grow." He who said this knew all the dimensions of the obstacles, and could, because of his experience, evaluate them and apply them for the Common Good. Construction in the name of good is untiring, careful, solicitous. What beauty is contained in this inexhaustible creativeness!

Peking, February 20, 1935.

OEUVRE

OEUVRE is a clear and at the same time almost untranslatable word. One could say "creation," but still that connotation in which *oeuvre* issued from the French literature remains to be understood.

People are accustomed to judge art in all its manifestations rather light-mindedly. Someone has read two poems and is prepared to judge a poet. Someone saw three or four paintings, or reproductions of the paintings, and is ready to judge the artist. One novel alone suffices to define the author. One book of essays is sufficient for making an irrevocable decision while having a cup of tea.

The proverbial "cup of tea" so often mentioned in works of literature does not entail any obligations. Possibly, also, the opinions uttered at the tea table should not be binding, and yet they often do have profound results. In these conversations, the "cup of tea" people do not stop to think that separate works are only petals of the entire *oeuvre*. It is not likely that an experienced gardener or a botanist would presume to judge the whole plant from one petal of a flower.

Everyone has had occasion to hear very definite judgments about authors from people who in reality have read but one volume of the works of that author. And how often are judgments pronounced solely on the basis of newspaper reviews without the trouble being taken even to read that which was criticized. Then, truly, for the appreciation of a whole creative work, no matter to what realm it belongs, the concept of *oeuvre* must be brought out particularly clearly. In order to form a just opinion of any author, not only is an adequate acquaintance with the entire scope of his creativeness needed but one should view the works in the chronological order of their creation.

The full scope of one's creativeness is like a necklace of gems matched in a definite order. Each work expresses some psychological moment in the life of the creator. The life of the artist is molded out of these moments. In order to understand the effect one should know the cause. One should understand why that particular order was followed in the creative process. What outer and inner circumstances accumulated to produce successive pieces of the whole creativeness? This would mean judging the design of the whole necklace from only one or two of its gems.

Decidedly, in all realms of creativeness—literature, music, painting—an attentive and solicitous attitude is needed everywhere. Everyone has had occasion to read and hear about someone's attributing to an author a great deal of something absolutely foreign to him, quoting only fragments from an originally unbroken flow of thoughts. It is not only unqualified laymen who attempt to judge. In every field of endeavor self-appointed judges are to be found.

I remember some fellow law students pondering how they would apply the acquired knowledge. One intended simply to practice law, one wanted to become an administrator, one was planning to become a prosecuting attorney; but one, a rather jolly student, said, "And I, probably, will have to judge all of you." Who knows? Maybe this jest helped to launch him into a judge's career, toward which, in the final analysis, he had no special inclination.

As in many professions, so, also, in judgments about a creative process, a great deal is molded quite casually. But because of this haphazardness almost irreparable results may issue.

It is said that values in general change thrice in a century—according to generations, as it were. To observe this sinuous line of valuations is quite instructive. How many extraneous considerations will influence public opinion! Rivalry of publishers, or greed of art dealers, finally, all varieties of envy and animosity are reflected upon the evaluations with such complexity that for a future research historian it would be almost impossible to discriminate between them. Many examples of this could be cited.

We recall two rival publishers who deliberately slandered an author in whom they were both interested so that they could acquire at a lower price the right of publication of his works. And these specific disparagements were recorded in some reviews. We remember an art dealer who by all possible means tried to reduce temporarily the value of the works of a certain artist, in order to buy up a sufficient quantity of his works and afterward to commission somebody to restore the reputation of the forgotten artist.

There is no need to recall certain episodes from the world of collectors, where rivalry drives people to most unworthy actions. It is important to remember, however, that the appraisals of creativeness are particularly convoluted and personal. We remember how a certain music lover one day warned a well-known musician not to play on that day because an influential music critic had a toothache.

But when to all these ways of life one adds the desire not to study thoroughly an *oeuvre* in its entirety, then the situation. becomes verily tragic.

Let us think of any prolific writer. Could one form an opinion of him without knowing all his works successively? True, one may judge separate works of an author, but such an opinion should refer to one work and not to the entire creative *oeuvre*.

It is most important to evaluate a great personality not only from his biography but by surveying the accumulative processes of his creativeness and all the ways in which it was expressed. Hence, one is reminded once again of this word *oeuvre*, so apt in its true meaning. It impels one to think quite broadly, to encompass an entire manifestation and study broadly its influence and consequences.

Leaving the consideration of personal *oeuvre*, history also evaluates the *oeuvre* of an entire nation, an entire epoch.

If a historian does not learn to appraise the small accessible facts, by what means could he approach and embrace broad tasks? Prior to thinking about these broad tasks, one should think about the conscientiousness of private and personal judgments. He who chooses to remain always within the boundaries of truth, will learn to discern the quality of all that is incidental, and will cautiously compare causes and effects. It is one thing to simply rejoice at a certain work, but it is quite a different matter to rejoice at a beautifully strung complete necklace in which are to be found many precious stones in unusual combinations.

Just now, when there are so many ruptures and confusions, the clear-cut, honest, and heartfelt grasping of each subject is especially urgent and timely. We read that recently Stokowski gave a definite opinion about the harm of mechanized music for true creativeness. Stokowski justly pointed out that even in the very vibrations there is a vast difference between those transmitted directly and those transmitted mechanically. And certain instruments are altogether not perceptible in mechanized transmission.

At this time, when music, the stage arts, and painting are subject to all sorts of machinations, precisely now the evaluations of creativeness should become still more exact, deep, and thorough. Precisely now, when the contemporary way of life strives toward brevity, abruptness, and chance, it is especially essential to aspire to evaluations based upon the entire *oeuvre*.

Although translatable with difficulty, *oeuvre* is an expressive word.

Peking, February 25, 1935.

THE MOST SIMPLE

PEOPLE come for the most simple. At times one may think that there is a demand for something more complicated. One may think that much is already known and therefore, naturally, one should avoid repetition. But after reading a lot, people nevertheless come for the most simple. How to work? What thoughts are conducive to work? What time is best for work? What is fatigue? Should one fear diversity of work? How deeply should one immerse one's self in the study of the monuments of antiquity? Are the postulates of antiquity applicable for contemporary life? Is construction possible? Where to find fortitude against all kinds of worries? How to be free of fear? Should one harken to one's inner voice? How to remember what it says?

An endless amount of questions—many times explained, many times touched upon; but everyone wishes to have an answer to the question put in his own way. Indeed, it is presupposed that the answer must be precisely the one that is expected. This is again very old, and, it seems, known to all; but people in their questionings will prove to you that this is absolutely not known to them or, better, they have quite forgotten about it.

When you see numerous volumes of commentaries and repetitions accumulated about scriptures which are most brief, clear, and simple, do you not wonder about how and for what all these explanations are piled up. The very simple stimulant and again, the most simple questions. These questions are seemingly about the very same thing, but in different connotations, and call for explanations, yet in peculiarly personal expressions. And so the wheel of life becomes more complex, starting from the very simple.

A man comes, asks that which has often been mentioned. He did not read that which was mentioned or had it in mind to do so. He wishes to hear an answer expected by him. If the most thorough answer does not conform with his already inwardly presupposed reply, then all that will be said will be regarded as not convincing. This happens rather often in life, and yet it relates to a certain type of people who put questions. And behind these there is a formidable mass of those who are altogether too lazy to formulate questions even for themselves alone. Sometimes they attempt to excuse this laziness by seeming modesty; but when the heart is aflame, man does not become subject to inert modesty. He seeks, knocks, even bursts in, all for the sake of being admitted.

It is remarkable to recall those flaming hearts who at times in spite of unusual difficulties conquered them and found the key to the most cunning locks. I remember one experienced worker who spoke thus to his young co-workers, "If you wish, convince me." Listening to the proofs offered, he shook his head and smiled sadly, "Still not convincing. As yet you did not stir me. Invent something more significant." Later he listened to some more and again shook his head. "You see, you did not even make me jump from my chair. You did not even prompt any exclamation of delight on my part. This means you should find such a convincing word that it will overcome all other considerations and become unalterable." And then, in a whisper he added, "Probably this will be the most simple word."

In all life's reconstructions, especially at present, people's souls long precisely for a simple and hearty word. If people come with questions about the most simple, the answer must also be simple; simple not only in meaning, but also in the expressions used. The very same sunlight, the very same basic striving toward Good, the very same smile of encouragement must express itself in a simple answer to a simple question.

In a voluminous book such an answer may be given more than once and in various forms. But books are often read somewhat abstractedly. In the very printed word there remains somewhere the ghost of an abstraction. At limes people themselves seek to find a sort of self-vindication, blaming a somewhat unclear form of exposition. There are known cases when people renounced their own words, which did not fit the particular occasion. All this is not simplicity by far, for now, as never before, a simple answer is needed that grows out of love and the best quality. Precisely in his heart man fully understands what simplicity is.

Precisely, the heart will knock once again because of various unneeded adjuncts.

Simply! Simply, with a good word! With a good action!

Peking, March 3, 1935.

LIGHT REALIZED

LIGHT does not become extinguished. Radiations and lights, earthly and supermundane, always remind people of their existence. People went to see physicians and begged them to stop their unbidden visions. Many efforts were needed, so that even crude apparatus could vindicate the gift of human sight.

When people insisted that they saw light, they were scoffed at. They were called schemers. However, the near-sighted person does not trust the far-sighted one. Radiations of the human body were denied, and were attributed to the realm of mysticism, or ascribed to faulty eyesight.

To the ancient knowledge, to the one cognized in times of yore, new paths were opened. Above all fanatical forbiddances thoughtful observers perceived convincing testimonies.

"In a German medical journal 'Fortschritte der Medizin' appeared a detailed article by Prof. Paul Dobner, about the radiations of the human body. Prof. Dobner found a reagent which made it possible to establish, although indirectly, the evidence of human radiation. This is a common aluminum plate. Aluminum possesses radioactive properties, and a plate from this metal, when brought in contact with a photographic film darkens it, as if it were emitting light. Prof. Dobner established that human radiations have the ability to increase for a short period of time the radioactivity of the aluminum: if one puts the aluminum plate first over a hand, and then over a photographic film, it will darken it with a considerably greater intensity than will a plate out of the same metal, which was not subjected to this previous operation.

"According to the degree of darkening, one can judge the intensity of the aura of that part of the human body with which the aluminum plate was in contact." Prof. Dobner established that the flow of human radiations is strongest from the finger tips and directly before the eyes. This conforms to the theory of magnetic "fluids" which issue precisely from the fingers and the eyes of the hypnotist. Another important circumstance has been revealed by Prof. Dobner: "The character of the radiations of the human body depends upon the condition of the blood. In illnesses of the blood the intensity of the radiation of the body falls off, and in cancer patients the aura disappears completely.

"The aura of a healthy person spreads to a distance of forty meters around the body."

This is not a discovery but an affirmation. Yet proofs are needed. How many unknown listeners will be grateful for this affirmation on which they insisted long ago and which caused ridicule and derision to be directed at them.

The physician says also: "The ideas of Hippocrates which governed medicine for a span of almost two thousand years had great influence on it. Medicine, as a scientific discipline in a contemporary sense, was originated only in the second half of the last century in connection with the study of anatomy and with the appearance of the sciences of physiology and biology.

"Only when the causes of certain illnesses became known, was fighting them put on a scientific basis, and medicine walked out of the darkness in which it stayed through the entire period of its history, especially during the medieval epoch when the chief means of cure were prayers, and conjurations of those evil and impure spirits who were regarded as the instigators of various ailments."

In stressing the immutability of the basic idea of Hippocrates, expressed over two thousand years ago, mainly that the human organism strives to cure itself from various diseases, the professor pointed out that the role of medicine is that of assisting the organism in this battle; however, this help must be rendered not to the one or other sick organ, but to the entire organism. In this respect psychological factors—faith of the patient in the physician's skill and his knowledge—carry great weight in medicine.

A physician observes correctly the deep significance of psychological factors in medicine. How many times one has heard remarks of wise doctors during the successful outcome of a cure, "You yourself helped me to cure you." In this one must consider attraction and repulsion, magnetic currents and rays, and, in the final analysis, all that enters into the concept of this very same light. People approach with various intentions the very same, the deeply fundamental, which penetrates and unites all that exists.

In the Paris Observatory experiments in the sonorization of the starry sky are taking place at present. As is known, every light ray can be transformed with the aid of the so-called photoelectric cell into sound, and back again. Moving pictures with sound are founded on that. The light of a heavenly body caught by a telescope and directed at the photoelectric setting gives a definite sound. The star, in the literal sense of the word, is singing. Out of all stars tested the most melodious sound is produced by Vega. Its light, out of which this sound is born, must travel twenty-seven years before it reaches Earth.

Naturally, light and sound are inseparable. Indeed, the sounds of heavenly bodies must direct thought toward the greatest realizations. The language of sound and the hieroglyphics of light are incalculable in space. When it is proposed that we think about far-off worlds, not only astronomical problems are presupposed. What great expansions of consciousness will resound and radiate! Even by crude means it has been found that the organism stricken by illness does not emanate light. The same can be observed not only during illness, but during all other obscurations caused by malice, anger, irritation, or depression. All this was known from time immemorial. Many a time this has been uttered in beautiful expressions by the best thinkers.

Therefore, speaking properly, there cannot be a discovery of that which is long since known, but there can be a cognition not yet discerned by all. And for that knowledge deep gratitude should be expressed to the scientists. They introduce considerations of deep significance to the broad masses in the language of the times and within the scope of accepted evidence. If people would think again and again about light and sound, if they would hear luminous sounds they could advance upon the path of expansion of consciousness. Not the simple accumulation of information, but the broadening of world outlook and striving to the most high will bring the people out of the gulf of the routine way of life.

The odors of the kitchen will be replaced by high spatial aromas. Instead of a smoky bit of candle the radiations of light not of this world will glimmer more often. And silence will resound. All this—the high, the boundless, the incalculable—will restrain humanity from shameful denials, and will lead it toward the lofty creation of benevolence.

It is so needed!

Peking, March 5, 1935.

CAREFULNESS

IF success depends, more or less, upon our inner suppositions, how should one learn to watch oneself, so as not to poison space? Such care will teach true cautiousness. We have no right to impose upon someone else's energy— to willfully squander another's value. This is not permissible on the material as well as on the spiritual plane. And yet, out of seemingly good intentions the squandering of another's forces often occurs. Thus people think that they took something from someone, whereas the willful loan really took place in some other way. People think that they safeguarded something, but in reality they increased it and created a burden.

Many a time one could observe that friends, because of ignorance, sent very poisonous arrows at the most tense moment. Maybe, on the eve of a most responsible action, precisely a friendly arrow let fly rashly caused a dangerous scratch. True, the sending of the arrow was to have been in another direction, but the sender did not take into account all the inner links and involuntarily grazed just that which had to be safeguarded. And the more the cooperation was already cemented, the more dangerous could uncalculated blows have been.

It would seem that sentiments of love and devotion should sufficiently warn careless bowmen. The feeling of trust, as a basis of cooperation should remind one of caution. The innate feeling of good will should have created a prudent magnanimity. But, apparently, all these combinations are not sufficient. Perhaps, besides heartfelt care one should develop within oneself that which is called carefulness.

In each rash action there also is certain to be hurt for others and for oneself. If a man has not fully learned to exercise care toward other people, let him be cautious at least in regard to himself. Each attempt to usurp someone else's value will be a robbery, and it will be as harmful as each usurpation of someone else's property.

Cautiousness or carefulness! These two concepts are definitely connected, although at first glance they define different actions. Learning to understand cooperation helps to realize the touching significance of carefulness and cautiousness. When cooperation is comprehended, respect toward the actions of one's co-worker will be developed first of all.

If someone does something, it means he has sufficient grounds for precisely this means of expression. A co-worker, before suspecting the action as being imperfect, will first look upon it with full confidence and magnanimity. And when, after the well intended investigation of the action, the co-worker will think that something could have been done differently, he will in the best possible way try to explain why his considerations are more efficacious.

Are expressions and exclamations of animosity or wrath possible among co-workers? How can they be co-workers after this? If in one instance there can be malicious thunder and shrill cries, it means this could happen also in other instances. Who knows? Perhaps amidst the most responsible actions the very same tongues of crimson flame may flash out. It means the wine is not yet ready. It means the cooperation was not yet achieved. If a great deal has not yet been crystallized and steadied, is a responsible action possible? A test always comes on a small thing.

There is an ancient fairy tale about a king who announced that he would set forth some serious tests. All were preparing and expecting them. And then they showed surprise as to why they were postponed. Or perhaps they were cancelled altogether? But quite unexpectedly all the co-workers were summoned and a new system of labor was announced. It appeared that the tests had already taken place. People had been tested upon the daily occurrences least noticeable to them. It was noted down when and who became irritated, when inaccuracy and wastefulness took place. In short, all had been weighed at the time when people were still expecting that their tests would lake place in some pompous gatherings.

For such an occasion people learned some well sounding formulas, studied by heart some sayings, committed to memory formulas and calculations. And at the same time, in their daily life, not even noticing it, they themselves revealed their inner nature and qualities to a sufficient degree.

Not in vain is unexpectedness spoken about in narratives and lofty teachings. Preparedness for such "expected" surprises can be achieved only through constant vigilance and carefulness. Safeguarding a friend and co-worker, people safeguard themselves. When will it be understood that each groundless judgment is already a sign of unpreparedness for responsible actions? And yet one action, twisted or infringed upon, drags behind it a multitude of distortions. To straighten out these distortions is far more difficult than not to admit them altogether.

Friends! Let us be very cautious. Let us be very careful.

Peking, March 8, 1935.

WILD ANIMALS

IN China it was regarded as special good fortune to be eaten by a tiger. It is told about quite a remarkable way of hunting a lion in Africa. One trails the king of the desert, and approaches him without a gun, but with a large pack of small, furiously barking dogs.

The lion, hiding in bushes, endures the barking for a long time, but finally amidst the branches his threatening paw appears. The experienced hunters say, "Now he will leap." Indeed, the dangerous beast leaps high and lands in nearby bushes. Then to the first dog pack is added a new, fresh pack. The barking increases. The experienced hunters say, "Now, it will not be very long, he cannot stand it." Then comes a strange moment when the dogs, completely infuriated, rush into the bushes. The hunters say, "Let us go in, he is finished." The king of the desert cannot stand the barking at him, and he expires from a rupture of the heart.

I had occasion to observe a monkey court in India. On a high cliff seated in a circle is a whole "Areopagus" of very old grey-bearded judges. In the center of the circle is placed the accused. He is very alarmed, apparently tries to prove something with his gestures and screams, but the "Areopagus" is inexorable. Some sort of decision is arrived at, and the accused, with his tail between his legs, emitting a pitiful squeak creeps to the top of the rock and throws himself into the rushing torrent below. So it happens in the foothills of the Himalayas.

Verily, if one but listens to the stories about the big monkeys who live near the snow mountains, complete books may be compiled. We had an opportunity to see these mountain dwellers, sitting in an orderly family circle, on a platform near a cave. The onlookers commented, "Perhaps they even have flint implements!" They are very much like men.

Also there is a feeling in animals akin to man. During a time of cold winter on the Tibetan hillsides the grazing lands disappeared under the snow. The camels were sent three or four days ahead on a path where there was supposed to be grass. This hope also proved to be futile for there was a deep snowfall and no fodder could be found. In two weeks all the camels perished. I recall a bright winter morning in our camp. Upon a distant, glistening, snowy hillside some sort of animal is moving. A camel! Without a man. Slowly and majestically a lone camel, weakened by fasting, approaches our tents. His gait is sure, and using his last strength, he hastens to where he was fed before. He recognized the camp as his home and was not mistaken. Of course, he was fed the very last remaining grains. The packsaddles were ripped open in order to get a wad of straw. And in spite of everything he remained alive, this one faithful camel. He lived and later crossed with us through all the passes, upon narrow edges, up to Sikkim. We gave him as a gift to the Maharajah of Sikkim, and he may be even still alive on his land. This was the first two-hump camel which came to India from Tibet. All the people from the neighborhood rushed to see him, and he calmly shook his head; his wise eyes, the color of dark agate, were deep and brilliant.

Most likely, the eyes of a roe deer, clouded with tears, are full of expression when the hunter hastens to finish her, already wounded by shot. Sensitive hearts, once looking into such eyes and seeing those tears, will never again raise a knife over an animal.

If people would but decide to kill animals only when extreme necessity arises, a necessity for food! All sorts of appetites for killing must be abandoned sometime. Medical statistics about the spread of cancer indicate that this scourge of humanity is especially prevalent where meat eating abounds. An experienced physician will always warn that sooner or later eating meat will have to be abandoned if gallstones or any such unpleasantness is to be avoided. And from the point of view of nutrition one reads almost constantly in the scientific journals convincing articles about vitamins, which are superior by far to a meat diet. One should hope that those times have passed when animalistic physicians prescribed raw meat and blood. What a horror! To prescribe even the drinking of blood.

But, if even the problem of the preservation of health, if scientific experiments and physicians' advices do not convince one, would there not at last be a final proof if one were to look into the eyes of the animals?

The dog is the friend of the house. The eyes alone of a faithful dog can tell a lot; besides, they see more than the eyes of ordinary people. How often it can be noticed that a dog senses something invisible, sees, bristles, and warns by its growling. One recalls many stories about such sensations of the animals. It seems to us that dogs sense more than other animals, but maybe it only seems so, for we observe dogs more than other animals. The dog has entered more closely into our daily life, and people are more used to dogs' means of expression.

One sheep dog asked for coins, collected them in her mouth, and later, entering the bakery, spit them out, thus asking for a sweet roll. We knew a dog in Paris who went for a paper. Outside of any daily acts, so much is known about the self-sacrificing actions of dogs when they were ready to freeze to death in giving their warmth to their owners.

Many animal eyes can be recalled. Again and again, humans could learn a great deal from animals.

Today a new dog, "Nohor," appeared here. It means "friend" in Mongolian.

Peking, March 8, 1935.

THE INVISIBLES

HAVING read the published letters of a certain thinker someone wondered, Why does the author return, as it were, to the very same subject? The reader did not grasp that the letters were written at different times and addressed mainly to different people in quite distant localities. For the reader, these invisible correspondents became fused into one; apparently for him they remained invisible people. The reader probably imagined that these letters were written for him alone, not taking into consideration any extraneous conditions. Invisible friends, invisible listeners, invisible co-workers—all this relates to the realm of fantasy just like Fortunatus' hat.

Not so long ago any such invisibility was either altogether denied, or called charlatanism, or attributed to the realm of hypnotism. The most difficult of all for an average man is to get used to the idea that he may be surrounded by some "invisibles." When guardian angels were spoken about, it was preferred that this be limited to old wives' tales. Yet from time immemorial it was usual to speak about iron birds, about a word heard six months before a journey, about ironclad fire-breathing serpents.

Likewise, an idea about Fortunatus' hat persistently lived and lives in various folklores. In the best fairy tales and epics the idea of invisibility was carried out quite persistently. During a war a smoke screen was used as a means of invisibility. This was a very crude resolution of some legends and tales. But now, in small type, the newspapers report the following: "A young Hungarian scientist succeeded, apparently, in realizing and turning into reality the fairy tale about Fortunatus' hat. The demonstration of the invisible rays took place in one of the public squares, before a statue. After the apparatus was set in motion, the statue suddenly disappeared from view, and its presence could only be established by touching it. In a few minutes the statue appeared again before everyone's eyes, as if coming out of a fog."

Thus, prophecies or recollections out of folklore again enter life. Just as iron birds already fly, and people are carried by iron serpents, words resound thunderously throughout the whole world, and likewise "the invisibles" enter life. One can imagine how these newest discoveries bring about a transformation of everyday life.

Only recently a story was told about a man who played a joke on his good friend, a lady. Moving into a new house he saw, in the window across the street, his friend who apparently just got up from bed. In that same room was a telephone. The jester telephoned to her and in the conversation mentioned the progress of television. The lady was skeptical. But then he started to describe to her, her night dress and other details, and she, in terror, hung up. This joke, in a somewhat different manner, was reported in the newspapers when, learning about the progress of television, certain inhabitants of London became seriously worried about the inviolability of their house. Workers connected with television had to explain that there was no danger from this direction. In other words, at that moment there was no danger, because entering the realm of the invisible, one may presuppose that anything may result from invisibility. It is important to establish the principle.

Let us recall the primitive daguerreotype and the contemporary growth of photography. For instance, even now in some countries, instead of the easily falsified copies of documents, the simple use of the photostat is still unknown. On the other hand, in some courts a photostat is already regarded as a document. Or let us recall the primitive railroad train, a sample of which was exhibited at Grand Central Terminal in New York. It most assuredly has nothing in common with contemporary achievements. Thus, if the principle of the invisible is discovered, the most stupendous improvements may be its results.

To fence off such mechanical achievements is impossible, sooner or later they will penetrate into life. It means, one should think about other, natural means through which equilibrium could be achieved. Let us again remember the very same thing—the natural benevolent properties of the human spirit. If a dog senses something invisible, how much more could the watchful human spirit know. And how naturally this knowledge could come! At first it will be an unconscious intuition, then it will pass into a realized sensitivity, and later, out of it will develop definite straight-knowledge. Thus all mechanical "invisibles" will be envisioned, and the entire daily life will change for the better, the higher side.

When you read the works of the hermits of Mt. Sinai and of many other hermits and dwellers in caves, you marvel at the lofty, fiery knowledge contained in them. In their entrusted teachings they disseminate broadly and generously the fundamentals of life. Centuries pass, the methods of expression change, but truth remains unalterable. All that is taught about so-called "wise actions," and about the "heart's prayer," which is noted in the ancient book *Dobrotolubiye*[2], is acknowledged by its followers, but they confess they do not fully realize where the place of the heart is. Because of this misconception all kinds of disturbances take place. But the great elders, hermits, and dwellers in caves knew unerringly where the heart is, how to treat it, and how to evoke its benevolent action.

What a wonderful word—Benevolence!

Before these lofty, natural ways all sorts of mechanically produced rays appear to be poor, limited, and not achieving anything. But for those who do not wish to know greatness, this lesser thing will already be the beginning of the path. If someone writes about this to one country,

---

[2]   *Love of good.*

he probably will feel the need to write to other countries also. In different languages, in other words, in different formulations of thought, people are impelled nevertheless toward consonance in the epoch. It means that all who hear about this consonance are obligated to create a truly benevolent resonance out of it. It is instructive to see that a very important achievement takes place, not in one particular nation, not in one particular country, but sometimes in the most unexpected one.

Thought is propelled in certain universal outlines. Where, because of ignorance or misery, people shy away from the high, spiritual paths, they encounter the least, the mechanical paths. But even these paths lead nevertheless to the same achievements. And yet spiritual gates are so needed. There is so much to remind one about this inescapable way. Take the very strange ailments of recent times. All the sort of burns of the organism, all the poisonings through gasoline and other substances and through thoughtlessly provoked energies—all this is already knocking at our doors.

We read: "One hundred years ago, in June of 1835, Baron de Morogue, a member of the Superior Council of Agriculture delivered an address at the French Academy of Sciences on the unemployment and social ills which threaten France and the whole world because of the introduction into industry of more and more new machines." The Paris newspapers dug out of the archives of the Academy this prophetic paper and published excerpts from it which are truly quite interesting.

"Every machine," wrote de Morogue in his report, "replaces human labor, and therefore every new improvement makes superfluous the work of a certain number of people in industry. Taking into consideration that workmen are accustomed to earn their livelihood freely and that most of them have no savings, it is quite simple to picture the irritation which the mechanization of industry will gradually arouse in the working masses."

Dr. de Morogue foresees that "in spite of the technical

improvements in production, the material conditions of the workmen will worsen. Hence, moral, social, and political dangers will arise."

De Morogue's report made such a strong impression on the Academy that in 1835 they dispatched to the King a special memorandum on the necessity of regulating the mechanization of production. This paper did not prompt any action.

And so, in different ways people again arrive at considering the regulation of mechanical achievements. This will not be a cry of protest against machines or ignorant grumbling against improvement, but a summons to sound co-measurement. After all, so many former "invisibles" have become visible, and at the same time things seen and accepted long ago have become invisible.

Crude treatment of invisible energies may cause numerous calamities. How much real knowledge is needed, in order that the millions of unemployed may find a useful and joyous occupation ordained by life.

If "Fortunatus' hat" can hide something, then the human spirit can reveal Truth in all its glory.

Peking, March 11, 1935.

NEW LIMITS

THE question has been raised, When does life cease from the legal point of view? From London someone writes: "When is a man dead? When the heart action and breathing have ceased, it must be considered that life has abandoned the human body."

The strange episode of the fifty-year-old gardener from Arley (England), John Pickering, who is at present recovering from an operation during which heart action and breathing stopped for five minutes, brings about an entire revolution in the medical world.

The case of John Pickering has upset the criteria in the medical reference books. All those present at his operation attested to the statement of the physicians verifying his death.

Any physician, in fact, would certify death upon complete absence of pulse, breathing, and heart reflexes, as was done in Pickering's case.

In *Principles and Practice of Medical Jurisprudence*, Taylor says:

"If no sound of the heart is perceived during an interval of *five minutes*, a period which is many times as great as that which observation warrants, death may be regarded as certain . . ."

There is every reason to assume that if the heart absolutely stops beating for a period longer than two minutes, death is certain. The same observations also apply to respiration.

The contradictions which arose in the Pickering case indicate that the medical manuals must be revised. They were written before the discovery of adrenalin, that life giving stimulant which restores people to life from that state which in the opinion of medical authorities has been called death.

The consequences are quite far-reaching, and it is even difficult to foresee them. In the first place, relatives will require further measures of their physicians in cases of apparent death.

Questions also arise in the social and legal fields. For example, what about the last will and testament in such a case as that of Pickering? Will life insurance premiums continue to be demanded? Could marriage be terminated by such a death?

Indeed, besides these questions which arise, there can be enumerated many others no less significant. In general, the criteria for the moment of so-called death become extremely conditional and in reality they are subject to revision.

Thus, for example a case has been cited, when, under hypnosis, a death that was pronounced inevitable was considerably deferred. Likewise it is explicitly related that a quasi-dead man uttered some words under the influence of suggestion. Most likely some will say that this is impossible. And yet precisely the author of a widely used medical reference book assumed that the above cited case from London would have to be recognized as terminative death.

Let us not return to all the erroneous or mediocre conclusions which in their time have led humanity into error. It could be recalled how at one time people scoffed at experiments with steam, with electricity, and with many inventions which have now become matters of common knowledge even in primary schools. It can only be regretted that now, the same as in days past, negation obviously predominates and much is made difficult by this destructive growling.

Many times people have been advised to keep diaries or written records in which to list known authentic facts. Just as meticulously as meteorological observations must be persistently carried out everywhere, many other facts also must be noted down in all their unusualness.

One occasionally reads about the birth of quadruplets and even sextuplets. The fact in itself is an unusual one. But when all such facts are gathered together, observations based on them can be very instructive.

Generally speaking, one must steadily go on learning to keenly examine reality without any negations. When timid people exclaim, "This is impossible!" such negative outcries should be referred to more than cautiously. All these new limits which are seeking recognition in the everyday life of contemporary humanity must be realized, and primarily for the sake of good.

Even when we speak about new limits, can we affirm that they are new and that they are limits? Who has the presumption to insist that this very thing was not known some time ago? Peraps that language has been forgotten in which these same facts were enunciated, but no one can assert that in essence they were unknown.

It is cause for rejoicing to note how recognition of the past, and together with it a prognosis of possibilities, become broader and deeper. The authentic written record of the ordinary, inquisitive man can be of immeasurable benefit by lessening superstition and ignorance, and by fortifying true, searching investigators.

Peking, March 14, 1935.

FRAGRANCE

GARDENS have ceased being fragrant." Thus said Mrs. Eiskaff in her lecture to the American Women's Club.

She continued, "In ancient times the wealthy men and administrative officials of China cultivated gardens in order to create around their homes the illusion of the natural hills and fields of their provinces."

Taking pleasure in this recreation and change of atmosphere within the boundaries of the city, they furnished enjoyment to their wives also. Especially for Chinese women, obliged to lead a secluded life, these gardens added beauty to their existence.

In constructing the gardens, the Chinese strove to come as near as possible to imitating that scenery which was particularly pleasing to them.

These gardens did not occupy a large space. The Chinese valued the land too much as an area suitable for agriculture. Yet on a comparatively small plot of ground the art of the Chinese gardeners enabled them to create true works of art.

Speaking about Chinese women, she expressed regret that at present they have become as changed from what they were as the old gardens. Strange as it may seem, though the Chinese women are incomparably more emancipated now than they formerly were, nevertheless they have lost much of that influence which they had in the life of the country. Formerly, though almost without exception leading a secluded life, they still knew how to exert a desired influence on their husbands.

Mrs. Eiskaff's lecture takes on still greater interest in that she is a well known translator of the ancient Chinese poets, occupying the post of honorary librarian of the "Royal Asiatic Society," as is noted in a newspaper.

Once when I was asked, "What is the difference between East and West?" I said, "The best roses of East and West are equally fragrant." We have had occasion to read very condemnatory books about different countries. Each such condemnation has immediately provoked a rebuff from the censured country. A new book, sometimes very hastily written, appeared, full of the most extreme judgments.

One book-collector displayed in his library a special shelf of varicolored books, saying, "Here is a collection of condemnations." Thus the books were set apart in an order according to negations or condemnations.

The collector-philosopher noted quite appraisingly in this sequence how widespread is the poison of condemnatory judgment. Chronologically examining these peculiar accumulations, one can see that these authors hastened to immerse themselves in only negative values. Let us even admit that they did not wish to tell lies intentionally, but only to compile an odd lexicon of negatives. Occasionally such censorious collections remind one of a certain jocose critic who counted how many times the negative *no* was used in a certain book, and pathetically concluded, "Well, can this be a good book, in which the word *no* has been used seven hundred times?"

Indeed, in his condemnatory mood, the critic did not try to count up how many times the word *yes* was said in this book. In any case, when you see an entire section of a library composed of negations, it becomes frightening. Indeed, negations alone will not be comforting; it seems that without offering a panacea we have no right to criticize.

In the complexity of life there can be found new monstrosities, and yet let us not be in the position of pronouncing any general condemnation. Take the case of *The Good Earth*, the author has tried to set in opposition two, us it were, mutually excluding currents. This is not passing a judgment, it is comparison. In general, we ought not to say simply that something is bad without saying what is good or how it can be made good.

In each garden there occur periods when the blossoms have not yet opened and when leaves and buds are not even visible, yet the gardener will tell you that within three months you would not even recognize the garden. Everything will blossom, open up, take on new forms. The experienced gardener provides a multitude of examples which are applicable in all life. A winter's tale about summer gardens will always be expressed in particular words. Especially in winter does one dream about summer.

And speaking also about woman's task, about the destination of women, often more and more is required of woman in view of the fact that in an inner sense she bears a special significance. Right now, equal rights for women are spoken about everywhere. Already this formula sounds somewhat old-fashioned. Already it becomes impossible to speak in generalities about it. And how otherwise? Where can equal rights be inadmissible? Sometimes it is customary to say that grandmothers knew something better than their granddaughters. And this comparison will be absolutely conventional. The best roses are equally beautiful. Here, outside the window, the trees are budding, the cherry trees are already covered with their floral finery, and there can be no garden without fragrance.

Let there be a garden, let the deserts bloom, let the life-giving underground streams again rush forth.

The gardens will be fragrant.

Peking, March 19, 1935.

WAVES OF LIFE

IT is related as follows: "In the life of every man there are so-called lucky days marked by an unusually good mood and success in all undertakings. But, along with these, there also occur 'dark days' when disappointments pour down as if from a horn of plenty, ill luck follows every step, and all seems to be painted black."

"On this seemingly quite casual factor, Riese, a German scientist, built a complete scientific theory. Everything in the world, from great to small, says he, is subject to the law of undulatory fluctuations. Likewise, in the life of every man there exist certain rhythms of rise and fall in all his physical and psychic qualities.

"Through experimentation Riese has established that human life is determined by three kinds of rhythms: masculine, which has a period of twenty-three days and which regulates the physical processes in the organism; feminine, with a period of twenty-eight days, which deals with manifestations of the soul; and, finally, the rhythm of the sympathetic nervous system, which governs the mental processes. These rhythms form special curves—either rising, and then all our faculties and qualities manifest them selves most vividly, or falling, when body, soul, and brain work haltingly and unsatisfactorily.

"These fluctuations do not depend upon any external factors, even illnesses do not affect them, and they always, for everybody, preserve their lawful order. Riese even attempts to calculate a life curve for every person and foretell in advance those days when he will be what is popularly called, lucky, and those days when it is better not to undertake anything.

"Riese, with the assistance of a well-known sportsman, Trossbach, tested his theory upon people who are active in sport, and with its help he formulated why certain sportsmen, not depending on any training, either suddenly reveal great attainments and beat all records, or just as suddenly fail and lose to their far more weak rivals. Riese calculated the life curve of the famous German runner, Peltzer, and proved that during the sports competition in Germany, which preceded the Olympic international games, this curve indicated a definite rise. As is known, Peltzer at that time established a record. Yet, at the time of the Olympics in Los Angeles, Peltzer's curve went down, and therefore he ran much worse than usual.

"Scientific circles as yet refrain from forming opinions about Riese's theory, but sports circles in Germany are greatly interested in it and intend to start mass experiments for its verification."

Of course, Dr. Riese's reports are of interest not only in relation to sport. These waves could be studied equally from the standpoint of the influence of thought. In this, not only is the thought of the subject himself of significance, but also the thoughts of surrounding people.

There probably could have been found whole groups of volunteers ready to continue the initial observations of the researcher, and also observations from the standpoint of reactions to thought. With certain attentiveness and, of course, absolute honesty it would be possible to record remarkable mutual reactions. One can see curious interactions affecting the rise and also the fall. At someone's entrance, the moods of those present droop or perk up. In this maybe thought is acting, and maybe there is another influence.

* * *

"Father, it is impossible to live. It is becoming much worse." The priest-confessor said, "I will help you. Go and buy another goat. Then come and see me in three days."

At the appointed time the unhappy man came, completely out of his head and crying, "It is impossible to live this way."

The priest said, "Now, sell those goats."

In a few days the man came and told him that the goats were sold.

The priest asked, "Well, is it better now?"

And the man replied, "Now, we can live."[3]

* * *

And so, because of the counter tactics a psychic relief was brought about.

Now is the time of wide observation of human thought. A multitude of factors, disturbing and complex, invades contemporary existence. If physicians now ponder about mechanical causes, one will likewise ponder about psychic causes.

Peking, March 16, 1935.

---

[3]   A Russian story

SOURCES

WHO named mountains and rivers? Who gave the first names to cities and sites? Only at times dim legends reach us about reasons for establishing foundations and giving names. Furthermore, the names often relate to some already obscure, unused language. At times the names unexpectedly correspond to a language from some other country. It means that settlers or prisoners impressed their names on the way.

The question of geographical names often raises unsolvable enigmas. True, if people usually do not know how the name of grandfather's homestead came to be, then how impossible it is to grasp thousand-year-old reasons. The change in languages presents equal tasks.

If we but take the dictionaries published even in our time, the most unusual changes can be seen over scores of years. New words were formed and invaded the language. Former words were dismembered. Even the explanation of certain concepts fluctuates in the course of one generation. When people speak about preserving something old, one should clearly understand precisely what kind of *old* is meant.

Similar instructive observations are obtained from songs and folk melodies. If innovators themselves in creative forms often involuntarily turn to the lessons of antiquity, then similar expressions of sentiments are quite natural. If we look at the history of ornament preserved in samples of pottery which have reached us from ancient times, of course, we see in the embellishment a similar natural expression of human feelings.

Researchers have often wondered why during the Stone

Age in different, separated continents there existed the same technical skill and the same methods of ornamentation. Indeed, there could not be even a conjecture about the communications between these ancient aborigines. We simply witness a similar expression of human feelings. In comparing these analogies one may obtain instructive psychological deductions about the similarity of human expressions. And that means that the ways of calling forth these expressions had to be alike.

This was sent from England about a great discovery in the musical world: "Melodies that resounded thousands of years ago amidst the hills of Wales are now reproduced on harps and other modern instruments. Perhaps these are the very same melodies that rang out around the fires of ancient Britons before the appearance of Caesar's legions.

"This primitive music was preserved in an ancient manuscript, and Arnold Dolmetsch, who already for half a century has been working on the revival of ancient music on ancient instruments, now reproduces these melodies.

"He speaks about a recent find of a manuscript which contains more than ninety pages of these melodies as the greatest musical discovery ever made. It is especially interesting to note that the present national songs of Wales, and those of other English provinces as well, differ little from ancient melodies.

"The precious document discovered confirms that Wales hundreds of years ago already had its incomparable music. If not for the discovery of this ancient manuscript, then, indeed, the ancient melodies could not have been confirmed."

Truly, these ancient documents are exceedingly valuable. They could have been preserved only by pure accident. We have had the opportunity to see musical and also other historical documents completely eaten by worms, with dates and other concrete information forever lost. Besides, certain nationalities denoted an instrument and the voice in a curious manner, for instance, in wavy lines.

One can establish their exact meaning by listening to the still existing folklore.

However, in many places folklore is preserved no more, unless it has fallen into the static divisions of museums; then a musician or a writer may by accident stumble on it when wishing to bring to life these parchments and scrolls. We all know how in our time the most valuable musical rough drafts and historic letters were destroyed.

The same neglect shown toward artists in the family was indeed evident at all times. When we, at one time, wanted to see the family in which a grandfather was a remarkable painter, a wise friend of ours said, "Do not waste time searching in the families. Probably nothing remains there by now." Naturally such a judgment is not always correct, but the bitter truth about the careless attitude toward a close relative regrettably is known in many countries. Therefore it is so difficult to search on the spot, and each and every unexpected happy find is especially prized.

Just as people uniformly express their feelings in ornamentation, just as shouts of joy or terror are everlasting expressions, likewise the melodies of mankind bear testimony to eternal truths.

Since the beginning of this century, in different countries fine societies have appeared dedicated to research of ancient music and ancient literature. All of us have had occasion to hear splendid orchestras rendering age-old melodies upon ancient instruments. This was not a purely archaeological occupation, it was a joyous contact with the soul of peoples.

Just as is our modern ornamentation the involuntary repetition of the most ancient combinations may be indicated, so also in ancient melodies and writings there is often no sound of the "primitive," but a subtle and convincing expression of sentiments. These testimonies compel us to look with still greater solicitude into the past and observe purely psychic tasks and expressions.

Only a few ignorant people will say, "What do we care

about our putrefied forefathers?" Yet a cultured man knows that in being immersed in research of the expression of emotions, he acquires that convincingness which is close to all ages and peoples. A man who studies about reservoirs, should first of all learn about sources. Likewise, he who wishes to contact the soul of a people should search for sources. He should seek for them not with haughtiness and prejudice, but with a complete openness and joy of the heart.

Peking, March 18, 1935.

FORWARD

YESTERDAY, the scientific organizations in Peking feted Sven Hedin on his seventieth birthday. Such recognition from China and other participating countries is beautiful. Precisely in this way of mutual understanding and recognition is broadly welded the cooperation of whole countries. In the entire life of Sven Hedin, in his whole striving and indefatigability rings out the wonderful calling word: "Forward!"

Let us take Sven Hedin as a collective concept. The great explorer reached his seventieth birthday. It was recently announced that he was invited to make a large aerial survey of Brazil. Of course, Hedin does not reject such a possibility. Now he is departing for his own Stockholm. But no one thinks that he departs only, as it is customary to say, to settle down. This trip will be for him only a halting place.

Is it not because of such a wonderful adjuration, "Forward!" that the explorer looks so hale and hearty? Does he not conquer difficulties and dangers by this command? No one will deny that Sven Hedin is at present the most unusual, evocative example for the young generation. Think how many serious and captivating books he has written! What unforgettable discoveries were given by him to humanity! The majestic Trans-Himalayas will be linked forever with Sven Hedin's name.

Like a true Viking he was constantly striving toward valiant, peaceful conquests. Indeed, in these evident richest results rings out the blessed command, "Forward!"

Everyone who will trace the discoveries of Sven Hedin from their inception will be truly amazed by the invincible quality of this unique spirit. Where an average mind suspects some sort of finality, the epic saga of a Viking proclaims but the beginning of the next brilliant chapter. In this incessantly ascending path one does not wish even to speak of details, or mention numerous individual discoveries, or enumerate dangers and difficulties which were overcome. This entire unusual scientific conquest is given to humanity with untiring generosity. Into every travel of Sven Hedin is put some great idea.

Untiringly a great mind indicates new possibilities, new paths, a possible future flowering. A great scientist can only be a great humanitarian. The broader the mind the more fully flows the river of life before him. It is a cause for rejoicing that the beautiful explorations of Sven Hedin are valued. But one can equally rejoice at the very fact that such a vast strength is working now, in our time. When so much confusion and doubt cloud mankind, the Viking of light untiringly points to alluring, wondrous vistas and speaks about fabulously broad ways.

True creativeness is always full of optimism. A creator cannot exist in depression. A builder is full of knowledge in choosing the best materials. A living heart understands how necessary it now is to give to people the possibility for construction. In this inspired help there is a great humanitarian task. He who can with his incalculable labors inspire young hearts can also create vigorously himself. He will have no symptoms of fatigue. He will suffer no doubt or despair. He will say at all times the thrilling, bright word "Forward!"

This key cannot be given to those who have not attested it by their labors. This command will remain unconvincing when timidity and wavering are expressed. Therefore so valuable are all those manifestations which in their conclusive reality can unfurl the banner of the enlightened command, "Forward!" To this banner people can bring the best flowers. To this call they will send their best smile. Even amidst grey daily routine people will rejoice and strive to some kind of new and useful labors. If the explorer after completing his journey of seventy years is vigilant, joyous, and looks brightly toward the future, it means that the luminous "Forward" was his guiding sign.

Legends and fairy tales tell us about heroes, miraculous builders, creators of good and glory. Sagas also disclose white-winged swans, swift gerfalcons, and bold eagles. Scientists clarify the myth as a reflection of reality. Myths tell about true life heroes who have performed their deeds here on Earth.

If we could convince ourselves that the achievement is not anything abstract, but beautiful earthly deeds, then every reminder about the beautiful path of earthly achievements would bring to us the joy of the heart and would inspire and instill new strength. It is right to be grateful to all those who on their earthly journey clearly said the great word *Forward.* He who does not fear or humble himself, but renews himself, becomes ever stronger from his new contacts with Earth like Antaeus of mythology!

And so let us rejoice, when we see here, among us, a living example of resplendent invincible labor.

Striving lives in the sacred call, "FORWARD!"

Peking, March 19, 1935.

EASY DIFFICULTIES

IT is especially difficult for people to change their mode of living. One cannot help remembering an old proverb that "old furniture ought not to be moved." And this saying wisely states that something old should not be moved. That means that all difficulties are relative only in regard to our consciousness. Verily, people often speak of difficulties when they create them in their own imagination and have affirmed them with a prejudiced consciousness.

The city dweller, being surrounded with the conventional city comfort, considers that life in tents or in *yurts* would be the most dreadful existence. And should he find himself with such prejudice in the conditions of desert life he himself will actually build up all sorts of terrors. But if he will enter various conditions with the firm belief that people live everywhere and that they themselves create the conditions of life, then all the frightful phantoms will be dispersed. Not without reason do children who are uncontaminated by conventional superstition yearn for traveling, for knowledge, and they easily adapt themselves to different conditions.

Who knows? Perchance the migration of nations as a result of the great war was nothing but a lesson—a trial, for the renovation and broadening of consciousness. I remember how an enlightened and highly spiritual lady was terrified at the thought that she might have to spend all her life in the well organized confines of city life. Truly if one only imagines that all inhabitants of Earth have reached but a little well-being, then in that petty limitation is contained the great danger of petrification. And so a divine fate has pointed out that people should again travel and again shake themselves up for the acceptance of new profoundly conceived structures.

It has become clear after all these years to everyone who has seen many people that two distinct types of people always existed. Some have always come up to the surface amidst unbelievable difficulties; and not only did they come to the surface but they also brought much help to their surroundings. Despite various family and property complications, they always remained alert, cheerful, and friendly. The other type, even with outside help, always went down. They could not reconcile themselves to the change of conditions and even of nomenclatures. They not only considered themselves unhappy but they carried that grey unhappiness into their surroundings.

Every journey was for these people like some punishment from Above. They not only were unable to understand the new local conditions but they became engulfed in baseless condemnations of everything which was beyond them. One of the greatest consolations for them consisted in mutual condemnation and mutual belittlement, as if through demeaning someone they hoped to raise themselves. Instead of learning how to adapt themselves, understand, show compassion, and move on, they preferred to slowly sink to the bottom, as it is said in an old Ukrainian proverb: "Don't spend your forces in vain, brother, sink right to the bottom."

Such cases as we have seen during recent years did not concern only one nation. They were of a purely international nature from which those who are alive in spirit could learn in life the advantages of an active optimism and the horrors of an ignorant pessimism. Of course these two types of humanity, one leading, successful, enlightened and the other deadened, ignorant, and deteriorating, are always with us. But the years of extraordinary world disturbance have only brought them more clearly into focus.

Experienced educators have always understood that children should not be separated from nature, because only in it do they retain mobility, resourcefulness, and decisiveness. A wise physician always advises city people to keep closer to earth, and the results of such wise advice are often evident in life. All sorts of organizations—Sokols, Scouts, Pioneers, hikers, guides, and other healthy movements that bring city dwellers out into nature are the most healthy manifestations of recent years. Everything that calls to the friendly bonfire, around which all must be done by the people themselves, strengthens the spirit. And not only has everything to be done by themselves, but everything has to be thought of in a new manner and perhaps in a better way.

Inventiveness must be exercised. Who knows whether such a giant of inventiveness as Edison could have appeared if he had grown up in the narrow comfort of a city! Every one of us has seen many examples when even more or less outstanding personalities were overcome by surroundings of vulgar well-being. I remember that a brilliant educator, who on sending his wards into life used to say to some of them, "I regret that your parents are wealthy. I hope you will not get into a gilded cage." And to others he said, "No metal weighs down your wings. Fly high and far!"

As if to justify this advice, all conventional values were suddenly shattered. Even such strongholds as real estate values were struck as if by an earthquake. A certain inhabitant at the time of an earthquake rushed out of his house complaining, "And this they call immovable property!"

Many such maxims are offered by life itself. Some people are doomed to fear and are terrified by them; and others take things sensibly as they are. Some are unwisely attracted by mirages and others understand very well the difference between a mirage and reality. But in order to find one's way amidst mirages and illusions, one must first of all perceive these mirages. One cannot help remembering the Indian parable about the seven blind men who describe an elephant, each from his point of view. Likewise you cannot describe in words the impression of a mirage to him who has never seen one. But in cities mirages do not appear. In order to see them, one must visit the desert and there learn on the spot to distinguish reality from illusion.

Convinced of their infallibility city people have great difficulty in distinguishing true impressions. I remember how a member of our expedition, who was in the desert for the first time, decided to explore a beautiful illusionary lake. All my persuasion that this lake did not exist was of no avail. The deluded traveler summoned two attendants and to the surprise of everyone said that he would reach that lake within an hour and that he believed his eyes more than our contentions. After many hours the poor fellow returned exhausted and angrily refused to further discuss the question of the existence of the illusionary lake. And one must recall with what self-assertion he criticized our order to stop at a small well, instead of going an extra hour to the "splendid lake surrounded by trees!"

Mirages are always quite instructive. Only personal experience can teach the vanity of illusionary conceit, and the experiences of life are obtained best of all amidst nature.

But one cannot go out into nature only theoretically, deciding upon the usefulness of such an experiment. There will be small gain in such intellectual decisions. Nature must be understood. It must be entered into as a co-worker, not with condemnation, but in admiration.

Everyone remembers the beautiful legend about the mines of Falum, so picturesquely narrated by Hoffman. The owner of the mines is very stern with the miner, who, not from love of the work itself but from other, personal motives, comes to carry away the hidden treasure.

The voices of nature sound for those who enter it with an open heart, benevolently. Antaeus contacted the earth for the absorption of strength, in order to renew the might of the spirit. Indeed it was not from intoxication that he fell upon the ground, but he touched the earth consciously and then the earth conferred upon him a healthy renewal. Antaeus was called a mighty giant. Is it not from these health-giving contacts with the earth that he received this mighty name? And could those trials, those confusions which overcome one in closed cellars, under vaults, and between narrow walls have appeared to him as great difficulties?

Probably Antaeus would consider such relative difficulties simply incomprehensible. Thus, from the point of view of nature, such "easy difficulties" become not a paradox, but really a definition. "Burden me more when I go into the Beautiful Garden." Is this not an exact indication of how and where difficulties are transmuted!

When the Magi gazed into the boundless sky, they saw the Guiding Star. If they had not looked into the vault of heaven, they would not have seen the Star. Blessed is he, who in his days had armed them with the knowledge of observing the laws of nature, and had awakened their vigilance, thus making them watchful and turning them into wondrous messengers.

Why should we deplore any difficulties when the Guiding Star watches over us! He who said, "Blessed be the obstacles, through them we grow" also knew the Guiding Star.

Tzagan Kure, April 2, 1935.

MYSTERIES

ON the Karakorum Pass, at 19,500 feet, on this highway, the highest in the world, the groom, Gurban, began to question me:

"What is it that has been buried in these heights? It must be that a great treasure has been hidden hereabouts, surely the way to this place is arduous. And having traversed all the passes, one may chance upon a smooth vault. Something tinkles under the horses' hoofs. It must be that here are great secrets, but the entryway to them we do not know. When will there be revealed in books writings about where and what has been buried?"

All around this majestic Karakorum Pass the white peaks glistened dazzlingly. And all around us, without any break, rose a most brilliant scintillation. On the path itself, as if for a reminder, were a great quantity of whitened bones. Were not some of these wayfarers going for treasures? Indeed, countless caravans have crossed the Karakorum for riches.

* * *

Here I am reminded about another narrative concerning treasure. In Italy, at Orvieto, I was told a remarkable legend about hidden art treasures. The story concerned either Duccio himself or one of his contemporaries. It was told in a lofty style which goes so well with the mellifluous Italian language.

"Just as it is nowadays, in olden times the best artists were not always understood. For the beclouded eye it is difficult to evaluate forms, particularly lofty ones. People have demanded only the observance of old rules, and often beauty has not been accessible to them. Thus it happened with the great artist about whom we are speaking. His best pictures, instead of touching the hearts of people with exaltation were subjected to condemnations and mockery. For a long time the artist endured this unjust attitude toward him.

"In divine ecstasy he continued to create many masterpieces.

"Once he painted a very marvellous Madonna, but the envious prevented the hanging of this image in its predestined place. And this happened not once or twice but several times. When the viper begins to creep in, it invades both palace and hovel.

"But the artist, made wiser and knowing the madness of the crowd, was not distressed. He said: 'It has been given the bird to sing, and to me strength has been given for glorifying a lofty form. As long as the bird lives it fills God's world with song. And so while I am alive, I shall also sing in praise. If the envious and the ignorant put obstacles in the way of my works, I shall not lead the evil ones into worse bitterness. I shall collect the pictures rejected by them, I shall store them securely in oaken chests and, availing myself of the good will of my friend the abbot, I shall hide them in the deep cellars of the monastery. When the ordained day shall come, future generations will discover them. But if by the will of the Creator they must remain in secret—let it be so!'

"No one knows in precisely what monastery, in what secret vaults the artist concealed his creations. True, in certain cloisters it has happened that old pictures have been found in crypts. But they have been found singly, they have not been purposefully deposited there and therefore could not belong to the treasure secreted by the great artist. Indeed, in the underground vaults they continue to sing "Gloria in excelsis," but the treasure seekers have not been lucky enough to find what was indicated by the artist himself.

"Certainly we have many monasteries and still more

temples and castles which lie in ruins. Who knows? Perhaps the tradition relates to one of these ruins already destroyed and leveled by time.

"From this time on, people thought that the great artist had ceased painting. But, hearing these suppositions, he only smiled, because henceforth he was not laboring for the sake of the people's joy but for a higher beauty. And so we do not know where this priceless treasure is preserved."

"But are you sure that this treasure is hidden within the boundaries of Italy?" asked one of the listeners. "Already in remote times people traveled to other countries. May it not be that these treasures have likewise been unexpectedly dispersed, or, in better words, preserved in different countries?" Another present added, "It may be this story does not refer to a single master only. After all, human practices are often repeated. Consequently we find in history continual seeming repetitions of human errors and ascents."

* * *

When we reached the middle of the Karakorum Pass, the groom, Gurban, said to me, "Give me a couple of rupees. I will bury them here. Let us, too, add to the great treasure.

I asked him, "Do you really think that treasures have been collected together there below?" He looked around, surprised, even frightened. "But doesn't the Sahib know? Even to us lowly people it is known that there, deep down, are extensive underground vaults. In them have been gathered treasures from the beginning of the world. There are also great Guardians. Some have been lucky enough to see how from the hidden entrances have appeared tall white men, who then withdrew underground again. Sometimes they appear with torches and many caravaneers know these fires. These subterranean folk do no evil. They even help people.

"I know for a fact that one local bey lost his caravan in a snowstorm and covered his head in despair. Then it seemed to him that someone was rummaging around him. He looked around, in the mist there appeared either a horse or a man—he did not know. And when he put his hand in his pocket, he found there a handful of gold pieces. Thus do the great dwellers of the mountains help poor people in misfortune."

And again the stories recurred to my mind about the secret magnets walled up by the disciples of the great traveler Apollonius of Tyana. It was said that in definite places where it had been ordained that new states be built up or great cities erected, or where great discoveries and revelations should take place, on all such sites were implanted pieces of a great meteor, a messenger from distant luminaries.

There has even been a custom of testifying to the truth of statements by a reference to such ordained places. Thus it was said: "What I have said is as true as the fact that under a certain site has been buried a certain thing."

The groom, Gurban, again raised the question, "Why do you foreigners who know so much not find the entry-way into the subterranean kingdom? You know how to do everything and boast of knowing everything, and yet you cannot enter into the hiding places which are guarded by the great fire?"

> "Man lives in mysteries
> and they are numberless!"

Tzagan Kure, April 3, 1935.

MONSALVAT

IT is generally assumed that the human organism can best be developed and kept fit by all kinds of sports. Exercises are of course necessary, particularly when they are carried out in pure air. However, opinions do not agree as to the nature of these exercises. It is also surmised that the main harmonious development should take place in the nervous system and not only in the muscles. Once the nervous system is balanced and the nerves have regained their normal tension, we can achieve much that muscular development alone could never accomplish.

Everyone recognizes that any highly specialized sport, which only exercises a certain set of muscles, is limited and therefore not the best form of training.

We have, first of all, to wisely use the prana present in pure air; also certain motion is necessary that is natural to the human organism. If such motion does not disturb the nervous system and flows without violence, it will be a most fitting means for the development of the body and spirit.

It is a well known fact that a man under nervous strain proves to be stronger and more persevering than the trained athlete. Artificial, limited tension tends to produce limited thinking. The "golden mean" of thinking can only come from the harmonious equilibrium of the whole organism. When one thinks of all the marathons of today, it is deplorable that in this or that absurd occupation hours and hours are needlessly used up.

It can be asked who is made wiser or happier by a situation in which a human being senselessly dances for seventy-two hours, or more, exhibiting signs of ugliness in such a performance? Who benefits from a spectacle consisting of couples kissing one another for hours, which also reveals signs of ugliness?

In analyzing these modern marathons one is convinced of a profanation of the classic ancient name instituted by the Greeks. Moreover the Greek runners after participating in the marathon were accustomed to frequent the Academy where they could listen to and hold discussions with great scholars and philosophers. Thus, theirs was no one-sided profession befogging the senses.

Many researchers will tell you that violent bodily exertion is not needed for a harmonious development of the nervous system. We know that the members of the Peripatetic school of philosophers during their walks discussed the higher sciences, thus harmonizing their physical and spiritual prowess.

If we compare the decadent games of the Roman circus with the classical sports competitions of Greece, we shall get some idea of the ugliness of all purely physical contests. The Greek games demanded neither cruelty nor blood, which were part and parcel of the Roman circuses.

Alas, even today a public execution would draw an immense crowd. In Germany they have again begun to decapitate women criminals, and although this takes place in the prison courtyard, yet if such a spectacle were to be transferred to the public square, you would find in this "civilized" age of ours that a space as big as an amphitheater would be packed with spectators. As a matter of fact, if admission were charged, the gate receipts would probably exceed all the sums that go to philanthropic works.

We once heard that some ladies were vexed because capital punishment by hanging had replaced that of being burned alive. Obviously it is evident that such monstrous sentiments are due to a limited development of only some centers and instincts. A great deal of the degeneration and savagery are the result of precisely ugliness and narrow limitations. Certain muscles have become swollen, producing an abcess of sadism and savagery, the pus of which has poisoned both heart and brain.

In opposition to such an ugly physical development there is a theory that with a proper education of the nervous system one can control and develop the muscles and all the organs. Indeed, it is thought that sets in motion the muscles and also all other functions. Yet there are many people whose thinking is so limited that they do not realize this simple axiom. Nevertheless anyone who wishes can become convinced. We have often met people who gave little time for physical exercises, but who were nonetheless in the full bloom of their mental and physical abilities. By aspiring toward higher matters and taking an active interest in life, their organism became well-balanced.

Value the gifts of life. In desiring to live a life of labor and usefulness you will have acquired a great impulse which will do more to keep you healthy than all the vaccinations and massages. Conscious mental massage can pump fresh energy into a weakened organ. The simplest pranayama, which consists in inhaling prana and directing it to any spot which is in need of strengthening and development, is a very instructive example.

Every day one hears of the most awful methods of prophylaxis. Someone fears insomnia and finding nothing better takes narcotics or alcohol. Another, because of some symptoms incomprehensible to him because of ignorance, begins to smoke or take drugs, oblivious of the fact that such indulgence will only prompt their increase.

We often hear about the joy of dedicating one's life to service, but what joy can there be in the agony of narcotics, nicotine, and alcohol? They will not help us toward the joy of growth and ascent, but will only lead to a shameful retreat into darkness.

Physicians are well aware of many illnesses which originate in an addiction to modern sports, and it is quite common to hear of this or that serious illness, often incurable, caused by overexertion in sports. Different organs may be stricken and one meets most of all with overfatigue of the heart. Cardiac neurosis and other serious heart diseases are experienced throughout the entire life and they may lead to a fatal ending.

Specialized athletes are hardly fit for average physical activity. They can be likened to hothouse plants which are fit only for a special way of life. If any profession causes a limited way of thinking due to specialization, it is more so with sports, which make thinking lopsided and ugly. If one listens to the interests of prize fighters and other similar professionals and seekers of prizes, one very soon begins to question contemporary civilization.

Lately, it would seem that bullfights are beginning to lose their keen attraction, but perhaps it is only wishful thinking, since crowds still gather and roar in pleasure as they applaud this cruel sport. Of course no one will associate these professional distortions with the healthy Boy Scout movement, in which leisure time can be healthfully employed. The golden mean has been often and variably reiterated, yet perhaps the valuable essence of it has been rarely understood.

As we rise steadily in our ascent toward the spiritual heights of Monsalvat[4] we shall find very few sportsmen or prize fighters among the pilgrims. Those who aspire untiringly to these heights are very different in character. Physical prowess is not enough if we are not to fear the mountain paths and overcome the hardships and dangers on the way. The aspirants to Monsalvat generally have the necessary physical and spiritual strength not to cowardly swerve from the determined path. And the required physical strength will not be drawn from a desire for prizes. All those whose hearts are aflame with Monsalvat will ascend these heights in beautiful equilibrium, without any harm to their spiritual growth.

Monsalvat is ordained. It is a name known to all languages. In constant growth let us avoid all that is ter-

---

[4] Montserrat, also called Monsalvat. In the Middle Ages the mountain was thought to have been the site of the castle of the Holy Grail.

minated and finite. But we shall err if we accept bodily achievements as the goal of life and the crowning glory. It has been ordained that spirit alone shall receive the crown.

Let us ponder how the idea of Monsalvat was conceived. The educators will not forget when and how this guiding concept entered life. As we approach it we are once again aware that nothing is finite in the great relativity. Many a time will every teacher have to repeat this simple truth to those who enter upon the path of labor.

To those engaged in life's daily routine the heights of Monsalvat may seem remote and inaccessible. Many will save up their possessions saying with tenderness, "They will be needed when I go there." These people are not misers infatuated with earthly possessions, they are falcons spreading their future wings. They know that when the time comes, they will be permitted to go. And, above all, in this realization they will have overcome the oppressive feeling of loneliness which terrifies all those who dwell in ignorance.

Lofty expressions alone are suited to the heights, for base, commonplace words do not naturally gather about lofty concepts. Those who desire to see behold many things. For those who wish to hear, voices are already ringing.

Monsalvat is ordained.

Tzagan Kure, April 14, 1935.

THE BANNER

IN the White House today the Pact[5] is being signed with the participation of President Roosevelt. Over our *baishin*[6] the Banner has already been hoisted. It will wave in many countries today. In many corners of the world, friends and co-workers will gather in solemn communion and will determine the next forthcoming means of safeguarding cultural values. We shall not tire of repeating that in addition to recognition by the government active public participation is needed. Cultural values adorn and elevate all life, from small to great. Therefore an active care about them must be evidenced by all.

No matter how many countries signed the Pact today, this day will be preserved in history as one of memorable cultural attainment. The government has lent its powerful hand, and thus many new ways have been opened for all active adherents of culture. Maybe some sinister attempts will also be revealed today. The choice between Light and darkness must arise unavoidably. This is not a division of opinions, but indeed a choice between the constructive and destructive, the positive and negative.

The success of the signing of the Pact, and any opposition as well, should equally encourage all co-workers to further achievement. Let us cherish this day in our memory as a sign of an enlightened future, as one more impulse toward useful constructive attainments. I stress that the expression "division of opinions" would be quite unacceptable at present. Light and darkness never unite and there-

---

[5]   The Roerich Pact and Banner of Peace.

[6]   Mongolian dwelling.

fore cannot become divided. But if darkness senses danger to itself, it roars, it yelps, and fights. It could never have separated itself from Light, as is generally thought, for its essence was always the opposite of Light. Likewise, it will be always a dark background upon which glowing sparks are even more brilliant.

Let no one think that precisely today, on this day of achievement and festival, it is, as it were, unfitting to speak about darkness. For if we understand it as the antithesis of Light, as something which is dispersed by Light, then indeed on the day of the Festival of Light it can be remembered that a certain portion of darkness was dispersed today. We have never concealed the fact that darkness in its sinister aspect is strong. We have never concealed the fact that each victory over darkness will be the result of a big and difficult battle. Therefore, great is the victory of Light over darkness. Only in the full realization of the scope of this battle can we truly rejoice at each victory of Light.

Everybody knows that the Light and darkness of which we speak are by no means abstractions. They are not only a reality, they are evident to every eye. Here on Earth we see the servants of Light in labor and struggle. And also here we perceive the evil servants of darkness, filled with hatred of all that exists. Here in life, we learn the ways of Light, and likewise we are convinced of the sinister unity of the dark legions. The latter should not cause aggravation since it is unfitting to worry and thus weaken oneself when all the legions of Light are summoned. On the contrary, one should always rejoice at each flash of Light, which like lightning clears the thickening clouds.

Verily, today, the fifteenth of April, will and must be a memorable day. One more beacon will come into being, which will bring friends closer in far away countries, beyond the oceans, beyond the mountains, scattered through all the byways of Earth. We shall ask them once again to express themselves about all the useful and undeferrable matters. In many countries, at least this one day will teach a great deal. If we were to collect all these tested findings, there would be a whole treasury of useful and undeferrable advices. And so, let us counsel each other, and share all our accumulations and observations. Even during ordinary days, when it would seem that nothing of special significance occurred, even then the most urgent considerations have appeared. And now, when indeed the important and the significant take place, how many new strivings should arise! If, during the ordinary days, signs of calamity constantly arose and undeferrable help was demanded, then the significant date should instill in all co-workers of the Pact still greater vigilance and perspicacity. Precisely perspicacity is necessary in the matter of safeguarding culture. One should foresee many consequences. The causes may be deeply concealed and painted in deceptive colors, but they could lead to shocking results. Yet, to discern where the claws are hidden will be an excellent task for all guardians of cultural values.

We have spoken many times about a multitude of dangers for cultural values these days. Now governments offer us a powerful helping hand. We accept this support as a great possibility of new achievements. The Pact should not remain static upon the shelf of statutes of law. Each memorial day of the Pact must become a practical means for raising and strengthening the guardian Banner.

And so, in the desert, over a desolate baishin the Banner waves. But the deserts can also be very diverse. If, somewhere, a crowd of dark ignoramuses is gathered, this will also be a desert—waterless, soulless, heartless.

Let the Banner wave also over the hearths of Light, over sanctuaries and strongholds of beauty. Let it wave over all deserts, over lonely recesses of beauty, so that from this sacred seed deserts may bloom.

The Banner is raised. In the spirit and in the heart it will not be lowered. By the luminous fire of the heart the Banner of Culture will flourish. So be it!

Light conquers darkness.

Tzagan Kure, April 15, 1935.

ESSENCE

THE essential nature of people is fundamentally good. The first time this realization was strengthened in me was during an experiment long ago with the projection of the subtle body.

My friend, a physician, had put a certain Mr. G. to sleep, and after his subtle body was projected ordered him to send it into a house where he had never been before. By following his subtle body, the sleeper pointed out a series of characteristic details. Then he was directed to go up to a certain floor of the house and to enter a certain door. The sleeping man outlined the details of the hallway, saying that there was a door before him. Again he was directed to go further and to tell what he saw. He described the room and said that a man was seated at a table reading. Then he was directed:

"Approach and frighten him.

"Silence followed.

"I direct you to go near him and frighten him."

Again silence, and then in a timid voice, "I cannot do it."

"Explain why you cannot."

"Impossible; he has a weak heart."

"Then do not frighten him, but as much as you can without harm, make your influence felt. What do you see?"

"He has turned around and lit a second lamp."

"If it is not harmful, increase your influence. What do you see?"

"He jumped up and went into the adjoining room where a woman is sitting."

At the conclusion of the experiment, we telephoned our

acquaintance, and without telling him anything indirectly led him to relate his sensations. He said:

"Today I had a strange experience. A little while ago I was seated with a book, and suddenly I felt some inexplicable presence. I am ashamed to tell you that this sensation became so strong that I had a desire for more light. Nevertheless, the feeling became even stronger and I went to tell my wife about it and to stay with her."

Apart from the experiment itself, which so clearly demonstrates the causes of many of our sensations, one detail in it had for me personally an unforgettable significance. In ordinary circumstances the man would not take into account that someone had a weak heart. Without considering, he might frighten, abuse, or cause him harm. But the subtle body, the one about which the Apostle Paul speaks so clearly, in its essence is inclined toward good. So you see, before carrying out the order to frighten, consideration prompted the sensing of the condition of the heart. The essence of good whispered that it would be dangerous to tax an already weak heart.

One such experiment, in the most ordinary everyday circumstances, already leads one beyond the boundaries of bodily limitations. There resulted not only the projection of the subtle body, but a remarkable testing of the essence of good. What a dark burden must weigh down the luminous subtle essence for people to reach such hatred of mankind! Furthermore, as St. Anthony has said, "Hell is ignorance." True, the whole dark burden derives primarily from ignorance. Then how needful are good thoughts, which, with their unseen wings, touch the oppressed, beclouded forehead.

When, in their ignorance, people say, "Why these concentrations of thought, why are these hermits withdrawing from the world? They are but egoists and they think only of their own salvation," there is great error in such a judgment. If even through the most ordinary experiment we convinced ourselves of the good and noble essence of the subtle body, if we say that a thought of good transcended all commands—usually so unquestioned in such cases—then how needful are these thoughts of good! What a simple yet touching solicitude is evidenced in the simple reply about the weak heart. Right now there are not a few weak hearts, and who has the right to overburden them? Right now there are many mortally smitten hearts, which could no longer withstand a careless impact. And this would be murder just as is killing with a dagger, bullet, or poison. Does not poison penetrate into the heart through a malicious attack? What an enormous number of murders, actual, intentional, malicious in their delayed action, takes place beyond the purview of any courts or decree! To poison a man is inadmissible; to strangle a man is inadmissible; this is true. But then why is it permissible to gnaw at and tear the heart of a man? Surely, if people would even sometimes, though briefly, reflect in the morning hours about something good, apart from their own selfish interests, this already would be a great offering to the world.

Of course, ignorant cynics will probably sneer, saying a thought is nothing; in any case it is no more than a blade of grass in the wind. Any cynicism about thought, about the spirit, about intangible possibilities, will be a clear example of the grossest ignorance. When these ignorant ones, grinning maliciously, say, "It is not for us people of small culture to plunge into an ocean of thoughts," this will be said not at all in humility or timidity, but will be the expression of the ugliest pride.

* * *

Often people dream in secret of encountering something, as they say in popular language, supernatural. As if in the great essence there can be the natural, and as its antithesis, the supernatural! Of course, this ordinary expression, found in common usage, does not lead to a true realization. But the root of the matter is that as soon as people chance to come in contact with even the beginning of such an unusual manifestation, they fall into such unrestrained heart palpitation that the manifestation stops short. It is discontinued for the very same reason as in the case of the experiment related above. It becomes clear that the uncultivated heart and the inexperienced consciousness cannot endure anything above the trivial routine.

Very often certain inexplicable heart palpitations are spoken about. People attribute them to the category of sex, to excessive work, or to some other excesses. But among these manifestations not a few cases could be found when some beautiful wings have already touched someone, expectant or unexpectant, yet at the first proximity to them he suffered a mortal trembling. This, too, so often results from the incompatible distinction between earthly language and the heavenly tongue.

So much good and compassion is contained in the simple consideration for the weak heart. If people, even in their everyday life, would more often permit themselves a humane thought about a neighbor's pain, about his over-fatigue and the weakness of his heart, then, surely they would become in many cases more humane.

Apparitions have been spoken of in all sorts of narratives. They are entirely beyond question. It is undoubtedly true that many times, even with a highly needed goal in view, departed relatives and friends could not impart their good news, solely because of that same animal terror on the part of those to whom they appeared. Cases are known, when, desiring to save a person from peril, the departed ones have had to undertake a whole series of gradual approaches in order to first of all free the person from fear. Precisely fear so often prevents receiving the best news.

These manifestations, these good messages, and wishes to help have been written about so much that it is impossible to go into an enumeration of the individual episodes. Beginning with theological and on through many philosophical, historical and poetic narratives, it is everywhere affirmed that there is no death, as such, and that the proximity of other worlds can be sensed even amidst everyday life. All this is past doubting. But malice and hatred, which have so taken possession of humanity in our time, make it imperative to recall once more that the essential nature of man is good, and that everything evil and hideously harmful is primarily a sediment resulting from ignorance.

The truly dark ones, those creatures that have fallen very low, exert their influence first of all on the ignorant. Their favorite expedient is intimidation in many ways. They try hard to so obscure and lower the consciousness of their victim that he feels himself isolated, alone, and finally he believes his fortune to be only in communion with the dark ones. And these likewise try to deprive the victim of all true joys, imposing upon him all the shameful surrogates of self-indulgence.

Man wishes to find forgetfulness. Instead of wanting to reflect more clearly and to take up arms in a spiritual battle, he is made to seek oblivion. In this desire for oblivion, it is easier to take possession of him and make him an obedient instrument, cajoling him into ignorance. Whereas only the thought of good which lies deep at the base of one's being can impel him to a thirst for knowledge. Then man will not lose a day or an hour in order to learn, to improve, and to make beautiful every possible thing. In this process, thought about good will be also thought about beauty.

Tzagan Kure, April 16, 1935.

PYRRHIC VICTORIES

NOT by accident has the expression "Pyrrhic Victory" become so deeply entrenched in the study of history. A deep tragedy was contained in the fact that King Pyrrhus, after a seemingly brilliant victory over powerful Rome, was compelled to exclaim, "One more such victory and we are undone."

On the lips of a conqueror such an avowal about the depletion of forces sounds particularly tragic. And other, similar victories are known in various epochs of humanity. They are known in the history of governments, and in public and private life as well. One can vividly picture the situation of an army commander who has defeated the enemy and cannot move forward because his own army has disappeared. Translated into contemporary language, a factory owner can defeat all his competitors by great efforts, and at the end discover that he has no means left to keep on running his machines. Such cases are easy to find in contemporary life. True, the modern army leaders may look for vindication in the fact that even the powerful King Pyrrhus could not foresee the amount of strength he might need for a victory over an enemy. But nevertheless, after the battle, in the quiet of his tent King Pyrrhus himself was probably tormented by the thought that he did not provide for more reserves which could have been used in urgency.

This all relates to mundane Pyrrhic victories; yet Pyrrhic victories are also possible in spirit. A doer intensifies all his inner strength to conquer dark obstacles. An extreme tension is achieved. The enemy is repulsed. But after the victory it is suddenly revealed that the inner forces are entirely spent. This might present one of the greatest tragedies.

Of course, you will answer to this, How could the spiritual forces be expended when the inexhaustibility of this source has been declared so many times? True, the source of the spirit is inexhaustible, but it becomes inexhaustible when realized. The eternal, never outworn, never dissipated spirit nurtures all energies. But again, for this action the spirit must be cognized. Psychic energy must be preserved as the greatest healing expedient.

When would a doer feel himself depleted? Only when he did not previously take cognizance of his spirit. Spirit always vitalizes the body; but in order to acknowledge it one must turn to it, and while expending it in struggle its inexhaustibility should at the same time be known without any doubt.

He who makes his spiritual life an immutable basis of his existence, will never, in a spiritual sense, find himself in the position of Pyrrhus the conqueror. Such a spiritual leader, first of all, will know that the battle he began is but a starting point and will be only a link in an endless necklace of spiritual battles.

With such a realization, at the beginning of each battle the warrior will give thought beforehand to the great reserve of strength needed by him at the completion of the battle. He will realize that the end of this one battle only means the beginning of a new one. This future, undeferrable beginning of a new battle will be welcomed by the warrior as one more possibility sent to him.

He will once again realize more clearly to what an extent the dark enemies are unavoidable, and also to what extent it is equally unavoidable to have precisely them as one's own enemies. From the very beginning of existence these enemies were actually formed with all the fury of ignorance. After all, the fury of ignorance is always the most violent. An ignoramus, in spite of all, is somehow tortured by his ignorance. He does not wish to recognize knowledge, because then he stands the chance of losing his dark service. Yet, even in the most darkened heart stirs the most bitter feeling of something unrealized.

He who battles for the light of truth, for enlightenment, cannot be aggravated by the evidence of dark adversaries. If those dark ones would not attack him, it would mean that he was not acknowledged by them as an enemy. This would signify that darkness did not consider him as one of the workers and warriors of Light. This would be truly distressing.

It is easy to observe various strata of consciousness. An inexperienced worker without sufficient depth of consciousness at times feels self-pity, perceiving an endless battle. But a deep consciousness, trained by the heart, rejoices at being called to an honorable battle.

Then, a Pyrrhic victory will not take place, but instead a true victory is destined, in which incalculable forces and possibilities are disclosed.

We had a chance to see such true creative workers, who, seemingly, at the most difficult moment for them exclaimed, "This is fine! This is truly useful!" Later, when circumstances became favorable to them and a former situation proved to be useful, they were asked, "At that time when it seemed hopelessly difficult, how could you know that this difficulty would give rise to a possibility of victory? At that moment when you humanly exclaimed about usefulness, could you have already known the flow of all subsequent conditions?"

The worker smiled and replied: "Perhaps my mind could not perceive the order of future circumstances, but my heart with all its straight-knowledge affirmed the final victory. When I spoke with such conviction about the usefulness of the situation, it was not sending an invocation into space; my heart not only knew, but affirmed the future."

Indeed one should distinguish between conjurations of despair and the straight-knowledge of the heart. All strength may be spent in despair, whereas straight-knowledge with all solicitude will safeguard the reserves needed for the future.

In the expression "Pyrrhic Victory" there is great irony. Truly, of what worth is such victory, which has prepared only the most terrible defeat? The defeat of Pyrrhus began with this victory, which means that defeat was already there while the victorious trumpets were sounding. Napoleon marching upon Moscow was already defeated, and the retreating Kutuzov was already victorious. Napoleon spent his forces because, owing to his well known error of judgment, he lost spiritual guidance. At the same time Kutuzov wisely calculated his entire strength and piled up his future victories. Moscow was burning and the reflected glow of its fire illumined the defeat of "ten and two tongues."[7] Such an event demanded vast bonfires.

But it is instructive to recall how many ignoramuses condemned the actions of Kutuzov! How many madmen and traitors demanded that he use up the entire army, thus creating future calamity. But the old commander simulating an appearance of the drowsiness of old age knew his path, and his unfading laurel wreath of a conqueror will remain forever a true lesson.

Amidst the lessons of life, amidst the studies of living ethics, let those who guide and those who are guided discern where is a true defeat, and where a real victory is preserved.

Tzagan Kure, April 20, 1935.

---

[7] A well known historic saying in Russia meaning that the army of Napoleon included representatives of a number of European nations.

THE TRUE FORCE

A MIDST the early uncontrolled experiments with suggestion there remain in our memory a few true episodes. It is told that a man, after drinking a glass of absolutely pure water, died exhibiting the actual symptoms of that poison, after it had been suggested to him that he had drunk a strong poison. A man put into an absolutely fresh and clean bed under a suggestion that in it a man died from a serious contagious illness exhibited all the signs of that infection. A suggestion was made about the start of a flood, and in his own room, a man almost perished from indisputable symptoms of drowning. It was suggested to someone that he was crossing a turbulent mountain stream, and in the presence of a large gathering he removed his shoes, took off some of his garments, and cautiously made his way upon imagined stones.

A certain physician told a strong hypnotist that the latter could influence only people with weak nerves, yet he, being a physician, would never succumb to such charlatanism. The hypnotist smiled and said, "Because of what you said, when you leave me now, you will fall flat on your back; maybe then you will begin to think differently." A number of people were present at this strange duel of words. The physician, boldly and full of indignation, turned around and walked away from the hypnotist. But after a few steps he suddenly stopped and attempted to move further as if conquering some obstacle, then stopped again, and gradually, in spite of all his efforts, fell flat upon his back. The defeat of this materialist was met with shouts of laughter from the audience. The defeated physician got up shamefacedly, and rubbing the back of his neck hurriedly left the hall.

This small episode of the demonstration of suggestion could be followed up by a number of facts about people performing that which was mentally commanded and not being able to explain to themselves what compelled them to act in this manner and no other. Aside from conscious suggestions, there are, of course, many more taking place and being received subconsciously, and also many being commanded subconsciously.

And so, it appears that symptoms of poison are engendered by thought. Symptoms of contagious diseases are created not by the contagion, but by thought itself. For a contagion or poisoning a period of incubation is needed, yet a thought calls forth the same results and produces them with lightning speed. Thus, thought is stronger than any poison, any contagion.

From another angle, if thought is stronger than the most harmful things, it could be naturally more powerful than the most healing reactions. There are widely known cases when a physician, for the benefit of his patient, is obliged to prescribe sugar water, and it gives excellent results. Naturally, not the pinch of sugar, but the thought of the recipient is so powerful. It would seem that the facts of the power of suggestion are sufficiently known to all, and yet, constantly in professional practice and also in everyday life the significance of suggestion is either forgotten or, even worse, is still denied. In this one can observe the eternal battle of narrow materialism with unlimited, highly cultivated spirituality.

It is sad to recall that often the smallest considerations exceed the salutary sendings. This does not mean that the sending was weak. Speaking simply, the recipient could not find any need for it. And so, instead of something very useful, the most minute, mediocre, and conventional suddenly prevailed. Usually this takes place amidst conditions where one does not ponder at all about thought. There exist entire families in which a discussion about thought, as such, would be altogether inadmissible and, in any case, ridiculed.

Therefore, often the most important impellent, and the spiritual principle itself are subject to furious denials and ridicule. It is narrated that a certain warring tribe, when preparing to receive absolution for sins from its spiritual leader, always abstains from attacks and robbery. But after receiving the benediction, the robber warriors become particularly furious and rush to perform any and all kinds of assaults.

Is it not approximately the same when you see people leaving church after praying and immediately indulging in all sorts of slander? The very same often becomes obvious when observing people just afflicted by a great tragedy or seemingly affected by spiritual words; nevertheless, they become at once immersed in insufferable mean gossip and slander. In all such deplorable instances one can observe a primitive state of thought. Indeed, actual ignorance compels people not to discriminate where and in what is contained true strength.

And yet, the realization of the true power of thought can come only voluntarily. No lectures, or books, if the heart is not open to them, can enlighten any one.

A certain pedagogue suggested to his students that they think in every possible way. Behind his back the unrestrained ignoramuses called him an unhappy old bookworm. If this episode could have been transported into the surroundings of the classic Greek Academy, what a powerful ostracism would have been imposed upon the ignorant who dared to cackle at the noble word about thought. Loftily and with magnanimity must the valued concept of thought enter the consciousness. And what a steadfast friend and adviser and true well-wisher will be revealed through purified and treasured thought! Real strength is attracted and assimilated where thought is ennobled.

Tzagan Kure, April 25, 1935.

ATTRACTION

LIVINGSTONE could be taken away from Africa only when dead, so much did he love that part of the world. Casati was forcibly taken away from Africa, the only country in which he felt himself at home. All the remainder of his life, passed in Italy, his native land, he felt unhappy.

There could enumerated a great number of diverse examples of such seemingly incomprehensible attachments to a definite part of the world or even to a definite place. There are Spaniards by blood who cling to Havana or South America. There are Britons who have become forever attached to India. There are Swedes, Frenchmen, Russians who can breathe only the air of Asia.

In human life there are so many inexplicable attachments, from the loftiest to the most ordinary ones. On the one side we see attachment to the place of one's birth. There are many explanations for this. But how, then, can we surmise an unexplainable overpowering attraction to some far-removed place on the earthly globe? Often people get there as if by accident. And suddenly they find themselves, as it were, in their native element. After all, no one has expelled them from their birthplace. No wrongdoings or crimes have driven them beyond remote seas and mountains. It means there must have been some other reason, some other magnet, which compelled them to strive whole-heartedly to a place which no rational thinking could have advised.

Such attractions are entirely distinct from the proper desire of youth to set out somewhere, to get away, to spread their wings in new air. In the hour of such decisions the youthful seeker does not even give a thought as to precisely whither he wishes to go. He only senses calls and perhaps cries of the heart, which draw him to learning something more. Usually in such seekers noble characters are revealed. They are voluntarily seeking some kind of test. These first days of independence will forever remain for them a beacon of vigor.

We send a mental greeting to one of our American friends, who, now in the twilight of his years, recalls with especial spirit and tenderness his first journey as a cabin boy on a ship. This wise old man has related to me how, in his turn, he sent his grandson alone on horseback from the Pacific Ocean to the Atlantic, in order to accustom the ten-year-old boy to complete independence. Probably somewhere on that marked-off route unseen care was arranged for the young traveler, but, for all that, he had to carry out his task, left to his own resourcefulness and intelligence. And yet, travel in America which is unusually complex and filled with movement can at times be full of all sorts of surprises. Besides, there was the stipulation that the young horseman not only preserve his own health, but that he keep his mount in good condition. Doubtless such a trip will remain in his memory as long as he lives.

We all have also read about young people who have run away to America in quest of a new life. And in such cases the journey itself drew them, the search for new solutions of life, and not only the desire to find the longed-for place in which they would like to settle and concentrate on their work and life.

Quite different is the story about a five-year-old Tibetan lad who repeatedly and unrestrainably went off to some home of his own. The boy would dress himself as if for a journey. He tied on his back a supply of food and a sacred book, and at a convenient moment he disappeared from the house. When his people rushed off to search for him, they would find him going along the mountain paths. They tried to talk him into returning home. They told him that he ought to get back to his own home. But the lad assured them that he was going precisely to his own, real home, that the house where he had lived up to the present time was not his, and that he must hasten to his real home, where he must remain. We passed this place just as the boy had left for the fourth time, and we do not know how it all ended.

In any case, there was some sort of irresistible attraction, and it is quite possible that if it remained unfulfilled, the little boy would wither like a blossom without moisture. It was amazing to observe a five-year-old boy explaining so seriously about his real home to which he must go.

And so also Livingstone and Casati, and all the countless travelers toward their real homes would have withered if they could not have succeeded in reaching their destination, so clear in their hearts. Besides, this circumstance is especially striking in that these aspirants were not seeking only salubrious conditions of nature, and were not striving for some well-ordered place of abode. On the contrary, their home, their real home, could involve many hardships. Such a longed-for home was often almost unendurable physically, but for all that, they rejoiced in spirit and felt themselves to be in a destined place.

"Beauty is in the eye of the beholder." This adage shows deep insight. In it is emphasized an inner significance which surpasses everything external. If such a wayfarer has found his home, it would be harmful to tear him away because of some external circumstances. No business advancements, no tempting advantages compensate a man for the home which he has finally discovered. He need not become a member of the nation or tribe among which this inexplicable home of his is located. He is attracted thither not so much by the people as by all the other circumstances of existence. When a man feels good, it is usually not even possible to explain in words why it is so. Sometimes this feeling of well-being arises even under very arduous circumstances.

Likewise, when a man encounters his fellow travelers or his antagonists, he often cannot rationally explain his reactions, but through his eyes and his heart he knows much that cannot be expressed in words. People ought to regard such attractions with all solicitude. They should grasp them at their very inception in order not to extinguish or shatter them by the fetters of reason. If such an attachment awakens in a man, even though his nature may be subverted and his mind may be forever distorted, nothing will succeed in ejecting from his consciousness that which his heart and his spirit knows.

We also know people who have been permanently wounded. Either someone did not admit them to their already recognized home, or someone or something deprived them of their destined fellow traveler. The ignorant consider such attractions nonsense, a preconception, which should be terminated by any means. These ignorant ones never ponder on whence and from what cause this knowledge emanates. On the other hand it is understandable what an enormous significance for the entire life of a man is produced by the discovery of this, his recognized home, by finding somewhere his destined, long-ago-encountered fellow traveler. Even if for some reason, for some good, the man should be voluntarily separated for a time from his home, from his companion, nevertheless all his activity in the course of the temporary separation will continue under the sign of the realization achieved.

The man has found his home, he has found his companion, he has been fortified by long-established magnets, and thus the more clearly and resoundingly he can benefit his fellow man. The heart knows when it is again able to make contact with some other homes, and when the hour has come to inspire some other fellow travelers. Such straight-knowledge of the heart does not weaken a man, it merely transforms his activity, and many will ask, Whence come such strength and such assurance? They issue from realization of the longed-for home, from mutual strengthening through the longed-for companion. The family and teachers must deal solicitously with each manifest attraction. The home may be very near or it may be beyond mountains and valleys. And the companion will be found when nothing is allowed to obscure the true destined attachments.

Tzagan Kure, April 27, 1935.

RUSSIA

THE first chapters of your work have already reached me in the Mongolian desert. Although I know that this message will not reach you soon, nevertheless I must write to you.

You feel Russia so deeply and so truly. I have rarely met definitions such as yours. In a vivid mosaic you have molded a many-faceted image of great Russia. And you have done it with magnanimity toward all its parts. You expressly crossed upon benevolent milestones. Only good signs denote the right path.

You say: "Russia is not only a state . . . It is a super-state, an ocean, an element which has not yet been fully formed, which has not yet reached its own predestined shores. It has not as yet begun to sparkle in sharpened and faceted concepts, in its individuality, as a rough diamond sparkles in the jewel. It all still is forebodings, fermentation, endless strivings, and limitless organic possibilities.

"Russia is an ocean of lands swinging over an entire sixth part of the world and holding within its spread wings the East and West.

"Russia is seven blue seas, mountains crowned by white ice; Russia is a furry bristle of endless forests, carpets of wind-swept and blooming meadows.

"Russia is endless snows, over which are singing deadly silver storms and on this background the kerchiefs of Russian women are glowing vividly, snows from under which dark violets and blue snowdrops come forth in tender spring.

"Russia—a land of unfolding industrialism of a new type as yet unheard of, as yet undefined.

"Russia—a land of fabulous, richest treasures, which are hidden in her deep bosom until the destined time.

"Russia is not one race alone—therein lies her strength. Russia is a union of races, a union of peoples speaking 140 languages; it is a free collective, unity in diversity, poly-chromic, polyphonic.

"Russia is not only the country of the instantaneous present. It is a country of the great past, with which it is linked indissolubly. In her sunny birch groves even today rites to ancient gods are performed. In her frontier forests even to this day sacred oaks and cedars rustle, ornament-ed with fluttering bunting. And before them are placed offerings, pitiful clay bowls with gruel in them. *Zhaleiki*[8] are mournfully crying over her steppes in honor of ancient gods and heroes.

"Russia is the land of Byzantine domes, sounds of bells, and blue incense borne from the great, dead heiress of Rome—Byzantium, second Rome. And they give to Russia inexpressible beauty, superimposed upon Russian art. Rus-sia is a powerful, crystal waterfall, streaming bow-shaped from the abyss of time into the abyss of times, uncaught as yet by the frost of narrow experience, sparkling in the sun with rainbows of consciousness, sounding throughout the world with a powerful affirmation of Pan-Slavic being.

"Russia is grandiose, unrepeatable.

"Russia is polar. Russia has a mission in the new era.

"Russia is the only country in the world which through its greatest festival glorifies the affirmation of life, a festi-val of resurrection from the dead, rejoicing at the dawn of a blossoming spring day, with the lights of religious pro-cessions beneath the fiery amber brocade of the morning sky."

Is it not strange that in my letter to you I am quoting your own words? But these words are so true, so heartfelt, so beautiful, that I would like once more to live through the images created by them. They must be not only real-

---

[8]   An ancient folk wind instrument.

ized but also loved. The more we absorb them, with all their sounds and colors, with all the hieroglyphs of existence on our minds, the more will truth be revealed; and it is so needed. So urgently needed.

In your further survey of the structure of Russian original art you justly mentioned V. V. Stasov.[9] And together with you I once again in thought paid a tribute to his memory. It was he who, so to speak, introduced me for the first time to the treasure house of the Public Library. He introduced me to the treasures of this storehouse and supported me in my first calls pertaining to Russia.

I remember my correspondence with him. I always wrote him in the style of ancient Russian epistles, and he always rejoiced that the style and manner were as of old. Sometimes he replied to me in the same true style. And at times he laughed good-naturedly saying, "Although your yellowed epistle smelled of fresh coffee, its spirit remained Russian, really Russian." I remember his article about my painting "The March" in which he understood so well my anxious and fundamental striving. Kurbatov had our photograph taken at his famous desk in the Public Library, covered with books. When you quote Stasov I recall vividly the Public Library and those fine, remarkable people who used to come to his hospitable desk. And that same Stasov also took me to visit Leo Tolstoy, after I painted my "Messenger."

And when you mention Moussorgsky, the uncle of Elena Ivanovna,[10] you awaken in me the life of all those related to and linked with our great composer. The tragedy of Moussorgsky's life was also a true Russian tragedy. Maybe I have already told you when we met that in a certain country estate, because of ignorance, many manuscripts of that great creator were burned.

I do not remember whether we spoke with you about the family of Rimski-Korsakov, about the members of the

---

[9]   Vladimir Vasilevich Stasov, renowned music and art critic.
[10]   The wife of Prof. Roerich.

renowned group of artists—the *Powerful Kutchka*—and about the *Peredvizhniki*[11] with whom I often met. Kuinji, Shishkin, Repin, Surikov, Nesterov, the brothers Vasnetzov—all this was dear to me and instructive. You also recall correctly the attacks on everything national. Whereas precisely because of its national character the art of Russia was so valued in the West. It would seem that this vivid example known to all should have been a sufficient reprimand for all those who attempted to divert the powerful river of Russian creativeness into an alien channel. You truly understand the words of Stasov, "Every nation must have its own national art, and not drag itself on the coat tail of others, upon a trodden road, at someone's bidding." There was no condemnation of foreign creativeness in these words. Stasov was a truly cultured man to say this; but, as a sensitive critic he understood that the Russian essence will be much more valued if it is molded in its own beautiful forms. And Russia does give the most beautiful and the most penetrating images. The told and untold, the written and unwritten, as in ancient *synodics*,[12] the majestic images remain unuttered. In this inexpressibility is contained that hidden national, undrained chalice which you sense so heartily.

I hope that your future chapters, even if slowly, will also reach me and bring still more joy. You remember my painting, "Three Joys": a wandering dulcimer player tells a villager a story about three joys—St. George himself takes horses to pasture, Nicholas the Miracle Maker himself safeguards the herds, and Elijah the Prophet himself begins to reap the rye. I do not know where this painting is. In the book by Ernst there was a small reproduction of it. All kinds of unexpressed joys live in the heart.

---

[11]   A Traveling Exhibition in 1871 started an entirely new artistic movement, the propagators of which called themselves "the itinerants," *Peredvizhniki.*

[12]   A Russian word for a list of names of the dead to be read during a memorial mass.

* * *

Tonight a strong frost and snow struck accompanied by a storm. It got cold in our yurts, even the watch stopped. And in the morning the radiant sun shone in the literal sense, and all the hillocks and mountains sparkled white, pink, and blue in a sudden snowy adornment. The surrounding country, viewed from the steps of the former temple, reminded me of two of my paintings. One from far-off Karelia, and the other from the Tibetan Chantong. The very same hills were in my painting of the year 1915, "The Calling One." All calls pertain to the very same thing. The majesty of open spaces is one. Thank you for your word about Russia, which is so close to my heart.

Tzagan Kure, April 26, 1935.

THE INEXPRESSIBLE

SCIENTISTS say that absolute zero cannot possibly be attained. Professor V. de Haas, of the University of Leiden, who in his laboratory experiments reaches a point one five-thousandth of a degree above absolute zero, has declared that absolute zero (the ultimate extreme) will never be attained.

"Absolute zero is –459.8 degrees Fahrenheit. At this temperature all gases become solid and all motion ceases."

Thus, still another absolute point has been recognized as impossible. Likewise there results a small difference during decompositions and inversely, compositions. It turns out that that which is mechanically synthesized loses something which it formerly had, and which could even be detected on the scales at the beginning of the experiment. A well-known experiment with the decomposition and mechanical recomposition of a potato shows that there remains something that eludes formulation.

Similarly, one can observe something inexpressible in all manifestations. Moreover, precisely in this circumstance which eludes formulation something essential will be contained. Again one is obliged to recall the fact that the weight of a man immersed in intensive thinking differs from his usual weight.

On the one hand, such a factor is disappointing to the investigator in its unattainability. But on the other hand, precisely this something, even when detected by our crude physical apparatuses, always remains both inviting and inspiring. Could one hardly be distressed or disappointed when such obvious possibilities are already accessible to earthly expressions? No doubt there will come into being in the investigations some new approach which in place of the imagined absolute will provide a new infinity.

* * *

It is related that certain outstanding military leaders, during their most crucial battles remained in their quarters, seemingly absorbed in some mechanical usual occupation. Those who do not know would advance all sorts of ironical considerations. Some would even assume that in these moments the leader wished to mentally absent himself, under the influence of fear. But those who knew these great men intimately understood full well that at this time some unknown process was going on, which could not be put into words.

The leader has done everything that was dependent upon his decision. At this time he could not rationally make changes where his orders were already being carried out. The leader wished to set aside the language of reason and to allow something inexpressibly profound to create a new influential process. A small mechanical occupation was not just a killing of time. On the contrary, this was one of the means of shifting his consciousness. It stands to reason that the consciousness can be shifted without any mechanical distractions, but for this, along with the art of thinking, one also has to be in full possession of the reverse art of arresting thought.

Though the art of thinking is not easy, yet the ability to arrest thought can sometimes be still more difficult. For this it is necessary that the process of thought must entirely cease so that a new formation may arise in the consciousness without being burdened in any way. And this is very difficult, for here again the absolute is not reached in such an experiment.

Very often people assume that they have ceased thinking about something, yet it still remains an illusion of theirs. They compel themselves forcibly to think about something else. But this very compulsion will leave behind some reflexes of the former thought. Yet in order to shift the consciousness it is surely necessary to attain some almost infinitesimal numbers having many zeros. And, nevertheless, this will be a relative matter.

But long ago it was said on the Heights, "If you wish to become a new man, breathe a sigh about the Inexpressible. In a single sigh transport thyself unto the verge of Infinity."

Thus, not by prolonged calculations but in a single sigh about the Inexpressible is the consciousness renewed. And where a rocky cliff appeared insurmountable and impassable, calling distances are unexpectedly revealed.

But everything must be voluntary. In this concept is contained the greatest law. No coercion, no constraint enables the consciousness to be loftily transported. Voluntariness usually remains a not very well interpreted concept. In the ordinary understanding any liberty is often considered not concordant with good, with a heartfelt concern for one's fellow men.

Indeed, all testings and vital experiments will sufficiently demonstrate how much a true voluntariness transforms all actions. After all, this beautiful desire emanates from the depths of the chalice of consciousness. It results in both self-abnegation and a desire for continuous creativity in all spiritualized labor.

Again, it is very difficult to discern where is true voluntariness and where some alien considerations have entered in. In military organizations there are also volunteers. But among them only a few will be true volunteers, while the volunteering of the others will be tinged with extraneous considerations. There are entire army units where the members are supposed to be volunteers, but in reality they are trying to evade or conceal this or that dramatic factor in their life.

In all thought processes voluntariness plays the principal role. Without it there remains only a crude mirage which never renews the consciousness.

* * *

What kind of luminous sigh about the Inexpressible can bring forth that which is unexplainable through relative formulas? What kind of transference of consciousness into the Inexpressible helps to change matter into spirit, or rather, one state of consciousness into another? Where the will terminates, where desire is extinct, where the command is wordless, a single sigh about the Inexpressible will regenerate everything.

The most refined pranayama may be ineffective where a sigh about the Inexpressible is borne into the great spaces.

People read bookish words about the most great. These words are beautiful, but where there is the Word, the best words require something else, the still greater—the Inexpressible.

It is asked, "Is it for me to think about the Inexpressible?" "Verily, precisely for you on all the paths."

Tzagan Kure, April 28, 1935.

RECIPROCITY

"RECIPROCITY is the basis of agreements." So many times has this old French proverb been quoted. It has been repeated in lectures on international law, and has been used during the conclusion of all sorts of | treaties. Moreover, it has been quoted in countless cases of many vital perturbations.

Not just a most immutable truth is contained in the words of this proverb. Each human mind, in all its aspects, distinctly understands that without reciprocity any agreement will be only an empty and disgraceful sound. Without reciprocity the participation unfailingly amounts to falsehood and fraud, which sooner or later produces all the consequences created by deceit.

We speak about good will, but reciprocity can flourish only on the basis of good will. In no wise is it possible to evoke so-called reciprocity if this beautiful flower does not blossom as the lotus of the heart.

Waves beat against the rocks. The rocks meet them without reciprocity. True, the waves can wear away the rocks. The waves can form whole underwater grottoes and in their ceaseless motion can destroy stone giants. But of course this will not be reciprocity or agreement—this will be an assault. This is violence, and any violence inevitably ends in destruction of one kind or another. He who uses violence will perish from violence.

In the example of the waves and rocks, two discordant elements meet, as it were. Yet even the rocks, if their structure permitted, could lead the opposing element into channels useful for existence.

However, it is hardly possible to assume that human

hearts are as little in concordance as are water and stone. After all, even water can be in a solid state and the strata of rock can produce moisture. Yet these elements lack consciousness, or, at any rate, their consciousness is inacessible to us. But there can be no human heart, which on the one hand could bestow the dew of benefaction, and on the other be incapable of adamantine courage.

The humaneness which is common to all ages and peoples is likewise ineradicable. No matter what narcotics, alcohol, and nicotine may do to kill it, it can somehow, somewhere, be awakened.

A great criminal may be a devoted family man. Consequently, if his good feelings are still capable of being aroused in relationship to his near ones, in the same way, by some increased effort they can be extended toward all that exists. At present people are not setting up as an ideal St. Francis of Assisi, who even addressed a wolf as "Brother Wolf." Not even accepted is the ideal of the ascetics who possessed the language of the heart, which is understood by both birds and animals. Aside from these lofty ideals about which people usually exclaim, "Well, we're not St. Francis," there can be the meeting ground of common humanity.

On this heartfelt basis, it is still possible to open even the most tightly sealed heart. Apart from all their business affairs, about which people have composed the saying, "No deceit—no deal," apart from all their multifarious trade people cannot avoid contact with the spiritual spheres. People who are unaccustomed to such contacts sometimes even experience pain instead of beneficence. This arises from being unaccustomed to such sensations. Indeed, a man who has never felt an electric spark always believes himself extremely sensitive to even the least discharge of it. "It burned me," or "It pierced me," says the novice, hut by and by, if they are repeated, he does not even notice greater discharges.

Actually, these outcries arise not at all from a heightened sensitiveness, but from an ingrained prejudice. Is there not also precisely the same absurd prejudice in human relationships when a wave of rationality and cordiality beats against a rock of hostility and stupidity?

It is also strange that people so often imagine reciprocity as a matter of some sort of official governmental agreement. But, surely, without family, friendly, and social reciprocity, what is there to be said about that of the government? Rocking the basis of social intercourse, people shake all the other fundamentals. The foundations of marriage could be shaken, and as a result the state would acquire millions of homeless, savage juveniles born out of wedlock. It is possible to make an odious jest out of the employment of all kinds of poisons, and to end up with the poisoning of almost an entire people. Do we not see examples of this?

In each of such cases, which have turned into a national calamity, at the basis could be discerned some stupid egotistical action. Someone thought only about his own self-indulgence or culpable self-interest, and from this single malignant small piece of coal have burst out conflagrations leading to national disasters. Verily, brutalized egoism is primarily the enemy of reciprocity.

Life in a society provides a multitude of opportunities for the cultivation of reciprocity. Indeed, all feelings have to be cultivated. But a great deal of true humaneness and tolerance must be manifested in order that the very idea of reciprocity may grow freely and voluntarily. Reciprocity also reminds about responsibility. Each one who rejects reciprocity offered him in the work for the general good takes upon himself a grave responsibility. In reciprocity are combined mind and heart. In benefaction the heart senses where it must extend its benevolence. On the other hand the mind reminds about that responsibility which will grow out of cruelty or ignorance.

Experiments by small groups of co-workers assembled for good works provide many tests for the cultivation of reciprocity. It is better at first to test everything in daily life. Observe how routine daily tasks and conflicts are transformed, and you will apprehend how, as in a megaphone, they will reverberate, to be heard by all. Egoism and self-interest can also be verified through the megaphone. What a horrible, harrowing roaring and howling can result from an apparently most negligible domestic misunderstanding!

Not without reason in the ancient schools of life did the teacher sometimes intentionally fling out a test of tolerance and mutual understanding. Those who could not understand with their hearts that which was necessary, at least through reason could be put on their guard about the impending responsibility. It is possible to strike upon some resounding object in one corner of a house and receive an echo unexpectedly in an opposite quarter. It is exactly the same in the creating of responsibility and reciprocity.

If people could only realize more quickly that for the good of the peoples' progress reciprocity must not be left within the confines of a proverb, but should become the basis for cooperation!

"Reciprocity is the basis of agreements."

Tzagan Kure, April 29, 1935.

ANTAGONISM

"TO write you about the same thing is not burdensome for me, yet it is edifying for you."

How much resounds in these words! This "about the same thing" alone evokes deep reflection. One is amazed at the adamantine firmness that produced this calm statement, whereas in other cases, on other lips, it would cause irritation. Precisely "not burdensome," because the writer of these words, wisely knowing various degrees of the spirit knew how difficult it is to turn the rudder into the right current of thought.

Among the many concepts subject to repetition, antagonism is known to all. Whoever shall prescribe and urge that antagonism not be cultivated will himself be within the ranks of the builders.

A justly founded indignation against the corrupting attempts of the dark forces is one thing, but an entirely different matter is an artificially created and light-mindedly nourished antagonism. The beginning of antagonism flows from a very small and shallow source. So often at its base there will be some tiny personal feeling, some tiny offense, or nonconformity in acquired habits. Usually the man himself does not notice precisely when this small viper penetrates into his Chalice. The course of antagonism is usually very lengthy. It is accumulated from all sorts of preceding thoughts and illusions. A man sometimes feels a small offense, and later on his own volition he begins like a madman to attach to this embryo a tiny tail, wings, paws, and horns—until there results a veritable small monster tenaciously living in his bosom.

Many times these self-made monsters have been

described in popular literature. Nonetheless, almost all those who read about them never ascribe to themselves what is being depicted.

At first, speaking simply, something has been unpleasant. This something has probably taken place in the course of the daily routine; then this everyday matter is transferred into a far broader scope, and eventually, like a cancerous growth, it is established as a most dangerous aspect.

The man reaches such a point that, not realizing it in the least, he will not even be in any condition to meet with anyone or encounter anything. Gradually, through auto-suggestion he convinces himself that precisely this small daily detail has always been for him the most essential condition of his life.

Each one has had occasion to encounter such woebegone, odd people who have heaped up around themselves impassable barriers of illusory rubbish. Each one can call to mind people who insist that their organism cannot take in this or that food. At the same time, when they have been given precisely this same food under another name, their organism has received it quite well, without any bad consequences. This means that originally an aversion was created, which through autosuggestion reached monstrous obsessive proportions.

From any worldly domain it is possible to enumerate a great number of similar examples. A man believes himself unable to walk along the rim of an abyss, but pursued by a wild animal he rushes over a still more dangerous place without even noticing. No doubt everyone has in store many like examples.

Nonetheless, the question of self-induced antagonism remains one of the most unwholesome problems in life. Sometimes people try to explain such antagonism toward something either by innate light-mindedness, or by indulgence, absence of discipline, or simply by age. All these explanations do not make it easier, because the monsters of antagonism will plague their creator just the same, and do harm to his surroundings as well. From daily, private life they scatter their poison throughout society and they have a blighting effect upon fundamental state and world problems.

No doubt each one has sometimes had occasion to ask his friends about the cause of their aversion to something. It is likewise probable that many of those questioned believed that this was simply an irresistible innate feeling. Yet in reality in all cases it was obvious that somewhere, somehow, a kind of habit had been formed, and then some circumstance had simply failed to conform to this habit. Sometimes a dish proved too salty or an expected flower did not bloom on a designated date. Even such trifles can gradually be spun together into an entire idiosyncrasy.

One should cure oneself of such cumulated aversions just as one should of the germ of madness.

Many times life itself shows that precisely that circumstance which was apparently an object of irresistible aversion suddenly becomes a most useful one, and that place which appeared emptiest proves to be the richest. Then very shamefacedly the man has to rid himself of all his untimely conclusions. Many times he inwardly regrets that he allowed the self-made monsters to take possession of him to such an extent.

Since antagonism is unjust, so also is partiality. The man who surrounds himself with worthless favorite phantoms deserves the same pity as he who engenders antagonism within himself. Of course the creator of partiality must sooner or later acknowledge his inconsistency with great shame. And of course in people who do not think deeply this shame will produce irritation and will create new harmfulness. Indeed, both self-made antagonism and irrational partiality are equally shameful, because they both have to be outlived. Walking in shackles is very burdensome. It is just as burdensome as any other violation of true justice.

In Roman law the distinction between canon law and civil law is studied. The process of one being engendered from the other is very complicated. One is amazed at those profound minds which have penetrated these subtleties of the formation of human relationships. If we have before us all the various examples of sound judgment and of a desire for the most just solutions, then, too, in everyday usage this must impel us toward a very consciously careful attitude regarding our conduct.

"A word is like a sparrow; it flies out, not to be caught again." Thus does the popular wisdom forewarn. Indeed, here is assumed not only the outwardly sounding word, but also the significance of the thought which gave birth to it. If each thought produces some sort of zigzag in space, then this hieroglyph will remain somewhere, and will always remind us first of all about how deplorable it is to litter space with ill-considered hieroglyphs. For each one of them we are responsible and will have to reply through the megaphone of space.

"From the fall of a rose petal, worlds tremble."

The radio whines monotonously, and something is inexorably piercing space. What is this? Partiality? Antagonism? Let us hope that there is being created one more spatial hieroglyph of justice.

Tzagan Kure, May 1, 1935.

DELAY

D ELAY is like unto death." Thus said Peter the Great. What is new in this? Why is this saying so often called to mind? Is there anyone who does not know it already? There is nothing new in this aphorism, nevertheless it is and will be remembered. It should be inscribed upon all state and public institutions. It should be on the first page of school textbooks.

It does not matter whether something which has been said is absolutely new or not. In general is not the new merely a matter of time and circumstances? But the point is that something which has been said in such an authoritative form must enter into all human works. And this is not repetition, because what was said is probably entirely original in the brevity and convincingness of its form. That which is needful, needful for everyone, needful for each day is expressed simply. It recalls what people try to put out of mind, as much as possible. They try to counter this with the cynical maxim, "Do not do today what can be put off till tomorrow."

In cynicism and laziness people try to make up tales and sayings in order somehow to put off work. It means that for them any task is a burden, an affliction, it means that for them labor is a curse. And yet is it not terrible when a destined joy is turned into a curse, into terror, into distress?

Delay is everlastingly uniform in its qualities. How adroitly it screens itself, so well concealed that even the experienced eye does not always discern where it has occurred. Endless reasons may be found for this. Yet each one knows that a madman may become resourceful and inventive to an unimaginable degree.

Delay occurs through lack of knowledge and due to a complicated character. It occurs because of credulity regarding others and from intentional maliciousness as well. In a word, almost all actions that take place can be classified according to this or that degree of procrastination. If only this procrastination would not finally inflict harm! But any imperfection, the same as any evil, must invariably reecho somewhere and somehow. In the history of every nation can be found striking examples of how a small delay produced great effects. Consequently this delay was not as small as it might appear to the earthly eye; it means that in it was already contained the entire embryo of what was to follow. If such delays were to be examined under the microscope, there could be seen a ready culture for all kinds of bacteria.

If all who delay would recognize the future being created by them, then, surely many of them would be terrified and would increase tenfold their promptitude and diligence. But people in general think little about the future. We have said more than once that in schools students do not learn to think about the future. Yet without thought about the future, man will be blind, as it were. Those who have become blind see what is past, but do not perceive their future. Blindness, as such, should be avoided by means of the best medical treatment.

Thus it is that people seemingly prepare themselves for the future; but when its signs draw near, they are not recognized. It was said long ago that a messenger was coming, but when he arrived, people did not recognize him. Because of this the most needed and urgent letters may have fallen into malicious hands.

In the last analysis, such non-recognition is also contained in delay. The very word *delay* sufficiently expresses that something has been put off, that is to say, it has come too late. One can be too late in setting eggs under a hen, and then one need not be surprised that the chickens do not hatch out. The example of the egg is very convincing, because in it all the elements for the succeeding evolution have been made ready. And from a simple delay or from careless forgetfulness something foreseen and prepared is allowed to rot. But does any one have the right to engender corruption through faithlessness?

The statement by Peter the Great is in reality a great and relevant adage. One has but to recall his life and untiring labor in order to understand how many reins the ruler knew how to hold simultaneously in his hands. There are people who know how to hold several reins, but there are others who hold on to one with difficulty because of not having developed this ability in themselves. What sort of driver will one be with one rein in his hand? Such comparisons would be laughable if they were not sometimes so sad.

It should not be thought that everything innate already exists in a cultivated form. Of course everything must be cultivated and tested. Moreover, testings cannot be accidental, they must be encountered in full consciousness and with full preparedness and rationality.

Such preparedness and keen-sightedness protect one against delay. Can there be delay in the flight of a meteor? Could the orbits of the luminaries admit of delay?

"Delay is like unto death."

* * *

"Leave not the honey exposed too long" is also a saying about delay. Each one has tested himself on how his entire destiny can be altered by a minute's belatedness. It has been said: "Being early is to be judged, but being late is already condemned." In this ancient maxim is also expressed a warning about timeliness.

Again, is it necessary to repeat any of the old warnings? After all, they are so old, and they have cautioned people for so many ages. They have forewarned, and urged, and proved their usefulness. Nonetheless, petty habits of life have been violently opposed to all the good precepts. To counter each bit of good advice an excuse has been invented.

Our days are bringing all sorts of accelerations. But all these prizes for swiftness still do not signify that the great maxims about delay are becoming unnecessary. One may let a date slip by and then no swiftness is of assistance. Conversely, each belated burst of speed produces only a deep sorrow.

Something already molded and only needing a last impulse has become benumbed in an artificial situation. And what can be more unnatural than the spectacle of a man left standing on one leg? It is impossible to remain thus for long. It is also impossible to drive with one rein, especially if it be weakly held.

The fluttering ones must somehow be persuaded that delay is dangerous first of all for themselves. Of course, they think, Let someone wait. But they invariably forget the fact that such waiting will cost them too dearly.

"Delay is like unto death."

Tzagan Kure, May 9, 1935.

ANONYMITY

NO matter how often we mention the rapture and amazement before the anonymous creativity scattered upon the entire face of Earth, nevertheless, we are enraptured every time we see new examples.

When, upon dangerous mountain passes, you find gigantic images upon rocks, hewed out by someone's loving labor, you are filled each time with reverence for such creativeness, molded by a primal force.

And in Mongolian deserts you will always pause before this nameless creativeness, so little understood at present. How many discussions have been provoked by the so-called "stone babas."[13] Only recently there were attempts to account for these monumental portraits as being reminders of those buried, as it were. The reason for this was in the historic details of the costume. Also, a chalice placed in the left hand of the statue compelled one to reflect about its origin. Sometimes such a chalice had a sign of fire over it. There was such an image in my painting "The Guardians of the Desert."

In any event, a chalice adorned by fire could not be connected with the concept of a burial ritual. In this detail was already contained a reminder about some cult. The more so since the chalice drew attention to itself, being repeated many times in statues, and always in a somewhat ritual manner.

Our attention regarding some sort of ritual or cult was also directed to small bronze figures, brought to us by

---

[13]   Stone sculptures of women.

Mongols. One of them was purchased and is in George's[14] collection. For another of these figures Mongols asked an exorbitant price and it could not be acquired. On each of these images there is a ring attached to the top of the head indicating that it was probably worn over the bosom. The state of polish, owing to use, indicated its great age as well as constant wearing. But the chief interest lay in that very same chalice which attracted such attention upon the images of the "stone babas."

Undoubtedly we deal with some sort of cult, and a very old one at that. A chalice with a flame over it reminds one of so many things that it would be an act of carelessness to offer some immediate explanations. In any case this question is of unusual interest.

There were also brought small bronze crosses, to be worn next to one's skin, of an ancient type probably of Nestorian origin. Not far from Batukhalka are the ruins of the old city, and nearby are the remnants of a Nestorian cemetery. Perhaps, this was the monument of a Nestorian Mongolian prince.

An unforgettable impression of anonymous creativeness is likewise made by the images molded out of white quartz which are scattered over the deserts. Among them may also be found definitely sacred figures, images of big suburgans, and at times some unexpected human-like figures, obviously of phallic meaning. Every kind of anonymous creativity, apparently needed by the originator, merits special attention.

You sense quite clearly that these creations are evoked by some deep urgency. Labor used for them was a sacred labor. Someone, unknown to us, needed to spend his strength and time in order to leave, at times in most unsuitable conditions, an anonymous monument for the instruction of some unknown travelers.

The inexhaustibility of learning associated with great antiquity is always enticing. We encounter such special

---

[14]   Nicholas Roerich's son, a well known orientalist.

psychologies, such demands so alien to our present time that every conscientious investigator will experience a special kind of joy because of this inexhaustibility.

Many works are published, but what a quantity of notes, records—sometimes fully completed—and important investigations, remain in manuscript form! Each one of us has chanced to find in private libraries, and sometimes in a flea market, very valuable manuscripts. At times they already have been appraised by someone. They merited careful treatment in beautiful leather bindings, with very illustrious *ex libris*. But, just as often, one has come across barbarously torn pages, with entire parts gone forever, maybe used for most lowly needs.

So much anonymous creativeness is in these manuscripts! They were of much importance to someone. If not in their entirety, then in some parts they express many significant and lovingly collected observations.

To these nameless labors we shall bring a flower in reverence to their inner meaning.

Tzagan Kure, May 12, 1935.

THE COMPLETELY NEW

THOUGHT transference over a distance—Professor Joseph Rhine of Duke University, after four years of experimentation, has stated that he is a decided supporter of the possibility of thought transference over a distance.

"He has performed over 100,000 experiments. A staff of young scientists at Duke University was placed at his disposal, and he was assisted by the well-known American Professor of Psychology, William McDugall.

"Prof. Rhine's early experiments consisted in working with students who guessed his thoughts. He succeeded in choosing a group of thirty young men who possessed a special telepathic receptivity.

"Later, with this chosen group he began systematic experiments whose complexity increased in the course of time. From guessing simple thoughts the group went to the solving of various mathematical problems suggested by Rhine, who kept them secret from the students.

"The early period of experimentation dealt with a special pack of cards—Rhine prepared a pack of twenty-five cards with a series of different designs. Taking any card, Rhine instructed a student who was sitting in the next room to draw the design of that card on paper. When the students began to pass this test, Rhine went to the next series; he mixed the cards and placed them on the table face down. A student behind the door was supposed to tell the order in which the cards were placed on the table; in a short while all thirty students began to name the order of all twenty-five cards without an error. Later, these experiments were repeated with students who were not in the next room, but in another house a few blocks away. The experiments took place in the presence of a controller, so that there could be no tricks.

"Later, still at a distance, the reading of thoughts began, and it went so far that poets, invited by Rhine to his laboratory, wrote poems, and the students, at the same time, from another part of town, read them aloud over the telephone to the professor."

From another source the following is related:

"The leader of a recent expedition to the Himalayas, Prof. Dyhrenfurth,[15] returned from Tibet to Berlin.

"Each one of the participants of the expedition, so the professor relates, felt upon himself all the time the influence of some hostile power, the influence of a demon who, according to the beliefs of the local inhabitants, guards the peaks of the Himalayas and punishes with death those daring ones who venture into forbidden parts.

"Further on the professor told about the unusual sharpness of receptivity of the inhabitants of Tibet. 'Telepathy,' says the professor, 'is as widely spread in Tibet as is the telephone in Europe. One of our porters died in the mountains. We sent a messenger to his village. He had to travel for twelve days. But before he reached that village, a messenger from it reached us—he had left on the day of the porter's death. He told us that they already knew out there about the death of the man from their village. Appropriate prayers were being held there, and he was dispatched to tell us that we should bury the dead man in the mountains.' "

The inhabitants of the Himalayas, according to Prof. Dyhrenfurth, can increase their body temperature through autosuggestion, during the most powerful frosts. Thus, for instance, they are capable of sleeping upon the snow without any garment, at any degree of frost, and all they need to feel warm is to cover themselves with a shirt. The temperature of their body is so high that the wet garments

---

[15] Prof. Guenter Oscar Dyhrenfurth, Swiss geologist and explorer.

which Prof. Dyhrenfurth covered them with became completely dry in a few hours.

It is also related that, "In the Swedish Parliament a special electrical apparatus for the counting of votes was recently installed. As soon as a member presses the green button, a green light appears on a corresponding board, which means 'yes.' A red light means 'no.' When voting takes place, as many lights appear on the board as there are members in the hall; the mechanical calculator makes an exact accounting of red and green lights, and on another board corresponding figures appear while an automatic photographic camera instantly takes a snapshot. The photographs are kept in the archives as the actual proof of voting. After the voting is completed, the Speaker presses his own button and all lights on the board are extinguished.

"The members of Parliament used this perfected apparatus with full confidence for some time. But recently a question was discussed which seemed practically incontestable. Forty-six green lights and forty-two red ones unexpectedly were lit on the board. A dispute arose in the Parliament. Then the Speaker announced: 'Our robot is apparently out of order. Maybe he calculated incorrectly. We had better return to the old means of voting by name.'

"The Parliament followed the advice of the Speaker and it appeared that fifty-three men voted for the resolution and thirty-four against it.

"Then arose the problem of checking all the results of voting, beginning with the day of installation of the 'robot.' It may well be possible that a whole series of laws was accepted by the 'robot,' perhaps contrary to the wishes of the members."

What is there new about it? In all three communications, it seems there is nothing new. It is already well known that the robot-machine cannot replace a human organism. The communication about thought transference over a distance is not new. It was known long ago. Also equally known is that which is related by Prof. Dyhrenfurth. And yet, at the same time, one does rejoice at all such communications. For some they may be very old, but the repetition of the old is always useful. For others these communications will be newer than new. And perhaps, for the first time they will compel one to ponder about the power of thought.

Many people find it necessary that the information come from a person with a diploma in science. So much the better if the professors, among whom are so many incorrigible, narrow materialists, will begin in the name of justice to pay attention to real facts. It would also be quite useful if the readers of such communications would not be too lazy to write, either to the authors of such statements, or to the editors of newspapers, the facts that they came across in their own lives. We urgently request, Do not be too lazy to write conscientiously, even if briefly, about the facts which you have observed. With your observations you may draw the attention of the most unexpectedly useful people. Besides, owing to such observations, the very mechanics of life will find their due place.

One should not deny, but one should always co-measure and apply in accordance with justice. Let us not forget that even such a great mind as that of Napoleon did not understand, and rejected, the first presentation of a steamboat and torpedo, because he could not understand the power of steam. Many errors have taken place, but it does not follow that these errors should continue so that one might later feel ashamed of them.

Let honest reality, in all its abundance, in all its loftiness, become the convincing, guiding concept.

Tzagan Kure, May 13, 1935.

IMITATION

USUALLY, people are quite distressed when imitations are uncovered. Whereas the entire life is full of all degrees of imitation. Each teacher if he notices that his pupil has fully mastered his subject and his method could also call it imitation.

A man has adopted some sayings. In them he also imitates the sources from which they derived. A man adopts this or that style of work—could one think that he imitates that style? In the final analysis imitation and emulation are rather close, and only an inner impulse can prove the true motivations.

Altogether, if one were to become distressed by imitations and perceive them everywhere, life would be filled with quite unnecessarily bitter feelings. What of it if someone is attracted to this or another method and the means of manifesting it? True, there may be also quite base and greedy goals. There may appear even a counterfeit in order to corner some sort of market. In such case it will be simply a preconceived criminal action; and every legislation takes such falsifications into account. Essentially, such striving for imitation only proves that the original product was really good and merited attempts to repeat it.

About these counterfeits, foreseen by law, there is no use to talk—their destiny is clear. But there are other imitations which are not subject to any law. There may be, for example, an educational institution with original and practical methods. Somebody evaluating the applicability of these methods will open a similar institution on the next block. Of course, it will constitute an imitation, but it is absolutely impossible to forbid such competition. Or, someone will write a book or compile a dictionary, and someone else, an adroit businessman, will turn this dictionary around or will use a third of the book in its entirety, tying it up by some flimsy proofs. There is no doubt that it will be a false representation, and there is also no doubt that the adroit businessman will escape condemnation. Even if someone should be aware of all the circumstances of such borrowings and imitations, no statutes of law will convict the cleverness of such imitation.

The dimensions of all kinds of competitions and imitations are without end. The main and wise rule upon their discovery is not to be embittered. They will always be found in the very same foam of life as will any slander that is the result of base and criminal thinking.

If slander is to be regarded only as a peculiar evaluation on a large scale of that which was created, then an imitation is also only a proof of the soundness and convincingness of that which was originally made.

Amidst the properties of ignorance one may also see coarseness, ingratitude, falsehood, and all kinds of betrayal. These dark qualities will cover up the real causes of any and all falsifications and imitations. A great many obvious falsifications have ingratitude at their basis. Therefore, gratitude was regarded in ancient scriptures as a lofty, distinctive quality. Often a man approaches hypocritically under the guise of a friend in order to spy out that which he regards as successful and convincing, so that he may eventually give it out as his own. There are many such cases! Sometimes a coarse savage simply wishes to do the very same thing that he admires, not even considering what he violates in this way. That which he sees he regards as his own. And such examples of deplorable vulgarization are very many.

True, there may also be betrayals which attempt to make out of everything useful just a crooked mirror, in order to demean or harm a principle dangerous for them. There are many kinds of betrayal. In the final analysis, which betrayal is better, a conscious or unconscious one?

They both are, in the end, the very same thing, because their consequences may be of equal value. The subject of betrayals is inexhaustible. So much that is valuable and unrepeatable is destroyed by a miniscule betrayal, self-love, conceit, pride, or simply a mood, and quite often those who have committed some sort of betrayal, will forcefully deny it and try to prove to themselves that something quite different took place.

Now, we wish only to note how one should regard all kinds of unavoidable imitations. We hear from different countries about the very same thing; we hear of perplexity and indignation because an unskilled imitation violates an already existing useful work. In such cases you can do nothing. The only thing one can advise is not to be embittered, and only to double the high quality of one's own work. If that which you are creating is of a high quality, you may be calm—any kind of imitation will prove to be base, vulgar, and will consume itself. But if the imitation finally exceeds your work, then it will become emulation and should, in a sense, evoke a certain share of gratitude from you, seeing the growth of seeds which you have planted.

And so, imitation, rivalry, competition, if it has no destructive envy in its foundation, will be but an unavoidable branching out of your own undertaking. Every sower must first of all rejoice if the seeds strewn by him grow into useful grain. Thus it always was and always will be; and let the works, even those arising in close proximity, compel each other toward the betterment of quality.

Work! Create!

Tzagan Kure, May 14, 1935.

VIDEBIMUS

HOW many shameful moments in humanity's history were accompanied by this exclamation, "We shall see!" How many already molded, wonderful opportunities were cruelly and mercilessly broken by the opportunism of this "We shall see." In most diversified languages, in every manner, in all intonations this deadly saying was pronounced. If *margash* or *mañana* are said instead, these expressions also will denote the very same opportunistic expectation.

Many rulers of countries, pontiffs, and leaders did not find it difficult to speak this word aloud. And they probably never considered that in this manner they pronounced a verdict upon themselves.

Who, then, trying to evade, will say, "We shall see"? Only he who does not know the way and wishes to cover himself by extraneous conditions. Moreover, everyone who so evades does not altogether know what he wants. It is impossible to build something solid on an unforeseen confluence of extraneous circumstances. It would be more just and honest to say simply, "Let us delay this matter." But he who says, "We shall see," wishes to catch something extraneous and make use of it.

He who receives such a pharisaic answer as, "We shall see," can justly say, "You're a fisherman!" or "You're a masquerader!" He will be quite right in using such appellations, because his companion probably wanted to gain time so as to either cover up something or fish out something irrelevant.

Isabella d'Este sent to Cesare Borgia a gift—one hundred masks. This significant gift revealed all her sharp resourcefulness, and remained in history as a just description of Cesare Borgia. Likewise, in one of the Eastern narratives it is related that a certain ruler sent a fish as a gift to his treacherous neighbor with the accompanying words, "Caught for you." Thus was shown knowledge of cunningly conceived plans.

"We shall see, we shall see," says he who wishes to delay some decision.

"All right, all right," remarks he who wishes to change the conversation. There is nothing whatsoever "right" in this desire to hide, to avoid, only for the purpose of delay. People even invented a self-consolation, "What is delayed is not lost." But, usually, what is delayed is already lost. And how much of the useful, timely, and necessary was delayed for the sake of absolutely unfitting considerations.

In order not to delay and thus spoil something, one must also have a heart's spark. We had occasion to hear of a wise ruler, who when learning of something undelayable and useful, confessed that he experienced a sort of tremor passing over his spine; his hair stood on end, as it were; of course, this was not because of a feeling of terror, but from a tremor of true feeling. It meant that the heart itself was knocking and reminding that not even a moment should be lost.

The daily routine most of all disposes toward delay and neglect. So many small routine-like circumstances arise, that each new creative process appears to be abstract and ephemeral. How, then, to conquer the burden of circumstances? The sparks and flame of the heart will indicate the true path.

Byzantine emperors carried a special emblem, an amulet with a bag containing earth sewed in it. It was called the *akakia* [goodness] and symbolized the personal acceptance of the earthly burden. Apparently there was an echo of something most ancient in this custom which also reverberated peculiarly in the myth about Antaeus, and in other legends of different nations. But should the earthly burden be oppressive, or does being charged with it comprise an affirmation of a foundation? The emblem, in its meaning, could not be just a symbol of a burden. It could only be a sign of affirmation. Likewise, anyone who knows duty and responsibility and his path will not plunge into the evasive debris of "We shall see." He knows his path and therefore is not in need of any conditional terms. He will say, "I see" or "I do not see," but never will he humble himself by avowing his blindness and hoping that circumstances created by others will help him out.

In history whole political systems are known based upon "We shall await" and "We shall see." But these epochs were never marked by a renaissance. In the course of such policies a chance for existence could succeed for a while, but each powerful structure demands a responsive affirmation.

If a ruler is in possession of some reliable facts for some reason as yet unknown to his companion, he will say, "I shall wait." There is no need for him to scout and look around. He will simply need a certain period of time for the maturity of the seeds already sown.

All this is relatively the same. Somebody will say, "What difference is there between 'I shall wait' or 'We shall see'?" But there is a vast difference. In the first instance there is a responsible affirmation, and in the second—a conventional avoidance. One can respect unknown causes that make one wait; but the classical, "We shall see" will always fill you with doubt as to the quality of the intentions of your companion.

Your companion, in the latter case, says, as it were, "If you are successful, I will be with you." Such a union is not worth much.

What kind of architect would he be who would say at the start of the construction, "We shall see what will be the outcome." Such a building would inspire little trust. Some will say, "Will it not be just a quibble to make an issue out of a casual expression, insisting on its unfailing meaning?" Yet words exist for the purpose of expressing a definite concept.

And so, not "*Videbimus*" but "*Vide*"

Tzagan Kure, May 16, 1935.

SERENDIPITY

DR. CANNON, a professor of physiology at Harvard University, recently gave a lecture in Peking about the meaning of success in scientific discoveries. After citing many examples of diversified scientific practice the professor came to the conclusion that "success follows only those who accept it."

An excellent formula, completely correct and applicable in all walks of life. Truly, in addition to conscientious, far-sighted work it is necessary to show the ability to perceive the symptoms of the germ of success. Many a time the occasion arose to write that success must be caught, realizing that it is an "easily frightened bird."

Many a time ancient proverbs have been quoted. "Risk not, gain not." Different peoples, each in their own language, interpret them in their own way, yet in the same direction. An endless number of fairy tales and legends tell about unlucky simpletons who, because of their dullness, lost the Firebird. The fool was warned, "When you pluck the Fireblossom, do not look back." But just at that moment something seemed to appear to him, the gaper naturally turned around, and all that had been found by him was lost. Verily, success must be seized—taken firmly, without retreat and in full striving. In this complete striving is expressed that faith which already borders upon great true knowledge.

In all these stories, which were warnings, there are always brought out many circumstances that aided the discovery of luck. Beginning with grey wolves or unknown benevolent beggars and passers-by many circumstances become helpers in success.

One should also pay great attention to this inspired assistance. Not only should one discover such prepared assistants, but in the social structure it is also necessary to create conditions that act quickly. Precisely, such conditions should be created.

The inception of success is not only a personal affair, it is a success of the state. Each private beneficient success is also the success of the government, which means the government itself must be consciously solicitous that such successes be attained. The attainment of all the best proceeds through all the highest. It means that the state, as such, should give to its citizens all of the best, all of the true culture.

As usual, we do not speak about quantity, but about quality. What of it if the newspapers come out containing many scores of pages, which because of their quality could be shortened successfully into half the amount! What of it, if all sorts of questionable restaurants and cabarets grow like mushrooms and choke up people's thinking? Not without cause did some Easterner confuse the difference between a *cafe chantant* and a *shaitan*.

Yesterday, in the middle of the desert, we listened to a radio. Listened for over two hours. We changed all possible radio waves, and visited the most diversified countries. And what did we hear? True, somewhere, it seems in America, a fragment from "Lohengrin" flashed out, but the rest was so much restaurant and fox trot music that once again we were horrified by what was filling space. After all, all of these sounds, manifested and not manifested, influence human consciousness.

It is sufficiently known that space is filled, but apparently it is not yet sufficiently assimilated that the filling of space is the greatest responsibility of humanity. The essence of quality is that very diversified building material, out of which is built the success of civilization and with it eventually that of culture. A man civilized by a fox trot will be lost on the paths leading to culture. For him these blessed pathways will already appear unattainable.

"This is not for us." "Aspirations are destined for us, but not their attainment." This is the kind of pessimism into which not even a bad consciousness can fall, but the one weighed down by the baseness of daily life can. He who utters these negative, pessimistic words will thus renounce constructiveness. No matter how many times one may show to such a man the means of salutary successes, he will shrug them off as something unattainable, and will go to drown his sorrow in the nearest bar.

In this "drowning" of sorrow is evidenced a very cowardly pessimism. You see, the two-legged one has an urgent need to forcibly "drown" something. He thinks that he is drowning his sorrow, whereas he drowns his achievement or lets it go up in smoke. If at present space itself thunders with the horror of vulgarity, is it not the duty of every government to replace vulgarity with actions of high quality?

Many a time we had occasion to say that the people are being slandered unjustly, in insisting that they demand vulgarity and meanness. Both of these are thrust upon them from an early age. But give beautiful harmony, beautiful singing, beautiful words, and the people will be drawn open-heartedly to them.

Dark forces are everywhere. Everywhere they conduct their destructive work, and they dream of depriving the nations of those achievements which are already destined. Of course, that which is destined can be considerably delayed, but nevertheless it will reveal itself. Each such delay is an abominable crime against mankind. Each one who wishes to drive someone into the darkness and deprive him of light is but a co-worker of darkness. But nations, as such, are by no means co-workers of darkness. No matter by what means the servants of darkness induce them to commit abominations and vulgarity, sooner or later they sober up. Whole masses arise and rebel against all kinds of "drownings, fumes, and poisonings." Blessings to that government which understands that one cannot keep the people on a low level, giving them products of low quality.

Then space itself will not roar and howl, but will merge into the Beautiful.

Whether successes be in scientific discoveries, whether they be in ennobling creativeness, finally, whether they be in simple daily life, which also is in need of good fortune, is immaterial—success must be perceived everywhere and accepted.

Sufficient is told in fairy tales about gapers and simpletons who let their luck slip. The age of building a new culture should be the age of successful people, who, each one in his way, will find his treasure-trove, his destined success.

"Success follows those who accept it."

Tzagan Kure, May 30, 1935.

COMPARISON

D R. HASSELMAN, a newcomer from Manila, justly complained to us about the tightening of means for scientific research. Quite correctly the doctor remarked that grants still continue to come for certain customary research, but each new problem either meets with rejection or icy silence. Whereas constant need arises in research, and precisely in new, not in conventional realms.

Quite new observations arise, and, likewise, new diseases. At that, new scourges of humanity become so interwoven, as it were, that special observations are needed to take them apart and find new methods for combating them. Besides, it is also observed with justice to what an extent certain ailments become fashionable and draw attention to themselves which should have been applied to other signs of distress.

We personally know and feel how true are these observations of a practical physician. We personally know that means for every modest research flow exceedingly slowly. As we noticed many a time, it is even difficult to obtain means for research to combat such a scourge of humanity as cancer.

It would seem that the patients themselves and also their nearest of kin should be interested if a new possibility for research opens. It would seem so. But in reality even measures that merit special attention remain in their conventional framework. Since institutions already exist that are fighting cancer, it is thought that no other studies should take place. Even when there are known examples of curing cancer in some special localities, even when this is testified to by physicians, conventional opinion puts obstacles in the way of new searches.

It will be said that now is a time of such crisis that one should not think about anything new. But even if someone pretends to be satisfied with such an explanation, will it not appear strange to him that tremendous, truly incalculable sums are ready, not for healing purposes, but for death-bearing ones.

The magazine "The Nation" gives, under the title "Dance of Death," a curious analysis of data regarding this year. It is disclosed that the military needs of this year in London call for 124,250,000 pounds, or 10,539,000 pounds more than last year.

In Japan the military budget for this year is the largest in the history of the empire. The army will receive 490,000,000 yen, and the navy 530,000,000 yen. And also the Secretary of the Navy, Admiral Osumi, warns the population of future sacrifices, "even if we have to eat rice only."

Moscow increases the army almost twice, and the military expenditures of this year will amount to six and half billion rubles.

In Washington $318,699,000 are allotted for military needs. These expenditures are recognized as the biggest since the war. In Paris they are forced to designate enormous outlays for new fortifications and building of giant warships. In Berlin a new army of half a million men is being formed which demands correspondingly huge expenditures.

Let us recall that also in other countries extraordinary expenditures correspondingly arise for the erection of fortifications, new military bases, and increases in armament. Thus the figures speak for themselves. Truly, if need for fratricide is being developed so speedily, why think about new ways of preserving human life?

At the same time, somewhere, armies are being already moved, and on some borders armed actions are ready to break out. And no one knows if it will be some "private episode" or a match for destructive world conflagration. If the world thinking hypnotizes itself by concentrating only on the need of deadly killings, then all other measures, curative and constructive, may appear untimely.

Some will regard it as altogether unfitting to condemn peaceful measures. But what kind of peace is it when the mouths of cannons are ready to spew out death, and all kinds of poisons are prepared, probably sufficient to stop altogether all human life on Earth. Recently a question arose, What is the purpose of marathons of speed if they do not contain within themselves a peaceful, constructive element?

Yet the figures quoted above sufficiently prove that speed will probably be used aside from peaceful tasks. Because of spiritual confusion are not the new kinds of sicknesses going to multiply? And what will happen if, for construction of a cannon, funds of any kind will be available, but a benevolent, cultural structure will be rejected, supposedly owing to lack of funds?

These comparisons and confrontations are not in need of lengthy explanations. One thing is clear, independent creative cultural activity should be increased in every way. The leaders of culture neither impede nor destroy; they build and create incessantly. For this tirelessness mutual understanding and real cooperation are needed. The harder the times, the more necessary are mutual trust and fine cooperation.

All comparative figures will only show how urgently is needed a return to the foundations of constructive culture. If there exists decisiveness of the spirit and self-abnegation, such strongholds will be created that no poisons, no cannons will destroy them.

In the name of construction let us send a mutual greeting.

Tzagan Kure, May 23, 1935.

GATES INTO THE FUTURE

THE quality of durability is always very significant for the epoch. In the final analysis probably no one wishes to purposefully understand quality. It is lowered because of the surrounding imperfection. This lowering begins quite imperceptibly. At times it takes place under a pretext of seeming improvements. Striking the eye, among many other deviations from stability, is the problem of lack of durability in art materials which causes creative achievements to be short-lived.

One does not have to be an artist or an expert chemist in order to observe when going through art galleries the sad changes in colors of the paintings of past and present centuries. Terrible impressions are made by the ugly oil-cloth-like, cracked canvases. As if chains were put on the painting in circular and longitudinal cracks. This is not the the noble "crackle" of the old Dutch masters. This is not the golden patina of ancient lacquers, but a sort of sad black veil which covers the human creation forever.

On other paintings we see new outlines becoming visible. Galloping horses prove to have eight legs. There were cases when a dark figure on a light background appeared to be light on a black-brown background. Where thick layers of paint were laid on, they fell away in whole layers, producing irreparable damage. All in all, when comparing painting of different centuries, anyone can see that the painting of the last century leaves an unusually heavy and dark imprint due to the decomposed oil colors.

Much thought has been given to these unfortunate oil colors. Inviting ads have come out constantly about new, especially lasting oil colors, but in reality they proved to be just as defective. Artists, becoming desperate because of this imperfect material, naturally began looking for better results and again turned to tempera, to the egg colors, and to combinations of glue and powder colors.

Although all these methods caused much inconvenience and demanded expenditure of time for preparation, nevertheless there was found in them that freshness of colors which forever has distinguished the luminous primitives. Naturally, in the final analysis everything is subject to change. It is only a question of time. And yet it is better to realize that paintings can become visions instead of black boots. We even see excellently preserved pastels of the eighteenth century. We see many excellently preserved frescoes. It means that the main defect of oil colors lies either in the oils or in the undiscriminating combination of an absolutely unnecessary quantity of unnatural tones. It is known that some artists did use a vast quantity of all kinds of colors. They put them on almost without mixing, yet in close proximity, and thus a reaction took place due to uncombinable substances. It is also known that for speedier drying the artists used all possible fixatives, and the preliminary drawing was covered by a most harmful combination of fixatives.

Lately, denatured alcohol has often been used as a fixative, or alcohol of quite a poor quality, and shellac of low quality. If one puts together all these harmful conditions, even a non-specialist would understand how harmful all these indiscriminately used materials must be.

Therefore the recently felt desire of artists to simplify materials as much as possible and to work with only tested combinations becomes quite natural. In this direction one is excellently helped by the study of Italian and Flemish primitives which have reached us in the best condition. They also help to understand the process of technique, especially in those paintings which reached us in an unfinished state. There are quite a few such unfinished paintings, which by the will of fate remained in the process of work, and one can notice especially clearly on them exactly how the work was done. On such paintings, for example, as those by Van Eyck, one can observe how unerringly the color was laid on, how very precise contours gradually were traced and the painting was brought to an astonishing perfection in clarity of thought and firmness of hand.

It is not noticeable in these paintings that the search for tonal qualities took place right there, on that very same, carefully prepared board. Creativeness was revealed in simplicity and clarity. The artist knew definitely what he wanted to give and how he wanted to express it. Of course, this very clarity of creative process did not involve the artist in unnecessary, complicated mixtures of color. After all, the sonority and harmony of tones does not issue because the vegetable and mineral substances were blended in an "unnatural" way, but because of that blending which was so correctly defined by the French in their daily life as *valeur*.

In his autobiography Stravinsky recalls the just words of Rimski-Korsakov that there are composers without the piano and composers at the piano. The very same should be said about painters. Some want to solve tonal problems in searching upon the finished canvas. And others solve these problems inwardly, clearly, with power of imagination, and sing their colorful song when already in possession of mastery.

Old Italian and Flemish masters, in creating their unforgettable artistic images, solved them from within, with the power of imagination, and then sang out their colorful song, clearly, precisely, and simply. In this combination was contained true mastery.

At present we see that many young artists are impelled to these clear and precise, incarnate visions. In these strivings they will unquestionably avoid that tomb-like black impress which hangs persistently over many paintings of the past century.

Clarity of creativeness and a developed imagination will allow the artist to be restricted to most simple materials. In these comparatively simple materials were painted the greatest works of art.

I had an opportunity to observe with what simple means the good icon painters even today attain excellent results. True, certain ancient qualities of materials nevertheless escaped them. Thus, for instance, the quality of drying oil used to cover the painted surface had tremendous significance. Every good icon painter, besides the contemporary prepared drying oil, had also in his possession a treasured vessel containing a certain amount of the ancient drying oil. The master collected it from the ancient ruined icons, being aware that nothing would give that penetrating golden luster as does this age-old drying oil.

It would seem that the formula of drying oil was more or less known and even mentioned in ancient instructions. And yet anyone could see at once the obvious difference between the most modern materials and these—the ancient. Some think that time itself influenced the blending of materials, but others surmise that the old masters had their secrets with which they parted quite unwillingly. The latter supposition is not without reason, especially since many instructions in icon-painting were written in their own incomprehensible way, which was strictly safeguarded in the family.

From Italian chronicles we learn that oil and other materials were preserved in monasteries in earthen pots for scores of years before they were permitted to be used.

I had occasion to express perplexity as to why at present paintings are so lightly subjected to investigation by newly discovered rays, not realizing what would be the results years after these experiments. Since we speak about the preservation of the monuments of culture, then the utmost attention should be shown also in all technical respects.

I read recently about a certain art teacher, who in examining the paintings of his students exclaimed, "Indeed, lasting colors are not needed." Such pessimistic exclamations must not be uttered at all. During all times there were masters and pupils, there were all stages of growth in work. But the master, from the very beginning of studies, repeatedly spoke to his pupils about the essential quality of the materials. The master established a system of art education in everything. The pupils became, as it were, his children, and often lived together with him, affirming the general principles of life. Creativeness and life are so inseparable! He who understands the order of things in life, who enters into the rhythm of consonances, will also bring the very same foundations into his work. In the name of harmonious foundations of life he will not want to do things negligently. In the bravado of ignorance he will not presumptiously assume that which he does not know. The master shaped men out of his pupils.

People who understand duties and responsibilities know what that quality is that is manifested in imagination and in technique. The realization of quality will also bring with it a good quality of technique.

It is quite understandable that in art literature as well as in general literature the question of quality of materials is very important. If the writer knew that the ink used to print his creativeness must disappear after a few moments, it would not be an encouraging factor. Likewise, in all other fields, if people think about the future, they must naturally think about all those qualities of which in the future they will not have to be ashamed. Good quality of thought, good quality of imagination, good quality in execution—all these are the very same good quality, or gates into the future.

Tzagan Kure, June 1, 1935.

THE GREAT IMAGES

WHEN great images reach us from remote antiquity, it is somehow very simple to accept them. Even if they are clothed in myths and legends they are very convincing. Behind a curtain of time all is possible. Writers and painters of all centuries will dedicate their best inspirations to these distant images. Whole generations will be guided by these inspiring distant heroes and heroines. No one is jealous of them, no one is interested in the manner of these achievements—there remain only the memorable milestones of human ascent.

Entirely different are images from the recent past, to say nothing of the present. Take the description of great people recently passed away. So many unnecessary, non-characteristic traits are emphasized which only show that the exact nature of their lives has not yet been weighed or evaluated. The most doubtful, entirely unproved details are brought up, and the conclusions, even though they are not necessarily negative, are at best belittling.

Of course, with passing ages the scales will be balanced. The judgment of the people eventually will remove much of the dust that fills the eyes of the contemporary observers. The justice of ages does not have to belittle. Even within the span of a century we see that many things attain their own balance. The printed sheets on which great characters were disparaged and treated with contempt have not yet disintegrated. Not only in the memory of our grandfathers—and we now witness the same—did people laugh cruelly and unjustly at certain individuals who in less than a hundred years became the pride of their country and even of the whole world.

We shall not name the many writers, poets, scientists, social workers, and leaders whose names and whose very images have been changed in people's minds within a very short period of time. Everybody knows of many such cases. Although our contemporaries severely condemn yesterday's ignorant critics, they themselves often repeat the same mistakes. It has often been pointed out that the dictionaries and encyclopedias should alter their evaluations with every new edition. We can recall a number of great people who at first were described in dictionaries and encyclopedias as charlatans and agitators, but later received most honorable mention. Such metamorphoses can be noted even within one generation. In the history of human thought is this not remarkable?

It is difficult to say what causes this, although the obvious fact remains. Is it wickedness, envy, ignorance, or perhaps some kind of inexcusable stupidity and laziness? Someone is even responsible for the most peculiar proverb, "Abuse does not cling to the collar." Probably this strange saying is attributable to some bully who wanted to justify his peculiarities.

Sometimes people reach such absurdity that a mere attempt to express a friendly opinion, even a reasonable one, is considered as something untimely and unacceptable. While at the same time any criticism that is scandalous and perverted will be listened to calmly and even with inner approval.

Meanwhile, so many beautiful, truly great images have been coming to teach humanity; and not in some remote ages, but right here, very near. It seems that these images, being so concrete and real, should have inspired even more people. But this happens quite rarely.

We find these unforgettable, inspiring images shining not only in officialdom and those who rule but also concealed in ordinary life. Only a few can realize their deep significance for humanity. In this also, somehow and sometime, the scales of justice will be balanced. However, it is strange that people benefit so little by what already has been generously given them, which could be widely applied.

Beautiful, heroic images of men and women pass before us; they are true creators of culture, and it would seem most desirable to know about them now instead of the unnecessary and unexplainable holding back of these images in archives and records for the imagination of people of some future day.

Before us passes a remarkable feminine image. From early childhood the little girl likes to retire secretly with a large heavy book. With an effort she secretly carries away from the adults the treasure to admire the pictures, and later on she learns to read it all by herself. From her father's bookcases, at an unusually early age, she takes philosophical treatises, and in spite of the noisy, distracting surroundings, a deep and complete world outlook is molded as if it were a familiar realm discovered a long time ago. Veracity and justice, the constant search for truth, and the love for creative work change the entire life around the young, strong spirit. The whole house, the whole family, everything is constructed on the same beneficient principles.

All difficulties and dangers are borne under this same invincible leadership. Accumulated knowledge and aspiration toward perfection bring indomitable solutions of problems, which lead all the others on one luminous path. Ignorance, darkness, and malice are painfully sensed. Wherever it is possible a physical and spiritual healing takes place. From early morning till night, life becomes full of true labor, and all for the benefit of humanity. A large correspondence is built up, books are written, extensive essays are translated; and all this is done in a remarkable tirelessness of spirit. Even the most difficult circumstances are conquered by true faith, which becomes straight-knowledge. And yet, astonishing accumulations were necessary for such knowledge! Such an unwearying life of labor, with daily deeds performed in benevolence and true constructivity should be the ideal for all youth. When all the difficulties, and the inspiring work which flowed amidst them is known, it is particularly valuable for youth to learn about these achievements. Often one may think that certain things are insurmountable, that evil cannot be conquered by good. This is the kind of delusion, which at times is reached by the confused human mind. At such times the true examples of the heroic life are particularly important. We may rejoice that we have before us these beautiful examples, so encouraging to all beginners in constructive work. All this must be known. It is necessary to replace doubt, negation, and retreat—to proceed inspiredly in the encouraging work.

Some may consider themselves driven away and forgotten, not suspecting that here, not far from them, over all obstacles and all the impediments of darkness, the unspilled chalice was carried. If one would realize this, how much new vigor, and with it new possibilities, would come! How much dark despair at night would be replaced by thoughts about creativity and constructive work, which is possible in all stages of life.

Is it absolutely necessary to be burned at the stake like Joan of Arc? Will the scaffolds still be necessary when we realize the true value of moving, guiding words, and exemplary labor? Sooner or later humanity will have to give up everything that holds it back, impedes, and hardens. The one who is able to find a maximum of good signs will complete a most noble marathon. A true marathon does not require standing on one leg, but precisely discovering the maximum of good constructive signs. In these signs will be found the real peace for which all churches pray ceaselessly.

In order to achieve this true peace it is necessary to exercise much care, solicitude, and magnanimity. Is it possible to talk about magnanimity as something abstract and inapplicable? Is it possible that there are such brutal hearts as could oppose every constructive benevolence? It is impossible. In every living heart there must be some wholly human benevolent approach. With such a good approach the great images will be distinguishable and their works will be justly evaluated.

Tzagan Kure, July 2, 1935.

FREDUM

FREDUM is the term given in the ancient laws of the Franks to the fine imposed for the violation of peace. In other words, this fine is the "cost of peace" or "price of peace." Together with other fines such as the price of man or the price of blood (*wergild*) or the price of vengeance (*fehde*), the price of peace takes on a special significance.

The people who considered it necessary to safeguard by law a peaceful state of life were reaching out for ethical legal codes. It would not be a bad idea if, nowadays amidst the numerous branches of international, criminal, and civil laws, the basic question of the violation of peaceful conditions were remembered. Such a law could remind people in everyday life of the significance of many considerations pertaining to peace. Everyone wants peace. But many definitely do not wish to approach it by peaceful means. Yet peace cannot be built on the foundation of abasement, belittling, or self-glorification.

Indeed, in all aspects of life the concept of human dignity should always be venerated and upheld. People should not only be conscious of, but they should learn to love the concepts of dignity, honor, and heroic attainment. These qualities should not be abstract, belonging only to the stage or the pages of a novel. They should be revealed in all the details of daily life. They should be vital, because only that which lives is convincing.

We hear many a time that the concepts of *honor* and dignity are considered nowadays to be already outworn. And around the word honor there infallibly seem to hover duels, bloody fights, and mutual assaults. Yet what has honor in common with a bloody duel? Human consciousness should of course outgrow the "price of blood." A righteous judgment need not be based on walking upon red-hot iron. It is absolutely impermissible to combine ever living concepts with medieval conventionalities.

It is quite possible that timid thinking is afraid to include in contemporary life many concepts which are, as it were, tainted by superstition and various prejudices. But could human dignity and honor be regarded as prejudices? Similarly, every defense of peace will be neither the sign of fear nor of superstition. In every manifestation of this noble striving there will already be expressed that love of peace that is ordained in all fundamental laws.

Withdrawal from peace and all violations of peaceful conditions certainly already contradict human constructive-ness. If a man is, as Plato says, a *"politikon zoon"* then in such a social structure veneration for all peaceful relationships should be contained first of all. This is not impotent pacificism but a courageous and conscious defense of dignity, be it around the hearth, a clan, or the state. How could the idea of the defense of dignity be non-peaceful? One can visualize peacefully guarding or standing vigil in the name of peace, but at the heart of such a vigil there should essentially live the idea of peace. This lofty peace will not be like an ill-wishing neighbor, on the contrary, it will be a good neighbor, who honestly knows his boundaries.

Conquest has truly become a medieval concept. One may convince a man in the name of honor, reason, or the heart, but every violent conquest will forever remain on explicit pages of mankind's history.

Persuasion in the name of honor and dignity is possible when a man is truly a "social being," and not a wild beast. But to arrive at such a seemingly simple deduction one has to exercise patience and tolerance to the greatest extent. No one requires self-humiliation, for it was ordained since ancient times that "self-humiliation is worse than pride." Of course, no concept of peace and honor can be established on superstition or hypocrisy. If someone heralds peace while at the same time sharpening a dagger in his heart, this will not be peace but hypocrisy.

In a Byzantine *kainourgion* the majestic emblem of the *nikopoia* was surrounded by inscriptions of prayers of parents for their children and of children for their parents. Thus, the most sacred and heartiest was brought into cold official halls. From the history of Byzantium we know that such inscriptions remained dead conventionalities. In their formality they could not inspire or convince anyone, and the complete downfall of the Byzantine Empire only proves that the dead word has nothing in common with life.

Innumerable hypocritical inscriptions left their traces on the face of Earth. Precisely these signs of hypocrisy turned many people away from the true understanding of such sacred fundamentals as peace, honor, and dignity. He who knows how to affirm honor would have the right to speak of real peace. Without honor and honesty what kind of peace is possible?

The "fine for the violation of a peaceful state of life"— this is an extremely precise and universal statement. It includes not only the violation of public peace as foreseen by police regulations, but can cover a much wider and more essential field.

When we speak about the protection of cultural treasures, this will also constitute a struggle against the violation of peaceful conditions of life. When someone puts a lawful restraint upon cruelty, this also will be solicitude for the same peaceful condition. When people speak about the elimination of everything harmful to enlightened human existence, this also will be the defense of the same sacred and beautiful peace, the striving for which still lives in the depth of human hearts.

Innumerable sayings about peace exist in the covenants and laws of the East. From the most remote, most ancient times there stand before our eyes the radiant images of great lawgivers—born peacemakers. And in the classical world one can point out many strivings to the same ideal.

Not without reason have we now remembered the *fredum* of the old laws of the Franks. The period preceding the Middle Ages always was considered the darkest epoch. But even from this epoch, together with the "price of blood," came forth solicitude for the defense of peaceful conditions.

In one of our former letters we spoke of peace for the whole world. For the realization of such a broad and lofty concept one must abide by a multitude of peaceful conditions, the violation of which, even from the viewpoint of primitive laws, would be considered a crime. Let us not be misled by the idea that such peaceful conditions are regulated only by international conferences. They exist in all our relationships. Therefore let us be a hundredfold solicitous toward each other. Let us realize the necessity of tolerance and patience. If we should mutually reiterate these foundations an endless number of times, it would not be in vain. From obeisance to these peaceful laws there is regenerated a concept of honor and dignity. These concepts can never be considered survivals, but will remain forever as the basis of a wise and enlightened life.

The true preservation of peaceful conditions will attract success of which so much is said and which is so little safeguarded. Nothing is easier than to break a vessel. But even if it is glued together, it will still remain forever a damaged object. Therefore, in inexhaustible creativity make beautiful and sound vessels. Adorn them with the best thoughts, and dedicate them in your innermost heart to the great peace of the whole world.

Tzagan Kure, June 7, 1935.

SIGNIFICANCE

SAFEGUARD all existence from idle talk. I do not quite see how you will translate into different languages this very exact and significant expression—idle talk. In some languages it has synonyms, but in others it would have to be expressed descriptively, which is not always desirable.

When we speak about all kinds of meaningful concepts, good and bad, often, together with dreadful words, such as *betrayal*, there may also be added those of seemingly small importance, such as *empty talk*. Someone may say, "Strange, that a concept of emptiness can have some importance, and be especially harmful."

But let him who does not ponder on what he says reflect carefully on the real harm brought about by nothing more than idle talk. The usual attitude is: "Just so," "Simply spoken," "Just at random." But it is not so simple. *Simply* is a good word, because any simplicity in all its applications is good. But the trouble is that he who utters this sanctimonious formula, "Just so," has nothing to do with real simplicity, and most of all does have something to do with ignorance.

Often it happens that a man remembers the most crude and primitive actions and motives and insists that through these he personally felt much more simple. But this was not simplicity—it was merely unsociability. Thus the fine meaning of enlightened simplicity is abused.

All kinds of slander are uttered especially often amidst senseless idle talk. From it results obscenity, harmful condemnation, and carelessness in general. When the whole world is shaken by confusion and convulsions, idle talk becomes especially unbearable. There is so little time, there are so few moments to express the most essential, the most significant and undelayable! And these most precious, unrepeatable hours are madly expended in crowding space with idle talk. Not rarely, those who like ignominious idle talk call it a rest. And they add, "One cannot always talk seriously, let us just chat a little." If you think about this superficial expression "chat a little," you will see that essentially it cannot bring quiet, but on the contrary will lead to irritation. It is good to stir up the water if this has some significant, benevolent meaning.

Prattle is contrary to sense and will not prove anything, it is also unseemly. Who can say when out of that which is not serious something serious will develop? Who will attempt to judge precisely which weed seed will most quickly choke the careful plantings? There is hardly a gardener who alongside careful, useful plantings will also strew weed seeds. It would seem that this is quite a clear example, but, unfortunately, idle talk is not regarded as weeds. Weeds grow near dirty roads and abandoned habitations, or near all kinds of ruins and dunghills.

If idle talk is likened to weeds, then the locations where it grows also are defined quite precisely. One prattles on dirty roads, and in a decayed, dusty daily existence. One prattles because of idleness, ignorance, dullness. Yet all stupefaction leads to coarseness, that most frightful coarseness of character which is not only contrary to all culture but also to civilization.

In coarseness man also loses the sense of justice, co-measurement, and tolerance. Coarseness begins from a very small thing, from almost unnoticeable licentiousness, bravado, from allowing many small traits to creep in which, if vigilance and solicitude were used, could not develop at all. From the growth of grass one can learn many signs of life. Observe with what amazing insistence all kinds of weeds make their invasion; and where there are weeds the place is already polluted in some way. In this everyday example one is reminded of the entire psychology, and perhaps, to say it better, the physiology of idle talk. Speaking briefly, idle talk pollutes existence.

Such nasty idle talk occurs in many forms. It pollutes family life, it makes hearts cruel, and, finally, it sullies space itself, because every sound not only does not die but changes and is carried far and high. It sometimes happens that in the life of a family a voluntary fine is imposed for using profanity. This is a good custom. Likewise it would not be so bad to also establish a voluntary fine for any and all idle talk. How can one lay down conditions on the limits of idle talk? It is not so difficult to determine. If one can crystallize that which is said as having a significant aim, then it is no longer idle talk. But if sanctimonious formulas are uttered—"Just so," or "I did not think"—this will be within the boundaries of idle talk, a speck of dust in human existence.

But should one be silent? This may be said by a man who wishes to avoid responsibility for what he says. First of all, it would appear cowardly, and each cowardice is primarily ignorance. It would seem that so much is given to all, so rich and generous is all Earth and the Supermundane that there will not be time enough to become mutually affirmed in these beautiful gifts. Not to waste time on empty prattle and nonsense will depend on one's habits.

On the whole, can there be a condition of non-thinking? Truly, to compel oneself not to think is far more difficult than to make oneself think. Thought is such an unalienable, constant condition of existence, that some sort of unnatural intoxication would have to exist in order for the organism to reach a state of coma.

When people from the earliest age are taught to converse meaningfully and to think constantly, they derive real joy from this natural capacity, and their life becomes filled with importance. Each day and each hour they can realize that something constructive has been accomplished.

Many times it has been said that a somnolent state is not the absence of thought. In sleep one contacts the Subtle World; in sleep one learns a great deal and one awakes not only physically renewed, as it is thought, but also enriched in spirit. Probably, many have observed that in falling asleep with some benevolent thought, they would awaken in the morning repeating mentally the resolution of this very same thought, quite often in a clear and new form for them. The work of thought is limitless.

If this realm of thought-energy is so exalted and noble, have we the right to obstruct it with nonsense and the weeds of idle talk? It would seem to be quite clear, and yet, it should be inscribed upon a scroll in every educational institution, and in all life, be it of the state, society, or family. The present is a difficult time. One should realize the more where all that pollutes and is harmful has been secreted!

The masks of pretense and hypocrisy are many-faced. Authenticity and simplicity must be applied in their true, responsible aspect. This is by no means an abstraction, but a simple responsibility in facing existence, which comprises the duty of every man.

And it is not difficult at all, in fulfilling this high task, first of all to reject idle talk—this litter, this devourer of valuable time. Such rejection alone will bring into life that significance which will co-resound with all beauty, with the Supermundane and the Eternal.

Tzagan Kure, June 6, 1935.

ARCHIVES

EVERYONE remembers what happened to Beckmesser in the opera "Die Meistersinger" after he stole a manuscript from Hans Sachs. The base mind of the thief, in his anxiety to use this song, mechanically put it together and later faced public disgrace and condemnation. It often happens thus when fragmentary notes are used, of which there are many left in all kinds of archives.

Not just once have I had occasion to examine private and public archives, and the thought would often come, What a confusion of minds would take place if all these fragmentary notes, already worn away, were to be published! Not only in private letters but also in the documents of public institutions there are so many involuntary cryptograms that if one glued them together in a purely mechanical way, one would arrive at a downright absurdity, even where a high public benefit was hoped for.

It is terrible to think that historical deductions are often based on such incidental fragments. A historian remarks with profound thought, "The chronicler does not mention this and this, consequently there never was such a condition," or, "The legation was received in a certain chamber, which means that an extraordinary recognition was accorded this legation."

Such conventional deductions can be cited ad infinitum. But in reality it could be quite different. It could happen that the chronicler did not write about a certain event simply because at that time he was called to a meal, or the legation was received in an important chamber because at that time repairs were taking place in the customary quarters. Just why sometimes the strangest, most inexplicable circumstances took place is hard to explain centuries later.

A case is known when a request for the royal approval was sent by a courier to the palace and was signed three hours later. Afterwards an investigator might have noted that the emperor was so deeply interested in that document and hurried it to such an extent that he signed it at once. But in reality that episode was handled quite differently. The courier, a relative of the personal *valet de chambre* of the emperor, gave the briefcase to him, and he in turn, seeing the emperor promenading in the garden, found it possible to give him the document to be signed at once, and thus the signature was obtained.

From personal observations many facts could be quoted which to the eyes of a remote investigator could be viewed quite differently and would evoke weighty and deep conclusions. I do not want at all to devote myself to the subject of the significance of an incident in the life of a nation. Episodes are known to all when battles were won or lost because of the sniffles of the commander in chief of the army. Also known in the life of a nation are violent commotions which took place because of the deafness of a certain council chairman. Who knows what may happen? In no way do we desire to occupy ourselves with a rejection of some conclusions of the investigators, who, as it is, are often compelled to change their opinion when faced by new facts.

I wish to write to you about something different. Archives should be preserved in great order. Not only in a mechanical order, but take care that there should not appear some uncertainties which could later cause confusion. When one pictures file cabinets full of correspondence with different countries, one can imagine how some historiographer depicting social trends will be perplexed before this huge quantity of seemingly diverse aspirations and appointments. Besides, for the sake of abbreviation, many names are written shorter or designated by letters alone—so many misunderstandings may occur merely because of a similarity between these letters. Therefore one should in some cases, before leaving the documents in the archive, at once clarify, even briefly, the circumstances that could present some kind of perplexities in the future.

There were cases in which one could notice how, as a joke or with evil intent, fragmentary quotations were substituted. Of course, one could, when one wishes, make the strangest combination of fragments even out of any document. Likewise, one should correct the accidental errors in writing, not only on the originals but also on all copies. I recall how once, because of one letter, a serious offense occurred. One "Sabaneyev" was called "Sabakeyev,"[16] and of course he perceived in this mistake a deliberate insult. Often mistakes are corrected in the originals, and they remain in the copies left in the archives, bringing someone into confusion. Besides, misprints occur even in governmental orders. Everyone could probably recall misprints in orders that could create personal as well as public embarrassment. There are plenty of such examples.

Do not think that I enter into superfluous details. On the contrary, precisely out of seemingly small things sometimes issue unlimited consequences. Especially at present when there is such an amount of international correspondence in different languages, subject to a quite varied, conditional understanding.

Thus, for instance, in one case, because of an insistent request, I had to replace in a translation the word I like so much—*culture*—with *civilization*. But this does not mean that someone should draw the conclusion that to me both of these concepts are of equal value.

Often a keeper of archives was himself called archaic. But this is quite wrong. Precisely in the hands of such archivists is to be found all living history, including that of the state. Instead of routinely prepared folders in the files, the keepers of archives should enter their notations

---

16   This name is close to the word *dog*.

explaining all kinds of conditional terms unavoidable in correspondence and in expediting business.

I remember a case when a certain document was signed not by the Secretary of a Department himself, but by the Assistant Secretary. And a conclusion was drawn, because of this, that the head of the department for some reason evaded participating in this matter. But in reality, the head of the department on that day suffered greatly from an attack of dysentery and could not participate in any work for the time being.

Another episode comes to mind, widely commented upon at that time, when a certain head of a government had to leave a festive reception immediately. Who knows what may happen in life! Nothing human is alien to people.

The main purpose of this letter is to remind about the necessity of high quality in the preservation of archives. One should not, even for a brief period of time, admit the thought about adding something tomorrow to that which one was not inclined to do today. Each sign of laziness and sluggishness should be excluded everywhere, and especially in circumstances that could bring a successor into confusion. If we have no right to squander someone else's time, we also have no right, because of carelessness or laziness, to bring anyone into confusion.

Clarity, precision, and cleanliness are achieved where negligence is not allowed at all. And what a pleasure it is to see these qualities everywhere! They cleanse all life and replace unnecessary complexity by precision, simplicity, and clarity.

Tzagan Kure, June 7, 1935.

KING ALBERT

A NEW communication from Belgium—King Leopold sent a greeting to our Institution in Bruges and gave permission to use the inscription "In memory of Albert I, King of Belgium." His name more than anything responds to my thoughts. Since the very beginning of the formation of our Pact, the memory of heroic Belgium and its knight-king was constantly in my thoughts and remembrances.

The name of King Albert, his entire creative achievement for the good of his country, his military heroism, his broad views and deep magnanimity were always precious to me. Verily in these disturbing times it is joyous to have before one's eyes such a clear image of a heroic knight, without fear and blame, brilliantly spending his whole life in indefatigable labors for the well-being of his people.

It is significant when a cultural and enlightened institution has a true reason to be forever linked with the name of a valiant hero. King Albert found time to investigate the most diverse needs for the people's constructiveness. In spite of his vast labors he always found time to listen to, and give expression to, everything worthy.

In the archives of our Institution in Bruges there is substantial proof of the benevolent attitude of the late King to our Pact. The chairman of our Committee, Mr. Tulpinck, justly recalls this fact in his message for the day of our Third International Convention in Washington. "Together with our Belgian Committee, with all joy of the heart, we unite in reverence for the unforgettable name of King Albert. We are enthused by the realization that this most worthy, unforgettable name will be upon the shield of our Institution."

Nations should possess the full possibility of having upon the shields of their institutions dedicated to culture the names of their rulers, leaders, and heads, who led the people on a difficult and blessed path of true progress. Happy are those nations which can do so in full justice. Where the name of the king or leader could rightly be used at the head of everything, on all paths of life, there is created an impulse to follow him into the future.

The news about the untimely death of King Albert reached us on the train near Genoa. It seemed absolutely unacceptable. We could not accept the fact that a hero had left the world, whose name alone was a pledge toward an affirmation of constructive achievement to which the late King was devoted heart and soul. Not just a good, highly educated man passed away. A hero passed away, and there are so few heroes now.

Humanity should safeguard its heroes. It also should preserve their memory, for in this alone will be a healthy, creative inspiration. Life is dismal without a hero. It is more valuable that such heroes do exist not only upon the pages of legends, becoming god-like myths, but they also are sent in our times. They labor, create, and battle for good in these days. People can see them. A multitude of their companions in arms sense the touch of their encouraging hand and hear the ringing word. Our times are not forsaken. The name of King Albert will remain beside these indisputable heroes, so needed not only for their country but for the honor and dignity of all mankind.

Heroism is not selfhood. Heroism is true altruism. In heroism lives and glows self-renunciation and sacrifice. Fame accompanies a hero; it is not an intentional inscription, but a natural coat of arms on his glorious shield.

In March of 1914 I completed a painting "Fire" Upon the background of a Belgian castle, near the sculpture of a Belgian lion, a knight in full armor stands on guard. The entire sky is flooded with the bloody, red fire. Upon the towers and windows of the old castle fiery hieroglyphics are already flaring up. Yet the noble knight stands vigilant on his unchangeable watch. Of course, four months later the whole world knew that this noble knight was King Albert himself, who safeguarded the dignity of the Belgian lion.

And formerly when I had occasion to be in ancient Bruges, we heard so many heartfelt stories about the royal family. The old lace-woman speaking about the wonderful court laces also spoke in hearty words about the king himself, the queen, their family, so simple, easy to approach, dear to the heart of the people. Many signs about Belgium passed before my eyes. And there was not even once a cloud darkening the great name of the King. Is it not remarkable? Is it not significant for a foreigner, who in his travels could hear anything? But the testimonies were only good ones. And this shall be an unalterable joy, linked with the name of King Albert and his family.

And now, in the Mongolian desert, there is also joy in having the possibility of writing down these words. After all, in every good inscription there is definitely something calling, unifying, and opening the heart. We should be grateful to a hero who through his achievement enables us to open the heart and look with friendliness into the eyes of our neighbor.

Tzagan Kure, June 9, 1935.

UPON THE FACE OF EARTH

ANNA Yaroslavna[17] was a Queen of France. Another Yaroslavna[18] was married to a Scandinavian, King Harald. Yuri, a son of Andrei Bogolyubsky, was married to the famous Georgian Queen Tamara.[19] Roksolana, the influential and favorite wife of the Sultan Suleiman the Magnificent, was a Russian from Podolia, "Hurem Sultan," she was called. Golenishcheva-Kutuzova was married to Czar Simeon of Kazan. Prince Dolgoruki was a highly revered personage at the court of the great Moguls. Genghis Khan had a Russian militia. During the reign of a Chinese emperor there was a Russian guard regiment and a few centuries later the Albasians.[20] There were Cossacks in America. The Foreign Legion has many Russians.

No matter what centuries we look at, everywhere one may find these unusual combinations of Russian people with the peoples of the whole world. We do not even mention the wanderers, travelers, merchants—we see Russian names in most influential posts; they are favored. They are entrusted with the highest defense. At present the terms "being dispersed" or "carrying a mission" are so often

---

[17] The Russian princess, Anna, daughter of Yaroslav I, Grand Duke of Kiev; born in the thirties of the eleventh century; married Henry I, King of France, in 1051; enjoyed great respect after his death.

[18] Elizabeth, daughter of Yaroslav of Novgorod; in 1042 married Harald III (King of Norway).

[19] Tamara, born before 1160, Queen of Georgia 1184-1212.

[20] A Russian Cossack volunteer regiment formed in the second half of the seventeenth century in the Amur River region. They guarded Far-Eastern Siberia and defended it from Chinese attacks. The regiment was named for the little village, Albasin, which still exists.

used. Unforgettable are all former, deep penetrations of the Russians into the public service of the nations of the whole world.

Again we see not only those "being dispersed" but also a multitude of Russian names linked with the honor and progress of great nations. France is proud of Metchnikoff, England of Vinogradov, Kovalevsky in Sweden, Mme. Blavatsky in India, Rostovtzeff and Sikorsky in America, Lossky in Prague, Metalnikoff in Paris. Bark is at the head of a vast financial enterprise in Great Britain. Yourkevitch builds the "Normandie" with its oceanic victory. Belyaev commands an army in Paraguay. In France, Yugoslavia, China, Persia, Siam, Abyssinia—everywhere active Russian workers can be found in very responsible and trusted positions.

If we look into the list of professors in European universities, if we examine the lists of various leaders in engineering, if we walk through banks, and factories, if we glance into the legal profession, everywhere we see Russian names. Among the foreign scientific works in catalogues, you will be astonished by the quantities of Russian publications. Recently I saw one such catalogue of scientific publications, almost one half of which belonged to Russian works.

I wrote before about the pantheon of Russian art and science. Great names were listed—Chaliapin, Stanislavsky, Stravinsky, Pavlova, Prokofiev, Benois, Yakovlev, Fokine, Somov, Remisov, Balmont, Bunin, Merezhkovski, Grebenstshikoff, Kuprin, Aldanov . . . and all the numerous remarkable leaders in art and science, widely scattered throughout the world. They cannot even be enumerated! Honored are the names of Pavlov, Glazunov, Gorki. Even in the remote islands of Oceania, the names of Moussorgsky, Rimski-Korsakov, Borodin ring out. There is a sort of noble, self-renouncing generosity in this universal contribution.

By no means do we wish to say, "See who we Russians are!" On the contrary, one wishes to record the immutable, historic fact. In future chronicles this Russian universal contribution will be noted. It takes place within truly planetary confines. There cannot be any accidental, small divisions. In such dimensions all political and social considerations fall away. The consideration of creativeness for good grows, and each and every one must and should adhere to it as an indefatigable worker.

I often had occasion to tell foreigners about the life of St. Sergius of Radonega, and frequently I heard in reply, "Now we understand whence you Russians have the striving to give and to work." Indeed, a life such as was ordained by the Educator of the Russian people will always be a reminder that from a small framework made by one's own hands grow bright focal points for people's enlightenment. Not with pride do we pronounce the names of builders and propagators of enlightenment. Again, this is an irrevocable historic fact. It can be explained in different words, but the basic, lofty expression of this serene service for the good of humanity will remain a strong quality. We also know many other great, enlightened builders in different countries. Among beautifully sounding names we only remember those which, in their unchangeable construction, in their untiring achievement, at present call so powerfully to human hearts.

Without pride, without boastfulness we recall the many Russians who occupy entrusted, responsible positions in different countries. It will not be pride to mention the trust that was inspired by many leading Russian workers through their achievements in the whole world. To evoke confidence is not simple by far; as we already have said, it must ring in the heart with full convincingness. And if, in different countries, this trust resounded, it means that one more pan-human universal value has been established.

Sometime there will be written a just history based on facts about how much Russia helped different nations at different times; and this help was not offered because of thoughts of gain; on the contrary, Russia herself often became the party that suffered. But help should not be weighed on a scale. And on what kind of scale should one place magnanimity and self-sacrifice? In any case, the value of such magnanimity does not rust, in centuries to come it develops into trust. Many, many nations see their friend in Russia. And this circumstance was molded not by some kind of craftiness, but by time, deeds, and giving.

It is a great blessing if we can evoke a smile of trust. In these large concepts will the appellation "being dispersed" be correct? Is it dispersing when since ancient times we can see everywhere the contacts of our ancestors with the life of many nations? Those bearers of Russian names: Anna, Roksolana, Yuri Andreevich, Dolgoruki, all written and unwritten, known and unknown, they certainly were not "being dispersed," but on the contrary, concentrated their forces, carrying their gift of magnanimity to peoples.

Life was hard for many of them. Read, at least, the narrative of Afanasy Tveryatyanin.[21] These hardships are so pan-human that they are erased in the historical process; but the unforgettable signs of magnanimity, perfectment, and benevolent offering remain.

The Russian language is now popular as never before. Also, as never before Russian writers are being translated; Russian plays and symphonies are being performed, and Russian departments are being established in museums. Is this dispersing? On the contrary, it is something different, far more harmonious and important. If many nations have confidence in the Russians, entrusting them with responsible positions, then we also become strengthened in magnanimity toward other nations. From a united cooperation of peoples grows a structure, and it will be beautiful.

Pythagoras says: "Harken, my children, to the description of what the state is to be for good citizens. It is more than a father and a mother; it is more than a husband and a wife; it is more than a child or a friend. The honor

---

[21] A Russian merchant and explorer from Tver, hence his pen name. His real name was Nikitin. Traveled in Persia and India 1466-1472. Author of *Traveling Over Three Seas*. Died in 1472.

of his wife is precious to a good husband, whose children nestle close at his knee; but much more dear should be the honor of his country, which safeguards his wife and children. If a courageous man readily gives up his life for his home and hearth, how much more willingly will he die for his country."

Tzagan Kure, June 15, 1935.

WELCOMED LABOR

OFTEN discussed is the extent to which welcomed labor increases productivity and quality. All agree that this quality of labor greatly improves all the results of work. There is only disagreement about the relative percentage. Some think that the results improve 20 or 30 per cent, and others even allow these improvements to reach up to 70 per cent.

Those who admit such a large percentage in the improved quality and productivity of welcomed labor do not err. The work done under compulsion cannot even be compared with that beautiful result which is attained under the heart's inspiration. The very same is decisively evident in all actions. Be it a creation of art, or be it the so-called daily task, a foundation of desirability will be everywhere a bright banner of victory.

Everyone frequently meets a special type of person who, as it were, always speculates on a fall. Like stock speculators who sell short, such people will in everything find and insist upon something definitely going down. Usually they bring upon themselves tremendous and irreparable harm, and yet they smile sourly at everything and find only defects. They do not worry about correcting these defects, because they do not possess within themselves the joy of creation. And the desire for any kind of labor is unknown to them.

Everyone has also met certain types of wage earners who seek for no responsibility. This quality appears, because of the very same lack of desire for labor. I speak about desired labor and I do not confuse it, in this case, with beloved labor. To love the welcomed labor is not difficult at all—this is no problem. Everyone encounters in his life all possible obligations; in order to fulfill them he has to apply labor. At times this labor will take place in a quite unexpected field. One may have to learn hurriedly, one may have to show a magnanimous resourcefulness. This can be attained only when the desire for labor as such has not become extinct in the heart.

I recall a story of long ago about someone who started to calculate the amount of holidays due him. His companion in conversation went along with him and began to suggest many more new holidays. Finally the lover of holidays himself became troubled at the length of the list, and when he added it all they amounted to 366 in a year. Then the entire question tumbled down by itself. There should be a holiday. A holiday exists in welcomed labor. If each labor is understood as a blessing for mankind, it means that it will also be a very desirable holiday of the spirit.

A marathon of quality, a marathon of aspiration, speed in productivity—all these are beautiful marathons. In them is tested the quality of the spirit. True, in each being there is the seed of the spirit, but their condition and quality are different. Just as one should not remain static in cosmic movement so also the condition of the spirit must change uninterruptedly. Let us wish to all, and to ourselves first of all, that the chalice of the spirit may not be spilled, that the heavy drops of chaos may not shrivel the precious accumulated moisture in the chalice.

One talks about droughts. Where are these droughts? Are they only on the surface of Earth? One talks about sun spots. Are these spots only on the sun? One could sully everything. The best purifier of such spots will still remain welcomed labor. The desire for it is not expressed in physical means. It will fierily illumine all darkness and will provide that bright smile with which one should meet the future.

Tzagan Kure, June 17, 1935.

"THIS, TOO, WILL PASS"

YOU mention the wise counsel of King Solomon, "This, too, will pass." You write that you are learning patience. You find many teachers for this. This is right. Even if the number of teachers of patience were to be multiplied in various ways and means, express to them your sincere appreciation. Without them, maybe you would not succeed in finding so many possibilities for exercising patience.

Everything needs exercise. Some kind of flint is needed to strike fire with. The impossibility of enduring something is often spoken about. Anyone not tested in patience naturally may stumble, even upon small steps. The trials by patience will always be also the textbooks of tolerance and containment. What can be more deplorable than an intolerant man who does not know how to assimilate. To contain means to understand; to understand means to forgive.

A test of sincerity is also very instructive. Sincerity is that directness which is always necessary if it is authentic. All hypocrisy is contrary to forthrightness. Right is he who truly applies himself to the foundations of good, and who impels his entire consciousness to understand these foundations in their immutable, primary completeness.

One can see how through the ages conventionality and someone's intolerance at times crept into the highest positions, and where intolerance exists, malice and condemnation could also easily be conceived. A multitude of the highest examples points out to us that the self-sacrificing spiritual toilers for humanity knew no malice, intolerance or any kind of corrupting ignorance. One should follow that path which is so beautifully depicted in the lofty images which lead humanity.

You write that you are learning patience, and having before you many examples of patience, it is easy for you to become imbued with invincible patience. How much new understanding and broadening of consciousness will be brought with patience, once established. It will not be a suffering patience, but the bright joy of containment and understanding.

You write well and warmly about your dear ones. In your letter there is no place for any censure. And this is so good, so necessary. Indeed it is necessary that no place should remain for condemnations. Attentiveness to this could attract so much good that darkness would simply be dispersed by the sparks of this benevolence. According to the ordainment the arms of Light must be borne in the right hand and also in the left, ever ready to disperse the darkness. And where for the sake of good an achievement can be performed, courage should be always at hand in order not to retreat.

The word *achievement* is at times feared and even avoided for some reason. An achievement is not to be conceived of in contemporary life, thus speak the timid and wavering ones. Yet achievement for the good in full armor was ordained in all ages. There cannot be an age, a year, or even an hour, in which an achievement could be regarded as unfitting. The creative process for good is so vast that it can be achieved hourly, in all its forms. In its unbridled flow this benevolent creativeness will fill up all time, kindle all aspirations, and banish any fatigue. Noticing dark spots you will always know that "this, too, will pass." The more deeply the creative process for good is established in the heart, the easier will seem the wise counsel about any kind of darkness, "This, too, will pass."

Of course you know that it will pass eventually, but you should apply all your efforts that it may pass more speedily. One should not keep dust and rubbish in the house. From old rags harmful insects multiply. Where there is cleanliness one must not allow layers of dirt to be formed somewhere near the threshold. A threshold has great significance, and you know how to watch over it. All kinds of dwellers sit at the threshold. And there also are seated the inadmissible traders in hearts, who, with their peculiar form of patience, flatter themselves in the hope that there may come an hour also for their entrance. But let that hour not come.

Vigor is needed for everything. Check all the storehouses and approaches that could fill you with bright, young vigor. You write that you did not receive an answer from somewhere to your needed good letter. You think that summertime has deprived someone of the possibilities for action. Let us hope that this is so. But why should summertime deprive a man of energy, justice, and responsibility? Besides, could a rest be expressed in lack of thinking and in a desire to keep someone waiting? To burden someone is in itself an unworthy deed. You know of whom and of what I speak.

Give to all friends our hearty greeting. Help wherever you can. Instill vigor wherever it is possible. Be vigorous and create benevolently. And to all kinds of obstacles say with a smile, "This, too, will pass."

Tzagan Kure, June 10, 1935.

LET US REJOICE

MANY of your letters have reached us. They all arrived at once and I would like to answer them to you all, also at once. In all your letters, in different forms, was expressed one good, constructive thought. Each spoke well of his co-workers. Therefore let this greeting also be read by you all, together.

It is well noted that our friend was filled with the idea of "rejoice," precisely at the very time when I dispatched this same word. Just as in ancient times a greeting was started by this wish, so we, too, should not be niggardly in directing to each other a good wish.

Let this greeting be always in your daily life. And when the days are especially tense, when it is confused and difficult, then strengthen each other with this benevolent reminder. It is hard for everyone. It cannot be calculated for whom it is harder and for whom easier. One feels it in one way, another in a different way; in all this variety of feelings and experiences some could be hopelessly hard, as it were.

Such illusory hopelessness will be dispersed by a sincere, friendly well-wishing. Each joy is already a new path, new possibility. And every depression will be but a loss, even of that small thing which we possess at the time. Each mutual obduracy, each growth of an offense will be actually a suicide or an obvious attempt toward it.

One does not save solely by crying out; one does not convince only by a command; but the bright "rejoice," like a lamplight in the darkness will disperse the heart's anguish and darkening clouds. For what are you meeting together? In order to create good, to serve good and

Light in every way. Amidst your communions let a constant desire grow to meet more often, to give to each other something encouraging and strengthening. Among these encouragements, so needed in daily life, the most fruitful will be the simple "Rejoice."

People often deprive themselves of joy. They submerge their thinking in such dark shadowy stagnation that to each greeting they will answer with suspicion, "We should rejoice?" Yes, my dears, precisely you. There cannot be any situation in which a valiant spirit would not see a glimmer of light. Not without reason do you speak in your letters about remaining vigorous. This vigor is built up in you. For its sake you read a great deal, and in order to make deductions from your observations, you affirm them in your gatherings.

I am sending you here an excerpt from a letter in which another distant correspondent writes about darkness and ignorance. You also are acquainted with such conditions. In this letter there is no evidence of a desire to deliberately slander someone by any means whatsoever. On the contrary, the sinister facts are deplored. The malicious ignorance had caused heart's pain. But to this you will also say, "This, too, will pass." You not only will live through such reality, but recognizing it, you will conquer it with valor.

For the inception of such valor you will exchange smiles in a hearty greeting, "Let us rejoice." We will know how to treat each other with solicitude, heartily, and again, very joyously. Some dark signs, even in their darkness, appear as forerunners of Light. There is an expression in the East, "the first glimmer before the dawn." You notice it does not refer to the sunrise itself, not even to the dawn, but to the first noticed glimmer. The more keenly you look around, the more glimmers of light you will find. "The morning cometh, and also the night," thus, in the words of the watchman, the prophet Isaiah answers. In spite of the night, he already sees the dawn. And the dawn can be greeted precisely by the best bidding, "Let us rejoice."

It is good that you do not complain at all. Useless complaints have caused so much harm to people, and most of all to those who complained. Truly, why should a man complain about the fact that at a certain hour he happens to be in a definite place, and in a definite condition? To begin with, he himself worked hard to achieve both; and, too, why should a man feel so positive that he could be more useful in another place?

Maybe in this very place where he is at present, he has to fulfill a great and beautiful mission. Maybe he is placed precisely in this situation to guard vigilantly and strongly. Maybe in this very place something so very important is entrusted to him that he could not carry it out in any other place. People often imagine in an illusory way that they have to rush somewhere, forgetting the great treasures which are entrusted to their guardianship.

What would happen if all good people were gathered in an isolated place? True, they could fill space with powerful thoughts. But nevertheless they would have to send trusted messengers for earthly tasks, for faithful and urgent work. And what would happen if these messengers would refuse to go on a journey in the darkness of the night, amidst icy storms? Indeed, to walk upon sharp stones, to expect an enemy's knife from behind each rock, and to hear coarse, sacrilegious talk is not pleasant. But how else would earthly tasks be accomplished? How else will the temple be built, and how else is it possible to bring joy to the people?

Therefore, it is so good that you do not complain, that you understand the meaning and significance of work in a definite place. Of course, you cherish in your heart the far-off journey into the blessed country. You see within yourself, in your consciousness, all the benevolent structures about which every thinking person should ponder. You preserve within yourself the readiness to cross over all sharp stones and to listen to all threats and roarings, because you know where you have to go and the purpose of it.

And now, when you gather for communions, you will fill these hours with genuine joy. You will strengthen each other in realizing that evil is transitory and good is eternal. And where there is joy, there is already the seed of good. A benevolent smile does not resemble the grimace and smirk of the masks of evil. True joy will beware of all kinds of obscenity and sacrilege. Because joy issues from Light!

In joy alone will you find inexhaustible strength to incessantly continue the creativeness for good. In joy people strive to get together. Precisely in joy there is no loneliness. In joy I am writing to all of you together, because I do not wish to disunite you in any way. Why should one tell someone secretly about joy?

Joy is in reality. Joy is in trust. Joy is in mutual strengthening. Magnanimity, of which we always speak, is not an abstraction. Difficult days are here. And in these hours let us especially remember and preserve joy.

Let us rejoice.

Tzagan Kure, June 18, 1935.

THE MIDDLE AGES

IT is reported that the well known image, "The All-See-ing Eye," so familiar since ancient times in Byzantine and Greek Orthodox churches, is recognized today as a Masonic symbol. And this heresy is reiterated by people who, it seems, should know the history of the Church and of the most ancient church symbols. Is it conceivable that history is so little studied that every premeditated, ill-intended lie is accepted naively? This would be more than distressing!

From one side it is heard that archaeology is a worthless science, because in the wake of excavation of ancient monuments the investigation of ancient burials also takes place. This version likewise brings one to the saddest reflections, as if human consciousness did not advance at all and remains in the darkness of the Middle Ages!

Yet already in the Middle Ages the study of anatomy began. Of course, from the point of view of the cruel Inquisition, such studies often were likened to sorcery. Whereas if we should attempt to take a stand condemning the most ancient church symbols and denying the benefit of science, then such a state of affairs would surpass by far the most fierce inquisition.

In the same way one could consider, along with the rejection of the study of anatomy, the harm of the study of medicine altogether. One might as well return again to those dark periods when the first locomotive was called the devil's horse, and the harmless potato was called with genuine fear the devil's apple. To this it can be answered that all such inventions befit only the Sandwich Islands or darkest Africa. But life proves otherwise. Alas, we meet even today with such an outlook.

True, brilliant discoveries are made every day for which in medieval times one could be condemned to be burned at the stake, or at least to torture. But it is also true that purely medieval, evil prejudices and ignorance not only do exist but like vipers they creep in and infect with their sinister poison everything on their way. In this one also should pay attention to the fact that all kinds of superstitious confusions are not even expressed in the form of a question, but are simply offered as a conclusive opinion. Sinister conclusions are affirmed. There are no words to express the thought that at present, before our very eyes these most harmful seeds could sprout! To many who have not had occasion in life to meet with such darkness, it will seem that these remnants of the Middle Ages, even if they do exist, are very insignificant and may be scorned in their senselessness.

Regrettably, this opinion could be erroneous. It would be comparable to a situation where someone, perceiving a dangerous infection or a germ of madness, suggests that no attention be paid to it. We are neither Cassandras nor pessimists, but in the name of prophylaxis one should not remain silent where an obvious, ill-intentioned infection is revealed.

In those same Middle Ages existed many methods of ridding oneself of enemies or undesirable neighbors. Poisonous snakes were surreptitiously cast about, rings containing poison were given as a gift, sweet pastries permeated with colorless and tasteless poisons were served, a goblet of poisoned wine was given to drink one's health. There are many stories about poisoned gloves, dresses, and all kinds of evil attempts. And they are not inventions. There are many undeniable, proven facts known in history. Poisonings were practiced even in the recent past, and cunningly fashioned rings and daggers, with receptacles for poison, can be seen in collections and museums.

Speaking of museums, one cannot help mentioning

that only recently discussions were held regarding whether museums are needed at all, and should culture be safeguarded altogether? You will say that such adversaries of museums and culture are in the minority; after all, the aurochs is dying out now, only a remnant survives. Be it as you say—sowers of darkness are in the minority, but they are so united, so aggressive and unrestrained in their mode of action that their activities produce most terrible results. Many people somehow do not think first about culture, museums, the significance of scientific research; and when some shocking ignorance is offered to them in a crude, persistent form, they may, because of a weakness of character, succumb to this first impression.

You also know how much the first impression means and how indelibly it leaves its traces upon the consciousness. Such an infected consciousness, were it ever to eventually take all measures to remove the harmful roots, might not succeed in doing so. Even a dentist will tell you how difficult it is at times to extract infected roots. And it is far more difficult to perform such an operation within psychic confines. Because of these infections, many waverings, many confusions are engendered in the world; and out of them issue a multitude of barely remediable misfortunes.

Where confusion is put in the form of an inquiry, the danger has not yet become final. It means that the unbreakable crust around this question has not yet matured in the mind of the inquirer. It means that the seed can still take on any form. But if, instead of a question, you are presented with an affirmed and already molded opinion, then all possibility of discussion falls away. We all are glad to receive any questions, but if an unyielding, anti-cultural opinion confronts us, all possibility of cooperation is ended.

There is a story about two travelers who noticed a deliberately set fire in the vicinity of a house. One of them, in spite of the lateness of the hour, was ready to give an alarm and even interrupt his journey, but the other one said, "What business is it of ours? And besides, the weather is rather damp and the house may not even catch fire." Everybody would justly condemn the second selfish advice. If someone notices an incendiary fire, he ought not selfishly continue on his journey and not warn someone.

Yet, if there are observed the symptoms of the darkness of the Middle Ages, still not outlived, it is hard to find a reason not to draw public attention to them. But most likely many excuses will be found. Someone will say, "It was mere prattle," or "It was only a joke." Maybe Caligula was jesting at the time when he expressed regrets that all the people had not just one head so that it could be chopped off at once. If it was a jest it was in very bad taste and impermissible. Especially now, when people know about the power of thought, about the significance of suggestion, there cannot be permitted such medieval and archaic schemes which leave a terrible mark behind.

All friends of culture, wherever they are, should remain on an incessant watch, so that nothing abusive of culture might be uttered and affirmed in life. Let no one think that jests and malicious gossip are worthy only of being ignored. Darkness must be dispersed without mercy, with the weapons of Light in both the right and left hands. And on the left side is the heart, which will prompt the best solution at all times.

Medieval times existed, but they passed. Not in vain is this period called the dark Middle Ages. Humanity could not remain in it too long; the best minds molded the time for the flowering of the epoch of the Renaissance.

Tzagan Kure, June 20, 1935.

PROPHECIES

W ITHIN a hundred years Mars and Venus will be
inhabited." Such a "scientific" prophecy was reported not long ago by the newspapers. We copy this literally
as we read it:

"A two-hour working day, the abolishment of old age
and in its place one's entire life spent as if in the interval
from the 22nd to the 35th year; the delivery of water to
Mars and likewise the provision of oxygen to Venus will
make them habitable. Such prophecies for the next century have been made by an American chemical society on
the occasion of celebrating a particular anniversary in that
country.

"Ten thousand scholars were present at this celebra-
tion.

"These forecasts were made by Dr. Thomas Midgley,[22]
a chemist and vice-president of the Ethyl Gasoline Cor-
poration.

"Dr. Midgley says that within a hundred years the
causes of colds, influenza, tuberculosis, and probably also
of cancer and many other diseases that are now regarded
as dangerous will be eradicated.

"In the synthetic house of the future century you will
discard bedclothing as needless, heat your apartment
instantly by merely pressing a button, and throw your
soiled pajamas in the trash basket, because cellulose products will be so cheap that it will not be worth-while to
launder them.

"With the discovery of certain hormones, indigestion

---

[22] Discovered tetra-ethyl lead.

will be unknown, and the taking of a single pill will give relief from all discomfort.

"Sleep will be undisturbed and bad dreams will disappear. There will be sleeping tablets that produce only pleasant dreams, or tablets of another sort which will rid one of the need of sleep altogether.

"The engineering profession expects from chemistry a fuel that will relieve it of considerations that have hitherto handicapped it. The invention of such a fuel will make possible interplanetary communication.

"The use of gasoline, explosives, and other materials will undergo such a transformation that a new supply of energy will have to be found, perhaps in radioactivity.

"I do not wish to create the impression that interplanetary communication will immediately become accessible to everyone. Many preparations are necessary for this. Mars needs water, Venus a new atmosphere; all this requires the labors of future chemists and engineers.

"The world will be more healthful. The better health which will be found will make possible the development of such conditions of life and of intellectual occupations that presently insoluble scientific problems will be solved in a single day.

"Age will be under complete control; it will be possible for each one to arrange for an interminably long life by freeing oneself from casualties and maintaining life on nearly the same level. As an example, life could be prolonged at the same level as between the ages of 23 and 35.

"Agriculture will become an exact science through the use of powerful fertilizers and synthetic hormones for producing the harvest. This will also signify a far larger and quicker meat supply. Chickens will grow to the size of pigs, pigs to the size of cows, and cows will attain the size of mastodons; yet in order to attain such growth they will not have to be fed any more than at the present time."

Once again we point out that these forecasts are taken from a scientific report published in the newspapers. Many alluring prophecies lead to particular reflections.

Thus, for example, a scientist who knows that more vitamins are contained in vegetables than in meat concludes his report with something presumably far more attractive to him, such as the growing of monstrous chickens—as large as pigs. Likewise amusing is the fact that a scientist is concerned about bringing Mars and Venus into earthly conditions of habitability. For some reason he limits his thinking by desiring to subject the other planets to the conditions of Earth, perhaps the least of their sisters.

Very likely it has occurred to the scientist more than once, while he dreams of subjecting the other planets to earthly conditions, that the beings who dwell on the other planets are at the same time probably thinking about how to bestow their best conditions upon Earth. Will it not be conceit to assume that the inhabitants of the other planets must go about in earthly jackets and caps? Is it possible for the grandeur of the horizon to invoke thoughts full of earthly conceit?

Indeed, it would be beautiful if the prophecies of the learned chemist relative to the eradication of earthly diseases were fulfilled within a hundred years. Of course, what could be better? But unfortunately it is not for chemistry, along with the engineering profession, to succeed in this direction. True prophylaxis will consist not in the swallowing of chemical tablets, but first of all in improvement of conditions of health in the mode of life. It is possible to swallow all sorts of tablets and still vegetate in extraordinarily filthy and slovenly conditions. One may think of discoveries in engineering and yet sully them with neglect, falsehood, and human hatred.

Surely all Earth dwellers would welcome the forecasts of the learned chemist if in them a fitting place for spiritual development were allotted, if the great psychic energy, which in the last analysis is more powerful than any chemical tablets, were appreciated. One might ask why longevity for people, why remain outwardly at an age of no more than 35 years, if even since childhood, one is spiritually decrepit?

Why should people violate their great gift of health-giving sleep, fastening upon themselves forced dreams, as do opium-eaters? Of course, all morphine and heroin addicts, and similar dope addicts, and drunkards, likewise, instead of leading a healthy thoughtful life, try to bring themselves by compulsion into an illusory state. At present all the governments in the world are beginning to grapple with the evil of narcotism. Consequently, not by means of forcible tablets, but precisely by a healthy way of life is it possible to attain healthy, heartening sleep. Surely people sleep, not for enforced dreams, but for something far more essential.

To propagate life by force is just as monstrous as are chickens the size of pigs. In this forced attachment of oneself to the earthly shells there is expressed an unwillingness to think more broadly, and particularly within the confines of those countless planets and heavenly bodies to which the learned chemist would like to betake himself, probably clothed for such a triumphal journey not in an ordinary jacket, but in formal evening dress.

One would think that the time had already passed when anyone could be dreaming merely about crude material solutions. True, there have been days when the severed head of a dog, under the influence of forced currents, began to bark, and the miscreants who contrived this announced that death had been conquered. Such conquerors of death show, first of all, that they themselves are much afraid of so-called death and that they limit their thinking to the earthly vehicles.

If people would glance more often at the boundless horizon and reflect about the relationship of Earth with infinity, they would not be thinking about chemical tablets alone. The power of thought, the power of psychic energy would indicate to them entirely different paths on which they will not need forced dreams and visions.

Tzagan Kure, June 21, 1935.

CATACOMBS

HOW far and wide are scattered all conceivable catacombs, caves, subterranean passages and all kinds of shelters, in which people have attempted to safeguard that which was most sacred and precious to them! If one were to analyze the whole psychology of catacombs of different times and various kinds, there could be composed one, common to all, touching page of devotion and self-sacrifice.

Somewhere there are also some robbers' caves, but such haunts are in lesser numbers by far than the shelters in the name of preservation of the good, in the name of bringing better and peaceful principles to Earth. Those who have visited the catacombs and different subterranean passages become convinced that the hieroglyphs on the walls remain in one's memory as touching symbols.

Amidst odd, human trials, for some reason either catacombs or imprisonments or persecutions are absolutely necessary. Actions for the good most assuredly call forth the fury of opposition. When you are in Rome, by all means visit the catacombs. Go through different ones, do not be averse to have pointed out to you the very long side passages, which, as you will be told, are dangerous to walk through. Examine in detail the signs and inscriptions on the walls. Feel upon your own body the penetrating dampness. Glance behind you at the darkness which arises from the mysterious, endless passages. Recall how the people, scantily garbed, almost naked, barefoot, fled into this dampness, to the stone beds, amidst the epitaphs on tombs. In such a safe refuge all conventional class distinctions were erased. Matrons of the nobility were crowded together with yesterday's slaves in order to preserve the kindled torch of the heart. Each sign of devotion and self-sacrifice pours new courage into the heart. Self-sacrifice has been manifested in all ages. These persecutions were definitely essential as the highest spiritual test. Heroic novels could be written in all languages about them.

Truly, treasures have been searched for in caves and underground. These treasures must be understood to have many meanings. It is also necessary to be reminded about these treasures, because catacombs existed in the past and exist at present. Someone may think that all catacombs have now receded into the legendary realm. Not so, by far. Honorable catacombs, honorable imprisonments, honorable persecutions exist in full measure; they only become more subtle in their many varieties.

It would be an unforgivable abstraction to state that honorable persecutions have come to an end. As before, they exist in the front ranks of the battle for good. And they must be accepted with all firmness and decisiveness as the stigmata of bliss. He who was not persecuted for the good did not manifest it. It is anomalous to assume that real achievements come without battling for them.

Only recently we read the following description of the character of a certain public figure: "Whether you liked him or not, agreed or disagreed with him, you never remained indifferent to him. There was near him that some thing which could not be ignored—a definite heroism, unlimited daring, joy of battle, and fire of conviction. No half-tones, no sugariness, no timid concession were in him. All was as light as day, indisputable as the multiplication table, convincing as the thunder of Sinai."

Yes, thunder, for certain ears, is unacceptable and terrifying; but in others—self-sacrificing souls—precisely this thunder and lightning inspire a new unconquerable courage. When kindled with such courage, people lose the sensation of pain and the longest journeys are shortened for them, as if on fiery wings.

My dears, I know how difficult it is for you, what wise

caution is needed, so as not to allow that which is most precious to you to be subjected to ridicule and defamation. What has one to do? One may have to live in catacombs, on whose walls will be many beautiful symbols. You will not feel confined under these vaults, but on the contrary, as if having wings. Your very cautiousness will be no more than that cautiousness with which a man tries to carry a small sacred fire through a bazaar without having it extinguished. True, the bearer of this blessed fire must walk very cautiously, so that he may not be shoved, the precious oil not be spilled, and the fire not be extinguished.

There will be neither fear nor selfishness in this caution. If a man knows that he should carry something in the name of the highest good, he will intensify his whole resourcefulness, his entire containment and tolerance, in order not to spill his chalice in vain. After all, he is not carrying it for himself. He is carrying it, having received a mission from somewhere, and he is entrusted to bring it there. To shorten the journey he will go through catacombs, he will pass the night in a cave, maybe without sleep, forgetting about food, for he is not going just for himself. Service to humanity is not some sort of presumptuous phraseology. On the contrary, this is a lofty and difficult task which everyone should set before himself as an earthly goal.

In creativeness, in help, in encouragement, in enlightenment, in all quests for attainments, the very same Service lies before a man. In it he only fulfills his duty. Again, he gives, not being forced, but quite naturally, because it should not be otherwise. And now, when I speak to you about special caution, I have in mind that your lighted lamp can be shoved with ill intent. There may be destructive attempts to cast you into darkness without any light. But you must cover this sacred flame with your entire garment and safeguard it with all your thoughts; you yourself see how vast is obduracy at present. If barbarism creeps in everywhere it can, do not allow it to overturn the salutary chalice.

Do not think that these times are usual. It is quite a special period. During such responsible hours one should apply all one's accumulations, all one's attentiveness. On the towers and in the catacombs, on heights and in caves, wherever you are on watch, be valiant and unconquerable. In the most ordinary daily life find a lofty word to encourage your friends. They will come to you for this encouragement. And you will not only tell them that the hardships encountered for the sake of the good already will be parts of this Good, you will tell friends that difficulties do not pertain to yesterday, but to the bright tomorrow for which you live.

The deepest catacombs will become the heights beyond the clouds. The most malicious slander will become for you a hearth of creativeness. The malicious laughter will become for you encouragement. If you have to descend into the caves and catacombs, you will do so for the sake of ascent, with all care and inspiration. You come together for inspirational talks. Let these hours of communion be a memory about the most sacred, the most joyous, the most creative.

How will you know when the messenger will knock? Will he find you on the tower or in the catacombs—you do not know this; and this should not be known, for then the full readiness would be infringed upon.

Be ready.

Naran Obo, July 1, 1935.

THE DROUGHT

THREE companions sat together in friendly talk. One recalled a recently told story of an eye-witness about the instantaneous destruction of Quetta. How the people who returned from the theatre sat on the veranda, and suddenly there was heard a kind of cosmic rumbling and roaring; they rushed to the top of the steps and before their very eyes, in one instant, Quetta was destroyed. In this instantaneous destruction of a whole city and of almost fifty thousand victims, in the opening up of a new volcano were revealed one more cosmic tension and a warning.

Another companion recalled ancient signs from the *Puranas,* which predicted how entire cities will be destroyed, how the earth will dry up, how entire nations will die out, and other nations will return to the worship of the forces of nature. The man who reminded them of these prophecies at the end of Kali Yuga—the Dark Age—said: "Should we not confess that at present signs that were regarded but recently as fantastic, appear before our very eyes. Are not whole nations dying out? Is not the rate of deaths beginning to exceed the rate of births, a condition with which many governments are already battling? Do not certain nations return to the worship of the forces of nature? Precisely at this period are not unheard of droughts appearing, combined with all possible devastations? We have seen in magazines pictures of terrible, destructive storms, drifting sands, and devastating tornadoes. Not without reason, the more far-sighted governments sound the alarm, attempting to prevent terrible future calamities! Forests are disappearing, rivers are dying. Grasses are engulfed by sands. A terrible picture of a dead desert begins to threaten. In a self-deceiving madness many as yet do not pay attention to this unfortunate evidence. But the more far-sighted already think urgently about preventive measures, or at least of reducing the calamities. Could you say after all this evidence, that what was foreseen some time ago was incorrect?"

The third companion reminded them about biblical prophecies: "When the terrifying voices of Amos, Ezekiel, Isaiah, and other prophets thundered, probably their contemporaries laughed and derided them. One can imagine with what abominable, jeering revilement were insulted those whose words were eventually historically confirmed. Even now we know of not a few previsions which in their sensing of knowledge foresee the future.

"True, madmen and ignoramuses even today do not pay attention to all that is beyond their understanding, to all that threatens their mercenary advantage. But the broader thinking, true scientists have already attained the knowledge of thought transmission over a distance; they have already brought benefits to mankind through many wonderful discoveries. Yet how the ignoramuses derided these inventions which are commonly accepted at present! Edison was called a charlatan, the possibility and usefulness of the work of steam was rejected, railroads were scoffed at. One cannot enumerate all that was derided by the ignoramuses. One could trace in history to what an extent these derisions became not only a positive crown of thorns but also, as it were, an attestation to true progress."

The companions recalled various quite exact elucidations of the prophecies of Amos; they quoted significant statements from the *Puranas*, and also from historical chronicles.

A fourth companion, who had been sitting silently all this time, spoke up: "You all are croaking with your decrepit prophecies. My prophecy is far more correct. I said yesterday that stocks will go up and so they did. When and how your predictions will be fulfilled is still unknown, but mine is already in my pocket. Of what importance is it that some Quetta is destroyed! Maybe it will help my cement shares to rise. And the drought which you so bewail is it not useful? The more deserts the better. Humanity will rush to the cities, we shall feed them with patent remedies. My shares of a moving picture enterprise will go up. Look at these benefactors! Perhaps you will even think of reviving the deserts! You will drive away our city dwellers. Look at you now! You are satisfied with mineral water, no whiskey and soda, no smoking! Such miserable people, it is a bore to be with you! Such a simple thing as the more deserts, the more profit you do not understand and wave your hands! The more the people become maddened in the cities the more profitable it will be. Don't you understand this? Even if all your prophecies are fulfilled, when will it happen? I am not so old that "old lady Earth" will not still be here during my time!

"And it was not just anyone, but royalty who said, 'After us, the deluge!' And about whom are you so concerned? About some future people? Perhaps they will be nothing but scoundrels! And why do you worry about someone, bowing somewhere to a stump? We will manufacture these stumps—ten thousand out of bronze! And if humanity shall drink or smoke itself to death, what upliftment will take place! I do not talk about your upliftments, but about mine, the real one! You, miserable people! Here you have a victrola, and yet it cannot be enjoyed. You have stored up such boredom that no human ear could stand it. You consider yourselves modern, and yet you have not provided yourselves either with jazz, or with the tango, fox trot, or carioca, in short, with nothing real. To be with you is an evening lost."

Was there a fifth companion joining this conversation? Did he tell why droughts or narcotics could be useful? I do not know. But the fourth one soon left, apparently fearing that he might lose time in making decisions for tomorrow. In departing he even became angry, noticing that his other companions not only were not aroused by his words but even made some signs to each other as if saying, "There is living proof!" That is, not in a practical sense, but referring to current humanity.

Is it not striking that the problem of droughts during recent years has become quite urgent? Even all kinds of historic data about formerly existing irrigation systems is being recalled. Quite sensibly the natural science expeditions begin to include archaeologists who, because of their study of ancient data, help with the discoveries. Among the discoveries there are many that in all justice should be called re-discoveries, because while all this was known long ago, it was forgotten because of negligence. A recent newspaper report about the Golden Fleece of Colchis or about King Solomon's Mines speaks about the very same thing.

Vast is the drought of the soil. But still more vast is the spiritual drought. Let us hope that in the "irrigative" worries not only the irrigation of the soil but also the inspirations of the human spirit will be taken into consideration. Without these spiritual irrigations neither forest planting nor grass seeding, nor discovery of real sources will take place. All these most essential conditions will only come about when people shall actually realize them and, above all, love them. In love the quality of labor will be transformed. In love the deserts will bloom again.

Naran Obo, July 10, 1935.

THE LETTER

IN your letter you write about the new cultural under-takings. It is a joy to hear that in these clouded, tense days new works in the field of enlightenment are possible. The tension of the present time induces a special discrimination in people, according to their inner consciousness.

It is truly remarkable to observe how those who have seen and participated run away and deny; and those vessels that were filled by one stroke of lightning became powerful messengers. Once again it can be seen how opportunely such vessels are filled. They cannot be filled forcibly. If violence is applied they begin to splash about with irritation, and in such moments there always is the possibility of an obsession. I think that in your life no one compelled you to seek knowledge. In spite of all life's complexities you were striving unwaveringly to all Light, and carried with solicitude the lamps you lit.

Consideration and solicitude can be only partially cultivated. They both must be achieved through many accumulations. Is it not astonishing to see at times, in those people who were raised in very hard conditions, an unusual consideration and striving!

We all have had an opportunity to meet little children who, full of inner burning, were eagerly impelled toward a new person to learn something more. They already possessed inner accumulations which only had to be crystallized. Each revealed flow of benevolence was indirectly propelled into the chalice of accumulations. Such children advance speedily! They succeed not only in mechanical knowledge but also in the cognition of all their surroundings.

Out of their ranks were formed unconquerable fighters on the true battlefield of Kurukshetra. There was nothing coarse or negligent in them; on the contrary, they were always ready for new assimilations, always valiant and vigilant, in the full glow of the spirit. This is certainly not an abstraction. Every one of us, during his life, has seen such examples and expressed astonishment as to how in some way, even in some forsaken hole, such bearers of enlightenment could be molded! Often, in big centers, with all facilities at hand and with the possibility of useful encounters, many remained simply vulgar people.

Truly, not because of coercion, but because of inner burning is success achieved. A possibility should be given, the windows should be opened, and the locked door opened to the knock, precisely to the knock, to the call. "Knock, and it shall be opened unto you." In this briefest expression is revealed the great principle of living ethics. No torpor will touch the living, exalted quest.

One often hears that someone became obsessed by darkness. These notions become rather commonplace. It is as if one learns that someone stumbled again, on the very same step, and put another lump upon his forehead. Of course, everyone will ask, Is he so forgetful that on the very same step he proved to be again so heedless? Does he like to get these lumps through his own efforts? And why, in general, exaggerate the successes of the dark forces? If we shall mentally acknowledge their special success, we will, by this token, give them new strength.

As it is, we do know that the dark forces are well organized and inventive. Nevertheless, let us not over-emphasize their omnipresence. The dark ones, in spite of their sinister attempts, are primarily limited. One should remember this property of theirs, because in it is contained their final defeat. They themselves are aware of their limitations and are quite afraid when this inescapable quality of theirs is noticed.

If someone insists upon the victory of the dark forces, suggest first of all that he examine that person who is being obsessed. Would it not be that he himself, due to his own irritation, or coarseness, or doubt—in other words, his own limitation—cultivated some thistles in which hide all kinds of devils?

You have a great accumulation of spiritual strength. You know how this reserve grew; how broadly, variedly, and courageously you sought these attainments.

Of course you will agree with me that it is harmful to exaggerate the qualities of the dark ones, even if it be only through mentally admitting the possibility of their influence. Therefore, let us set a task before us—to discuss the Forces of Light, ignoring all and any dark artifices. Involuntarily we will know about them and will even feel their jostling. But the fragments thrown around by them will be melted over again in the furnace of Good.

It is essential to dispel the darkness of ignorance. It is necessary to sweep out all rubbish. It is necessary daily to reestablish cleanliness—this is a simple law of hygiene. But he who sweeps out the dust does not think much about it, he simply removes the harmful germs.

I would like to emphasize that some people by exaggerating the impacts of the dark forces are trying, as it were, to vindicate themselves or their near ones who have fallen under the wing of darkness. However, there could be no vindication for this. One may regret and await the hour when he who was obsessed, suddenly, in the light of the sun or of a flash of lightning, will have a glimpse of consciousness, realizing that the union with darkness is, above all, perilous.

As soon as such a realization shall knock at the crown of the head, the obsessed one will begin to tremble and will rush to open the windows and knock with all his might to attain knowledge. Where he but recently was coarse and mute before all rapture, there his heart will begin in a new tremor to harken to benevolent and uplifting thoughts and words.

Chiefly, it is necessary to refrain from all prejudices. With all their torpor they impress upon the mind preconceived, unjust, limited considerations. If one were to write the history of every prejudice, its forefather would prove to be a man very weak, wavering, and frantically irritable. Prejudice, as such, is already something unjust. This is not, after all, prescience, but precisely prejudice—something devised, and devised only for some humiliation or distortion, because of selfishness.

Anyone who is impelled to distortion will not be a faithful person. And yet fidelity is so greatly needed, faith is so greatly needed, for transmutation and an approach to great reality. Fidelity is always a true adornment. Fidelity has been glorified by the best poetic symbols—benevolent fidelity, self-sacrificing fidelity, heroism.

Letters pass through all kinds of unfaithful hands. But let them read once again about fidelity, about good and the Forces of Light. In a recent letter from a very fine man precisely this thought was expressed. Let the letters be opened. Let someone else read the words about good, about construction. Perhaps, if he has sunk too far into darkness, they will only invoke in him a furious grimace of terror; but maybe his heart will not as yet have completely turned to stone, and it will sigh about Knowledge, about Construction, about Beauty.

Naran Obo, July 12, 1935.

REGENERATION

I AM very glad to hear of your hearty response to my musings about the true annals of Russian art. You told me some time ago that in some of my articles you read, as it were, your own thoughts. I could say the very same about some of your essays, which are not only close to me in spirit but also in their imagery. I can only quote here the thoughts from your last letter which are very close to me:

"Recently I was riding in a taxi on Mostovaya Street toward Kitaiskaya Street. I saw a couple walking on the street, a husband and wife. I looked at them, got out at the corner of Kitaiskaya Street, and got ahead of them. When I got out I thought, 'Now, I know the future. Just at this moment this very same couple will walk out of a crowd of strangers. And so it happened. It means that the thought I had on the corner of Kitaiskaya and Mostovaya Streets that I will see them—had become reality. It is an unimportant case, but it has clearly proved to me that the idea, i.e., *idein* (in Greek), is that which will be. From this point of view the writings of Blok are exceedingly profound—he saw that which was to be."

This is true, but difficult for the general public to grasp, just as it was difficult for Leibnitz to realize that the body, besides extensibility also possesses force. If the substance of the body were to be extensible alone, then every paper bag would be a stone. And yet, a stone is something different from a bag. Nevertheless, Descartes and others taught that the substance of the body is extensible; it was difficult for them to break away from a habitual trend of thought. It is everywhere the same—thought is very arduous.

"However, artists, who think in images, know this idea well; imagery is, as a rule, the beginning of knowledge, and therefore the history of Russia's culture is recorded in the magnificent images which actually have permeated the history of her art."

These are approximately the thoughts which have been burning in my mind for a long time, and which I recalled, reading your letter of June 6th. Life goes on, embodying ideas, and ideas lead it on. It is possible that the Idea of Ideas, according to Plato, is that good which is incarnated in life. But in the Russian, so-called intellectual consciousness, which lies in the domain of discursive, rending, atomizing thinking, an image is regarded as something alien. This is the reason why the Russian intelligentsia of pre-revolutionary type is estranged from the people who think in images. And the folk images in art, music, and literature are magnificent.

This is why "The Annals of Russian Art" must be created in a manner that will make them at the same time the annals of Russian history—history of the past as well as of the future. The West became walled up in its stone houses, Roman law, and other things. Only in Russia do unprecedented vistas resound in space and time.

What do we Russians need? The cognition and realization of that which is real, which lives in our soul. Otherwise we are "close to bread but without it."

Precisely, we should think about regeneration. No matter where we may be, everywhere we should unite in thoughts about renewal, about the best. These thoughts, arising simultaneously in different parts of the world, create a powerful atmosphere. But mutually devouring thoughts should not be allowed. And where the heart truly aspires to benevolent striving, there cannot be base mutual devouring.

Regeneration is natural evolution. Either suppuration takes place or the flowering of regeneration. If we know that one cannot stand on one spot, then each thought about renewal will already become a constructive stone for the future. Indeed, the annals of art, the annals of creativeness will also be the annals of culture. It cannot be otherwise, because creativeness is the expression of the meaning of life.

In thoughts about regeneration let us not burden each other with any kind of insistency and premeditation. He who thinks about natural regeneration, knows all the conditions that could bring it about. Natural conditions of good are uniform in their essence. Therefore there could not be any absurd, unfounded, groundless disagreements where the one and only foundation is spoken about.

Only to those who can feel alienated from each other is the sole, propelling basis of self-perfectment not clear. People who do not feel this foundation will never understand that the annals of creativeness, in other words, annals of culture must be thought of at all times. One should not think that these annals will be compiled only in complete well-being, and more so since the very concept of "well-being" is quite arbitrary.

A reflection about culture is a deposit into a treasury, a sacred testimony about the true achievements of mankind. Therefore these thoughts must always be evaluated, amidst all conditions. And when they appear amidst especially difficult conditions, then they are especially valuable. But who knows why each one is entrusted with being on watch in that or another place? We could suppose in a purely human way that it would be better "not here, but over there." And yet, maybe the watch is entrusted precisely here. Therefore, let us accept this watch in complete readiness, while aspiring in our heart toward the longed for regeneration.

Let us not think that that which we place upon the heart is far from attainment. If we shall not retreat, if we shall manifest courage in everything, if, in spite of all sorts of Judases and Pilates, the good and the useful shall be un-contestable, then all that is sacred in the heart will blossom in life. When we think about creativeness, it means that we apply our thought to the most practical.

And this, applied in life, will also advance ways of accomplishment. Because at this moment we do not as yet know where and how the annals of Russian culture will grow, this does not mean that we should not concentrate upon this thought. On the contrary, we should find within ourselves, and in our associations, in our cooperations, and in the whole world, the best ways toward it.

In the expanses of the desert, in the lonely crowdedness of the city, in the sandstorm, in the flood, in thunder and lightning, let us hold in the heart the thought that must be realized—about the annals of Russian art, about the annals of Russian culture—in the beautiful and authentic images of all the people.

Naran Obo, July 14, 1935.

SEALS

MUCH is said about the ancient Chinese seals that have been found in Ireland. The antiquity of these seals is attributed to several centuries before our era, and some even think several thousands of years. On the basis of these seals is debated the question of the ancient relations of Ireland with China. Others observe that there could have been an intermediary point in Egypt or Crete, who had longstanding dealings with both the Far East and the British Isles when the latter served as the source of certain metals.

Indeed, all such questions require many confirmations and additional facts, but, nevertheless, the discovery of ancient Chinese seals in Ireland again reminds us about the extent of long-distance communications already in the most remote times. Long ago we had occasion to find amber from Königsberg in *kurgans*[23] of the Stone Age in Central Russia. Thus are proven, already before the knowledge of metals, the relations over extensive distances in Neolithic times.

All archaeological findings, the uniformity of many discovered types, and, finally, the details of ornament, rituals, and other elements of the way of life indicate not only a uniformity of the feelings common to man but also unquestionable relations across long distances. The similarity of the alphabet discovered not long ago in Harappa, India, to inscriptions on Easter Island also indicates noteworthy international relations many centuries before our era.

---

[23] Barrows of the Russian steppes.

Without any difficulty it is possible to discern how periods lasting for ages confirm the development of international relations and then, as it were, there appears a strange tribal forgetfulness, a timorous immobility, and the memory of former relations is wiped away. In itself the memory of peoples represents an extraordinarily interesting phenomena. To contemporary man it sometimes seems completely inadmissible that entire peoples could in some way forget something already fully known to them. And yet the facts and allusions in ancient chronicles indicate the possibility of just such strange forgetfulness.

Many completely lost technical methods of Egypt, the existence of gunpowder in ancient China, the details of various lost techniques of Babylon, certain objects of the Mayan culture—all this reminds one that, incomprehensibly, very essential discoveries have been entirely forgotten at a later date. Moreover, such forgetfulness does not always coincide with epochs of renaissance or decline. It is precisely as if some other psychological or even physiological factors altered the flow of the current of the peoples' thought.

Amidst all the misunderstandings and presuppositions, the question of the most ancient international relations always proves to be very complicated, yet of special interest from a universal point of view. The discovery of objects of definite antiquity in remote countries is a material sign of some communication, and all the more so when the objects are found in ethnographically old strata, which actually belong to a former flow of life. Something extremely inspiring is contained in these substantial signs, which in reality are embodied in these seals of national relations.

And again, at present in certain countries inertness and immobility are so clearly evidenced that there are inhabitants of some cities who are proud of the fact that they have never had to go beyond the limits of their native city or that they have even succeeded in never crossing a river which flows through the city. There are all sorts of odd people. And among the strangest oddities such a prejudice against mobility always remains one of the most shocking. Yet what a great number of people exist who have never looked beyond the limits of their own country! Only in recent years has travel re-entered, as it were, the program of self-education. Whereas from remote antiquity voices have been borne to us calling out about the usefulness of travel and of international knowledge.

The celebrated, everlastingly mentioned Marco Polo must be looked upon as a collective name. Frequently, by this name are meant the infinite number of travelers who have been the bearers of international relations. The name of Marco Polo has become firmly fixed in history, but actually a great number of names of people traversing ancient beaten paths remain unknown. But that is not the point. Of course any historic name becomes not so much a name as a concept. In like manner, on the ancient discovered objects we see seals incomprehensible to us, which serve as conventional signs for us, yet which were formerly the private seals of some commercial houses or enterprises, or of definite individuals.

Each reminder about international relations is, as it were, a new seal upon a universal human peace treaty. Not so long ago in London a certain Spaniard, Madariaga, delivered quite a pompous speech about the price of peace. Such bombastic abstractions are not the material signs of peace, but are, principally, material seals of world relations.

People are actually thinking about peace; some self-interestedly, others selflessly. In all cases some kind of sign is required, the actual seal of the fact that aside from human violence and hatred peaceful relations have been possible in different domains of business.

The price of peace is determined by living human dignity, by benevolence of heart, broadly embracing and noble. Not by denials of cultural treasures but by recognition of the creativeness of good is the price of peace determined and established.

Archaeology, as a science based on material memorials,

is recognized at present as assisting in many scientific and social considerations. And, likewise, into the question of the price of peace archaeology can bring many most valuable signs. From long forgotten ruins, from abandoned burial places and the remains of palaces and strongholds material proofs of peaceful international relations can be adduced. In almost worn away historical writings, in an ancient hieroglyph, the story reaches one's ears about how, in fragile boats and on wearied horses, man penetrated remote regions not only in warlike fury but also in a benevolent desire for peaceful exchange. These narratives will be stamped, as it were, with material seals, ratifying human peace treaties.

In the creativeness of good it is always possible to come to terms; only in a paroxysm of malice or of dark misanthropy are peaceful advances impossible. Long ago it was said in various tongues that he who raises the sword will perish by the sword, and he will perish at a preordained hour which perhaps will be quite unexpected by him. And so it is in each quarrel and in each dissension.

The seals did not ratify quarrelsome contracts. The seals were affixed to a document of some relations, of some commercial agreement. Yet, in each true businesslike procedure there will be the element of peace. A victory through good will be a most radiant and striking victory. It is possible to kill with the sting of a serpent, but not to conquer, for to conquer should also mean to convince. Regarding such prices of peace, let us refer carefully to all material signs. It would have seemed inordinate to connect Easter Island with Harappa in India, or now Ireland with China. Yet what is impossible at present? A seal or a depicted hieroglyph is fully convincing. "Peace on earth, good will toward man" is also substantial, for good will is engendered in the heart. And what is more substantial than the human heart, with all its inspired beating?

Man should rejoice at seals of peaceful relations. Each sign of remote international agreements is a pledge of the possibility of future treaties, heartfelt and unbreakable. At

one time savage warriors devoured the hearts of the van-
quished, but now in each peaceful relationship let people
remember about the living heart. The seals of antiquity
are for the future.

Timur Hada, July 18, 1935.

ESSENTIAL NATURE

IN the ancient cathedral of Orvieto, on the frescoes by Orcagna, are depicted solemn, joyous ascensions of the righteous into the heavenly realm. Under them demons are dragging the sinners by the hair to the tortures of hell. Angels do not haul anyone into paradise forcibly, by the hair. Only into hell is one dragged by the hair, by force. The ancient proverb "one does not drag by the hair into paradise" has a deep and ever memorable significance. Verily, one cannot haul anyone by force into paradise.

All that is unnatural is contrary to nature. Likewise, this is so regarding the degrees of ascent. Only those can fit in who, in one way or another, have already accepted this order in their consciousness. If someone, for some reason, cannot breathe in the mountain air, you cannot force him to go against his nature. The oxygen tank will help only briefly. In any event, it will not help so much as it will give the illusion of help. As soon as the artificial oxygen comes to an end, its lack will be felt tenfold.

If someone's blood vessels burst because of the altitude, it means that he could not exist on these heights. His nature proved unadaptable to them. Maybe with the aid of lengthy, gradual, fully understood exercises, the circulation could adjust itself to the new existence. But one should not forcibly, suddenly burden a nature that is not adapted to many and lengthy experiments.

All artificial, or properly speaking, forced measures usually produce a crude reaction, a destructive rebellion which does not do any good. Naturalness lies in true co-measurement and systematic planning. Rebellions arise also because of various degrees of consciousness. True, one may observe quite conscious rebellions as expressions measured and planned for a contemplated goal. But more often this may be simply called a rebellion of crude matter which in general opposes the possibility of natural improvements. The rebel often will not give any definite answer as to why and, chiefly, for what he rebels and attempts to crush something not quite explicit to him. He simply tries to unsettle something which he thinks hinders him. But due to inexperience or rather, ignorance, he, desiring to break up something, inflicts terrible and at times deadly blows primarily upon himself.

It will be a weak excuse if certain exterior circumstances or some kind of heredity disturb the nature in its normal systematic growth. Self-vindication means self-deception. Not without reason did this become a proverb: "He who excuses himself accuses himself." There is also another proverb, for some reason referring to Jupiter: "Jupiter, thou art angry, it means thou art wrong." Of course, under this "anger" one should understand not just sternness, but jarring, foul-mouthed bombast.

When advice is given to carefully preserve one's essential nature this does not mean that one should avoid all danger, all possibility of achievement. Guarding the essence is not an impediment to self-sacrifice and heroic action. Under the preservation of one's essence must be understood the discovery of all possibilities for perfectment and for improvement. Indeed, in this procedure the essence will be directed naturally. Through all the subtlest means one can be reminded about this natural path. But it is unwise even partially to use force if certain matters contrary to ascent are not yet outlived.

A wise teacher will never compel anyone to read certain books. He may offer an opportunity to become acquainted with useful sources, but he will not force, even indirectly. And what good would it do if that which is read is accepted under a stigma of ill will or distrust? Proofs of this are book reviews. You will feel at once which review is unprejudiced, written with a frank desire to clarify the work, and also when the review was conceived with an obscure prejudice, to tell not what was written but precisely what was not written. Prejudice is an antagonist and a destroyer of the essence. If for some reason the heart, this treasury of the essence, appears to be sealed or filled with pus, then no natural, just judgment can arise. Darkness will whisper a multitude of doubts and perplexities which could be solved even by a child's brain. And darkness puts on a strong lock.

Of course, all kinds of narcotics, from the most deadly to the commonly accepted ones, are an impediment to and distortion of nature. The doses of such narcotics are indeed quite varied. You may often hear an observation that even a great quantity of narcotics did not prove to have a visible influence upon one's neighbor. To begin with, what is "visible," and for what kind of an eye is it visible? And in the second place, we do not know to what an extent this neighbor was armed with his own, different accumulations. In general, the use of narcotics proves that the will has been weakened, in other words, an unnatural condition of the nature.

The essence is disbursed quite systematically and justly. People themselves attempt to distort and demean it. The preservation of the essence is neither magic nor something supernatural. On the contrary, this condition is most natural. In it the will is strengthened in a natural manner, psychic energy is developed and applied naturally. Why turn to some unnatural conjurations where the most natural and fecund order of perfectment is possible? Above all, benevolent creativeness, in all its applications, will also be a natural expression of life. Furthermore, all liberation from coarseness and prejudice will be the best aid in the preservation of the essence.

The essence should not be understood only materially. Since matter is only one of the properties of the spirit, the essence appears to define all natural conditions. The heart works naturally when we do not notice it. All other organs, although performing the most complex chemical work, accomplish this unnoticeably. Likewise, the natural condition of the essence will be beneficent and unnoticeable. Like the highest tension of electricity, it will spread beneficially, but the ordinary eye and the ordinary ear will not notice it. Thus, it is obvious that all violence, all withdrawal from a natural condition are inapplicable.

Often considerable time, and striving toward an immediate improvement, are needed. Often there may occur flashes accumulated long before but forgotten in the recesses of matter; many possibilities are given—they should only be adopted! Often the very intensity of labor or life's obstacles bring the consciousness to the natural path. Not without reason is the benefit of the sweat of labor often pointed out. And yet, the sweat can be understood in different ways, crudely and also spiritually.

Doors and windows must be opened benevolently. The ways should not be barred by poisonous gases. Death-bearing missiles should not fall from the heavens. Not with cannon fire can the essence of good be brought back. It is a joy to think about the good essence—destined for good. One may join in a hearty discussion about all that leads to creativeness for good. Let us not fear accumulation and repetition of the definitions of good. Good is needed. Good is urgent. The vault of heaven is supported by good.

Timur Hada, August 5, 1935.

TESTS

YOU ask how one can reconcile one's consciousness to the idea of steadfastness and endless testing, and how to acquire that vigor of spirit which enables one to accept into the consciousness such a systematic realization day by day.

The obviousness and reality of testings, however, are inevitable in everyday life. Even inanimate objects undergo testing at all times. A house is checked frequently by the assigned architect. Every ship has to be carefully overhauled each time before it leaves port. Each machine when put into action has to be inspected to prevent the danger of accidents.

These daily examples would seem to fully confirm that man's spiritual condition should also be kept under constant testing. His physical condition is observed by a physician. People have their family doctors who explain that the condition of the organism should be watched not only during an already evident serious illness but also during a state of assumed health. It is very important for the doctor to be able to establish symptoms of illness in advance so that he can prevent the possibility of illness or infection. Prophylactic measures are taken to avoid possible infection.

"As in heaven, so on earth." As in the body, so in the spirit. The analogy of infection and reactions is a very close one, for just as a feeble and exhausted body is easily subject to infection so is a wavering spirit at once subject to a most dangerous attack. The body may by good luck avoid contagion, but the effect on the spirit is much more complicated because of unseen and inscrutable factors.

Any coarse food such as bloody meat lays one open to invisible approaches. Every coarse, furious word is a gateway admitting the dark ones, and every violent treachery is an invitation to the darkest entities. If the conduits of good are immeasurable, the dark conduits, although limited, are still quite considerable and extensive. After all, we do not summon by the voice at far-off distances. Radio waves, in accepted hieroglyphics, create bridges and attraction. It is the same in the spiritual realm where an invisible radio calls, attracts, and broadcasts its commands.

Someone immersed in evil will tremble convulsively at such benign warnings, but if he has already given himself as a concession to evil, he will with grimacing and trembling concede the field of action to the dark concessionaires. Thought and will are active every instant, and there is hardly a moment when man remains inactive. Some mistakenly imagine that when they are silent or motionless or mumbling outwardly unclear formulas, nothing is done by them. In their spiritual world, however, all sorts of important actions are taking place. The needle of a sensitive apparatus would probably show a continual palpitation of the spirit. It can be seen how the spirit, in its essence, is always striving upward, but dark and heavy weights and all kinds of talons get the upper hand and drag it down into darkness.

The unchanging labor of the spirit goes on amidst all our daily activities and trivial routine. If the workings of the spirit are constant, if the spirit vibrates and is atremor even at the very smallest incidents, according to human understanding, then naturally the testing of the spirit will be constant. Since it is said, "All worlds are on trial," we may consider all parts of the worlds, down to the smallest particle, to be subject to the same process of testing.

There can be nothing unfortunate or burdensome for the consciousness in such continual testing. It is said that our planet was exposed this year on May 26 to a great danger, which for the greater part of the planet's population remained unrealized and completely unknown. In a matter of seconds Earth escaped the thrust of a powerful meteor. Can there be even a moment when we are not exposed to danger? Nonetheless people continue to act, work, grieve, and make merry.

In the July number of "Twentieth Century" our friend Jagadisvarananda sketches a beautiful but justly severe outline of contemporary life. He shows that modern life is largely taken up with a search for pleasures and that these are gradually degenerating. As we have often noted, people are abandoning conscious thinking and crave some kind of narcotics which will relieve them from thinking about the fundamental questions of life.

Where there is a desire for pleasures and for gold, naturally there are also special testings. If even such coarse pursuits as money and pleasure easily dominate the human consciousness, these will likewise be intensely subjected to testings. Where coarseness and foul language dominate a man, the needle of the apparatus indicating the battle of the spirit fluctuates especially. There are many who do not like even to admit that they are undergoing testing, which they promptly consider to be a sort of inadmissible tyranny. And yet testing is nothing more than the application of one's own spirit to the measure of Truth.

If the spirit itself indicates one of the lower steps, this can hardly be taken as an extraneous intrusion or a compulsion. The spirit always indicates willingly and with absolute precision the measure to which it responds at a given moment. It has often been said that everyone is his own judge, and many times it has been repeated about the way man makes his own destiny. Hierarchy, too, has been repeatedly spoken about, and also constructiveness and co-measurement.

Self-testings definitely take place in everything. The normal-minded man knows what amount of food he requires, but he who is addicted to gluttony ignores it and thus harms himself. A healthy organism carries out its most complicated tasks naturally, but if the balance is disturbed man is warned through his senses. It is the same with the testings of the spirit. Anyone who has not ignored or rejected spiritual manifestations will sense and hear the little bell of his heart. A man will be warned provided he listens to such a warning and admits it into his consciousness. The heart moans, but not everyone will understand its urgent call.

A man whose ignorance is great can even become obdurate to the call of the heart. He may even force his heart to become silent, and this violence is one of the causes of many forms of heart disease. Let us not forget that by spiritual compulsion people can also harm those near them whose radiations are akin to them. If man has no right to harm his own nature, if any form of suicide is to be condemned, then the killing of others by a malicious consciousness must also be condemned.

If there exists the so-called deadly eye, there exists also the acutely sharpened will. Therefore, how many unintentional and pernicious glances are dispersed like arrows in space. Knowing this we will not despair, but on the contrary this realization will only reinforce the shield and create a new source of courage and vigor. Let us not fear, but even love testings, for we shall be strengthened by them. Blessed are the obstacles, and even more blessed are the testings which temper the strongest blade.

To love means that love has entered into our consciousness. To love means that we shall transmute a concept within ourselves and apply it to life. If any one notices that someone is drooping with fright in the face of testing, let him without fail invigorate the frightened one with his own joy, strengthened by the realization of a new, tested shield.

It has been said, "I shall receive all arrows in my shield, but I shall send but one." Everything is tested, all worlds are on trial. This is not a cause for terror, but a source of broadening the consciousness, a key to vigor and success.

Timur Hada, August 27, 1935.

[276]

IMAGES

A SEEKER of treasure gains the Fireblossom; the seeker passes by most frightful visages which attempt to hinder the destined fate. The young prince rushes after the Firebird and on this path must overcome the most hideous monsters. All folk tales infallibly compel all seekers of the miraculous and good to pass through the most extraordinary obstacles and show fearlessness before the most ferocious monsters. Achievement is always linked with the renunciation of fear.

The so-called "fears" often narrated in the lives of hermits refer to the trials through fear which definitely accompany the path of achievement for good. At times, also other, different, trials and temptations are encountered, but the tests through fears are especially stressed in descriptions of their lives.

It may be asked why it is absolutely necessary to pass by the most frightful images, why specifically these terrible trials? Yet the answer will be extremely simple. Hideous visages do exist, and one should know all that exists. Therefore, the more striking the revelation of all kinds of visages, the greater and speedier will be the experience created for future spiritual battles. You know that knowledge is essential, that self-perfectment takes place only under conditions of constant learning; and the many-sided images of life are among the most profound psychological accumulations.

You also know that the visages of darkness are full of deceit and cunning. They devise all sorts of concealments of their true intentions. Therefore the powerful blows of the creative chisel are so needed in order to actually reveal to human consciousness the real significance of these and other images.

Worst of all is a delusion. Therefore, at the destined hour the true visage will always be revealed. The servant of darkness himself will not immediately suspect that he is already revealed in his full stature, with all his excrescences and ugliness. For quite some time he may still imagine that his, as he thinks, most cunning burrows will not be disclosed. And yet, his darkest plots will be already revealed through the most instructive examples.

It is strange to see how seemingly slick plotters are suddenly revealed by all their sinister peculiarities. As if a certain force compels them to express unwittingly what was hidden within them, and to do that which so obviously proves their nature. Often they hide for years something premeditated, and then, to their own indisputable detriment, and, most likely, unexpectedly by them, they show their true faces.

This is called "the selection of images." People should not be horrified at the frightful masks shown to them, but, on the contrary, should accept the knowledge with full understanding. One should be grateful when this amazing selection of images appears opportunely for salvation and success. Every choice is in itself an orderly procedure. Each step toward order is already a practical advance. It is known that the inhabitants of the countries of the far north, who remain for long periods in twilight and who are awed by the midnight sun, await the coming of full light with great impatience. Let the night be even darker, but then let the sun shine in all its heartening life-giving force.

It is the same with the selection of images. It is worse to remain in confusion with undetermined entities. Let the most hideous masks appear, then a clear-cut selection will take place and become established. Only a timid spirit will beg to be liberated from the revelation of true images. Every courageous worker will say, Let not even the most frightful darkness be hidden from me—then the sunlight will shine more brilliantly.

The inexperienced worker will say, Safeguard me from seeing terrifying images. Spare my eye and my ear from the threats and roarings of darkness. But a worker with wide experience, on the contrary, will ask that there be no delay in showing him the true nature of whatever happens. Not for one instant will the real worker for good be aggravated when shown the true significance of all that happens. He will be filled with gratitude for the clear indication of truth. In no way will he be frightened when seeing great numbers of dark images. Because together with them he will also see good images. He knows firmly that quantity is nought before quality. Let entire legions of darkness pass before his eyes, yet he will always know that the legions of good are more numerous and ever ready to repulse darkness.

The selection of images is a most natural and practical action. In the final analysis it always takes place, but sometimes people cannot account for it when such a spectacle is shown to them. Because of a useless habit people often ascribe that which they see to mere chance, and yet they are being shown an entire complex. In one instant they could learn and immeasurably multiply their knowledge, if they could clearly understand it. If they only would judge their surroundings with complete impartiality! Take someone who seemingly was an adherent of Light and who suddenly reveals an obviously dark aptitude. It means that without justification he was considered to be a worker for Light, but his nature remained in the service of darkness. His benevolent smile was only a mask. "What a mask!" will exclaim he who penetrates the nature of such a man and takes into consideration this instructive discovery.

The disclosure of masks proceeds, based upon life's experiences, and may pass, as it were, into clairvoyance. Someone may be astonished at why and for what reason he who belonged to evil was admitted and tolerated. There may be many reasons for it. There also may be karmic grounds. There may have been an act of compassion which accords the possibility of improvement to the dark one. Finally, there may be a wise decision, precisely at the very last moment, when his nature blossomed with all its characteristic colors. Therefore, an experienced worker will not bewail the fact that he has learned something too late. By what kind of specific measurement will this be "too late"?

According to earthly measurements something may seem belated, but in the timeless, supermundane decisions this may have happened at the closest and best hour, according to a Higher decision. To fear frightful images means to show one's entire inexperience. It is not in vain, according to folk wisdom, that a true seeker must definitely pass by the most frightful monsters. If he makes this journey without tremor, firmly knowing his bright goal, he will find, and will also be able to accept, the sacred chalice. But if he trembles with doubt, if he wavers because of brutality of spirit, it will indicate that he is still far from the beneficent goal.

Fearlessness, of which so much is spoken, should not be some special, praiseworthy quality. Fearlessness is the most natural quality of a normal heart. Each fear is in itself a sickness, a convulsion, an infection. Best of all is to test fearlessness upon revealed visages. In cotton padding, in darkness and warmth, man will not see frightful visages, but he will dwell in the permanent depths of twilight. In what way then will his true knowledge be formed and affirmed? A hero not only does not evade frightful images, but, on the contrary, he boldly and resoundingly blows his horn, challenging monsters to combat.

Fear is unknown to a hero. He rejoices when he can see the evil monster and vanquish it. The selection of images is a speeded up education, and strengthening, and broadening of consciousness. Let us not fear, but rejoice at each knowledge. The images are frightful, yet the heart sings.

Timur Hada, August 30, 1935.

INVINCIBILITY

A FIRM foundation is needed for each construction. On all the steps of existence the very same realization of invincibility is needed. As in daily life so, also, in the biggest structures one should be assured of the stability of construction. Why then do all kinds of impediments leading to evil so often occur in all their absurdity? From where does the corroding chaos come the most easily?

Doubt and envy—these two most poisonous snakes attempt to crawl in wherever any kind of construction takes place. It would seem that people were sufficiently warned from time immemorial about these two monsters. It would seem that everybody knows to what an extent and with what diversity these progenies of darkness try to cover up themselves. One hears endlessly about all kinds of masks behind which hides the malign darkness which dispatches its destructive agents everywhere. Yes, countless times have people heard about the horrors of doubt and envy.

Not only in parables and legends, but in the very daily examples people were shown that one cannot advance while hiding in one's bosom these ill-smelling vipers. All admonitions, all sermons warn about taking a stand against the invasions of evil. People swear most solemn oaths that they will not fear, or retreat, and will not commit a betrayal. And later, after uttering the most lofty and solemn words, and mentioning all the highest and most beautiful Images, people with the greatest of ease admit the most evil vipers into their heart.

Verily, one wonders how incongruous are the solemn oaths and assurances admitted so lightly along with the smallest currents of the most criminal thoughts. It is indeed astonishing how the seemingly least motives lead wavering people into the most terrible and irreparable consequences. It seems that such a lack of co-measurement would be impossible for human reason. The most primitive mind obviously should resist such betrayal of the greatest and finest thoughts and creations. If one could depict graphically the scope and significance of oaths but recently uttered, and also the sheer groundlessness of reasons for envy and doubt, then one would be really shocked. The human mind will not even dare to picture such a lack of co-measurement.

How could yesterday's sun become as black as coal? For such retrogression some very powerful poisons are needed. How could a minute envy, a null doubt or irritation suddenly overcome all the best strivings toward luminous infinity? The poison of vipers spreads to such an extent that the infected brain does not want any facts. It is blind even to the most vivid reality. It wishes only to comfort its repeatedly accepted master. It is anxious to perform some sort of coarse, calumnious action. It feels a need to burst into obscenity. It desires to cause even a slight harm to Good and to Light.

If even such an obscured consciousness shall inwardly whisper that in spite of everything Light will not be impaired, the malign irritation will still try to strain the entire strength of the lungs in fruitless attempts, if not to extinguish, then at least to unsettle the bright flame. In these moments of dark madness man retreats from all logic. Everything more or less sensible, all the best examples, all the most convincing inheritances are, for the obsessed, only an occasion for irritation.

The obsessed one is ready to inflict the hardest blow upon himself. He is ready to subject his whole future to the greatest danger, fully merited, only in order to be able to utter slander and obscenity. In admitting the most evil blasphemy, the obsessed one attempts to somehow vindicate himself, as if the evil of destruction was not already brought into action by him. This obsessed one has already heard quite clearly that the evil created by him must be outlived without fail. The poison engendered by him has to be outlived, at best, with great sufferings. It would seem that it is so easy to understand about the harmfulness of evil and its nearest adherents—betrayal, envy, and doubt.

Ask any builder exactly what basic structural material he needs for a building. Even in these purely material, ordinary, daily examples you will see to what an extent the builder will seek for stability and indestructibility of materials. If we see the striving for invincibility in ordinary daily examples, to what an extent then are such foundations necessary in spiritual structures. One can build only out of good materials, fully resistant to destruction. Observe many examples when spiritual associations broke up because of such petty things and trifles, of which it is even a shame for sensible people to think.

Try to get to the root of doubt or envy. You will see such a minute cause that it would be difficult to observe it even under a microscope. Later if you were to show this tiny cause to this same man who became obsessed, he would be the first to deny in every way any possibility of such an absurdity.

Then by what oaths can one attain spiritual invincibility? Neither by oaths, nor by threats, nor by commands will it be reached. Only through the enlightened heart that has already reached the step of inviolability is steadfast cooperation attained. Through enlightened labors an inviolable degree of illumination of the heart is created. The heart is reared in labor. The heart realizes what is true cooperation. When the full degree of cooperation is cognized, then a man will not waver in doubt and be defiled through envy.

Inviolable cooperation—what wondrous bliss it is! How broadly it is ordained for humanity. Such beautiful delineations are given, in order to measure through them all the greatness of inviolable cooperation and the shameful mediocrity of evil machinations. In a most touching manner, people have reminded each other about an "Indestructible Wall." In vast dimensions, with the strongest materials people have attempted to strengthen the testimony about the "Indestructible Wall." Apparently, humanity must repeatedly speak about the blessedness of resplendent invincibility. Apparently, humanity feels that it must remind itself endlessly about the actuality of good and the shamefulness of evil.

But in what kind of almost invisible, nasty worms does evil crawl through the world? Not without reason do people themselves speak of a worm of envy, a worm of doubt, a worm of baseness, thus designating the shameful obsession through which all that is best and highest is trampled. But if people repeat so many times to each other about the shamefulness of bowing to darkness and all its engenderments, will they nevertheless freely admit the abominable worms into their heart?

Much is spoken about evolution. Yet from every point of view, from the lowest to the highest, evolution presupposes the thriving of the good. People know that impeding something good actually signifies cooperation with darkness. Why speak about it again? Yet if one does speak about it, this means that there are reasons for it. That which all should know is not simply repeated, it is reiterated because of obvious reasons. Crush the abominable worm within yourself. Liberate the heart from the harmful infection. In spite of everything, "Light conquers darkness." In spite of everything, Good is victorious. In the Good the true dates are known and in the Good co-measurement is born.

Invincibility is a stipulation for every creation.

Timur Hada, September 1, 1935

GOLDEN PRAGUE

THE present year is a memorial date for many things.
I am transporting myself back more than a quarter of
a century, thirty years; everywhere life's milestones, full of
inner meaning, are encountered. Some paintings and frescoes were conceived, and also these were years of public
activity—a great deal of everything.

Amidst all this diversity certain mementoes of special
significance to the heart stand out, among them the unforgettable year of the beginning of the foreign exhibitions.
Now we are used to traverse the oceans, to transport ourselves over mountains and vast spaces, but thirty years ago
people were much more immobile. Every trip was connected with some special decisions. How could one talk
about trips abroad or expeditions when Russia itself was
hardly explored, and to travel in one's own country was
almost regarded as a sign of bad taste. That was the period
when we asked in newspaper columns why the Russians
do not love their country and know so little of her priceless
monuments of antiquity and of her natural beauty. And
to these questions we received in answer cold glances and
shrugging of shoulders.

When remarkable travelers were met, such as Prjevalsky, Potanin, Mikluha-Maklai and other, one may
say, equal heroes of learning, they were looked upon as
peculiar people, almost as fanatics. However, the ponderous-ness of uninterrupted "settledness" was not akin to us
Russians alone. Occasionally we heard also about Frenchmen who said with pride that in their entire life they had
never left their native city.

True, everywhere was to be found a special type of people, the so-called wanderers. Even the homebodies grown heavy loved to listen to the fairy-like tales of wanderings to holy places and throughout the world when even every night's lodging became a vivid record of events. Let us but recall Aphanasy Nikitin[24] from Tver who exclaims in the fifteenth century, "Getting away from all our sorrows, let us depart for India." And he himself undertakes a journey of many years which was not talked about just as Marco Polo was not talked about; similarly one also did not speak much about Mendeleyev in his time. There are special reasons for this. Let us also recall from remote ages Prokopy the Blessed, who, from the high shores of Northern Dvina, blessed the unknown travelers as follows, "To the seafarers, to the travelers . . ."

Because of this unbroken circle of settledness, it was not so easy thirty years ago to dream about going outside of the boundaries—"Beyond the seas are great lands." But to all such far-off lands, to all the calling mountains, to the inspiring heights some kind of key must be found so that a messenger may knock and sound a call.

A letter came from the "Manes" Society in Prague, with an invitation to exhibit; they offered to transport all paintings, to arrange everything. In this invitation there is something hearty, which reveals Pan-Slavic, pan-human hearts. Thirty years have passed since that time, but I remember now, as then, all the joy blossoming from that hearty call. It was that door set ajar which at once broadened the possibilities, the quests, and the beautiful affirmations. This yet unrealized, but long inwardly awaited message came from completely unknown people—simply out of the blue sky. At that time I did not know the kind Milosh Marten. There, somewhere beyond the mountains, beyond the valleys, a new friend was found, and he called to the path longed for in the depth of the heart.

----

[24] A Russian merchant and explorer from Tver, hence his pen name. His real name was Nikitin. Traveled in Persia and India 1466-1472. Author of *Traveling Over Three Seas*. Died in 1472.

And the message came not from chance people, but from Slavs close in spirit. After all, we do consider them as brothers, and in every Slavic meeting the harmonies of a kindred soul are spontaneously created. The paintings went to the exhibition. And then came joyous news, a special issue of the magazine "Dilo," with an excellent, sincere article by Marten. F. Salda in "The Wave of Death" dedicated a powerfully ringing article. Hubert Tzyriak in "Modern Revue" called the exhibition, with deep poetic feeling, "A dream of the past." In this "dream of the past" I dreamt not at all of the past, but of the future. Therefore Golden Prague forever remained for me the gates into the future.

I recall that Elena Ivanovna, who was always striving into the future, rejoiced especially at this invitation from Prague. In every circumstance, aside from its outer appearance, is also contained the seed of the inner meaning. The seed of the Prague Exhibition contained something unusually friendly. True, Milosh Marten, F. Salda, and H. Tzyriak, and also others, who spoke about the exhibition, were very fine cultural experts. But besides this special knowledge in the domain of art, they were primarily men imbued with that pan-human feeling which makes possible the true advance of culture.

During the following years the unrestrainable progress of Czechoslovakia became evident. The great war itself was for the Bohemian people the gates into the glorious future. How many renowned Czech names were affirmed during this time of renaissance for Golden Prague! It was precisely Czechoslovakia which provided an unforgettable example for the world of the venerable scientist Professor Masaryk, who became a true leader of culture and proved that verily a leader of spirit, a leader of culture molds the people's stronghold. Since that time every meeting with the representatives of Czechoslovakia filled us with joy. Jan Masaryk in London, Osussky in Paris, Novak in New York, and many other representatives and scientists of Czechoslovakia only affirmed with their judgments that my joy of years ago about Golden Prague was not accidental.

We recall what was said in 1933 by Dr. Ferdinand Veverka, the Minister of Czechoslovakia in Washington, at our Convention of the Pact and Banner of Peace: "The main reason why nations reject war lies not only in its horrors, but in its stupidity, in its senselessness, in its unproductivity, economically and politically. War has turned from a profitable into an especially unprofitable undertaking. Rejection of war as a means of solving international conflicts—this new hypothesis which brings to the world a concept of peace as a basic social order—compels us to truly re-examine and change the very foundations of civilization. Peace is a state of mind, peace is a fundamental state of affairs, not the reverse side of war, not a free sigh between battles. When this realization shall become to us a reality, then the time will come when oppressed and harassed humanity will understand and accept the true peace, that of the Gospel—"Peace on Earth, good will toward men."

These words are the summons of a true bearer of the banner of culture. To think about such fully realized, operative peace can only be done by a nation that understands the entire practicality of the foundations of labor and the treasures of creativeness which will always be the true treasures. In such a direction of mutual magnanimity and understanding proceeded my relations with Golden Prague.

One more encounter—a stormy crossing from Le Havre to New York; not many passengers on the liner "Paris," and suddenly we meet friends of whom we had heard so much, toward whom our hearts were open for years. And this meeting took place during a storm on the Atlantic. This meeting reminded me of another one which took place in Paris, in the home of Princess Tenischeff. There, quite unexpectedly and simply, I met my as yet unknown friend Milosh Marten. And here, amidst stormy waves, we met his former widow, now married to General Kletchanda. She and the General were going to Columbia. We met as if we had been personally acquainted for years. That mutual trust rang out without which human relations have no meaning. God grant that every country may possess such leaders as General Kletchanda! Prior to the date of the thirtieth anniversary of friendship with Golden Prague, the meeting with General Kletchanda and his wife was a conclusive chord which once again affirmed the right feeling of joy about Golden Prague that flashed out already in 1906.

Memories can be of different natures. Sometimes they are only a necklace of facts, the collection of an observer. And these accumulations can be written down; they will also be needed in some mutual relationships. But in such a collection the heart may remain outside of the tremor of exaltation. Only where the circumstances merge into heartfelt rapture is there true significance in recording that which gave joy.

"Let us rejoice." It is easy to say, but not always easy to fulfill this summons. Therefore, let us value with a special solicitude all that can vitally support the joy of the spirit. That joy is real when in its foundation lie culture, friendship, and humaneness. Greeting to Golden Prague.

Urusvati, Himalayas, 1936.

DEFENSE

THE defense of the Motherland is the duty of man. Just as we defend the dignity of mother and father, so also experience and knowledge are offered for the defense of the Motherland. Slighting one's Motherland would be, first of all, uncultured.

Culture is true enlightened learning. Culture is a scientific and inspired approach to the solution of mankind's problems. Culture is beauty in all its creative grandeur. Culture is exact knowledge without prejudices and superstitions. Culture is the affirmation of good in all its efficacy. Culture is a song of peaceful labor, in endless perfectment. Culture is revaluation of values for the sake of the discovery of the true treasures of the people. Culture is affirmed in the heart of the people and creates striving for construction. Culture accepts all discoveries and improvements of life, because it lives in everything that thinks consciously. Culture defends the historic dignity of the nation.

Each opposition to culture is ignorance. Each obscenity against culture is a sign of a bestial state. Humaneness and service to humanity derive from culture. To carry the banner of culture means to safeguard the finest universal values. If a universal concept is close to the soul of mankind, how much closer and more penetrating sounds the word about the Motherland.

Declaration of the Motherland is not an abstract, nebulous idea. He who attempts to assert it will realize the entire responsibility for this act of affirmation.

People cannot be satisfied with abstractions. In the world all is real, and in the highest beauty the resplendent summits are real. The summit rests on Earth. Upon the crystal of thought rests the realization of the Motherland as it is universally understood. The defense of the Motherland is also the defense of one's own dignity.

The defense of the Motherland is also the defense of culture. Above the daily dust shines the concept of the Motherland. He who cognizes this beautiful and inviolable concept can consider himself a conscious worker for culture. In labor, amidst obstacles seemingly unconquerable, are found young forces. In love for humanity, in love for the Motherland the young hearts will find the uncontested radiant striving for achievement. In the Russian word podvig is contained a concept of motion, of advance, and untiring creativeness.

Great Motherland, all thy spiritual treasures, all thy unutterable beauties, the inexhaustibility of all thy vistas and all thy summits we will defend. There is no heart so cruel that it could say, Do not think about the Motherland. And not only during holidays, but in daily labors we will apply to everything that we create thought about the Motherland, her happiness, her national progress. In everything and above all, we shall find constructive thoughts, not in mundane dates, not in selfhood, but in true self-realization, and they will tell the world: We know our Motherland, we serve her, and we shall use our strength to defend her on all her paths.

"Above all kinds of Russias, there is one unforgettable Russia.

Above all kinds of love, there is one pan-human love."

Urusvati, Himalayas, 1936.

COMBATING IGNORANCE

THE conflict with ignorance must be a world wide manifestation. Not a single nation can boast that it is sufficiently enlightened. No one can find sufficient strength to overcome ignorance in single combat. Knowledge must be universal and upheld in full cooperation. The paths of communication know no barriers; so, too, the paths of knowledge must blossom in the exchange of ideas. It should not be thought that somewhere enough has been done for education. Knowledge is so much an expanding process that continual renovation of methods is required. It is frightful to see petrified brains which do not admit new attainments. No one inclined to negation can be called a scientist. Science is free, honest, and fearless. Science can instantly alter and elucidate the problems of the Universe. Science is beautiful and therefore infinite. Science cannot stand prohibitions, prejudices, and superstitions. Science can find the great even in quests of the small. Inquire of great scientists how many times must stupendous discoveries have been made in the process of routine observations. The eye was open, and the brain was not dust laden. The path of those who know how to investigate freely will be the path of the future. Actually, the battle with ignorance is as indeferrable as that with dissolution and corruption. Not easy is the battle with dark ignorance; it has many allies; it is sheltered in many countries and is covered with various garments. One needs to be supplied with both courage and patience, for the battle with ignorance is a battle with chaos."

Already five centuries before our era there came from the East the blessed words, "Ignorance is the most heinous crime." Later on the great hermits of the first centuries of Christianity decreed that "ignorance is hell." Truly, all fratricidal crimes have their origin in this dark abyss, and the world is filled with lies and darkness which further the most ugly, the most cruel, and abhorrent evil deeds.

To swallow food does not yet mean to live. Likewise, to be literate does not mean to be enlightened. Literacy is natural nutriment, but we see that just as food may be either useful or harmful, so can signs of literacy be used by both Light and darkness. Enlightenment and culture are synonymous. In both is contained readiness for infinite learning. In the furnace of such a constant renewal of consciousness the very essence of man is purified. Through this honest and unlimited labor of learning, people are ennobled and begin to understand the concept of service to humanity and to the world. A true scholar has an open eye and unfettered thought. But just as everything in life, the eye and thought must be trained. From the first steps of education, an enlightened approach and broadening of the horizon should be laid in the foundation of primary schooling. Knowledge must be freed from conventional limitations. Knowledge is the path to joy, but joy is a special wisdom.

The scientist and the artist know the meaning of the word inspiration. They know what perceptivity is, which opens to them new refined forms and reveals subtle energies previously unnoticed or perhaps forgotten. From remote ages came the realization that thought is energy, that thought is light-bearing. Very long ago certain people knew that thought can be suggested or, rather, transmitted. But even such an old axiom has only lately entered customary scientific thought, before the very eyes of the present generation. We all witnessed how quite recently the ignoramuses scoffed at so-called magnetism and hypnotism. It went so far that the same force under various names was accepted differently. Mesmerism was ridiculed and condemned, but the same force under the name of hypnotism received a certain right to existence. There are peculiar reasons why some pills have to be gilded and medicine vials have to be adorned with special labels. And it can be understood why some chemicals, which are now fully recognized, had to be veiled by the alchemists under the names eagle, phoenix, and many other symbols.

We all remember how when the Neurological Institute was founded by Prof. Bekhterev every skeptic ridiculed his experiments in thought transmission. The fact that the name of Bekhterev was widely known did not save him from derision and not even from all kinds of suspicion. Ignoramuses organized a whispering campaign, implying that a whole institution could not be devoted only to the research of the nervous system and thought. They whispered about some political intrigues, about some romantic infatuations, and even that Bekhterev had become insane. Such were the colossal allegations invented by spasms of ignorance. I remember how during this whispering campaign we sadly remembered the book by Gaston Tissandier, *Martyrs of Science*. Verily, where are the limits of patience when during the present generation a certain Academy called the great Edison a charlatan for his invention of the phonograph, and some universities did not admit women to higher education. I repeat that this happened not during the medieval ages, but in our time; and these actions were committed not by illiterate savages, but by people bearing the conventional official label of science. Let us not enumerate the endless row of true martyrs of science, but since we mentioned the persecution of education for women, let us also recall the case of the mathematical genius Sophie Kovalevsky, who was not admitted to the Russian university and yet received world recognition for her works in higher mathematics. And how many excellent scholars and physicians can be recalled who, being persecuted by their ignorant colleagues, were even compelled to leave their own country.

The world is proud of the name of the great physiologist Pavlov; everywhere are being affirmed his formulas of the teaching of conditioned reflexes and his genius in solving other problems. But even this glorious international achievement, crowned by the Nobel prize, called forth in certain circles a contemptuous shrugging of the shoulders. Among the latter one will also discover ignorance. Verily, no robes, no dead scholastic labels can cover human hatred, envy, and dull bigotry. It is far easier to combat illiteracy than to annihilate the sinister hydra of hatred of man with all its attributes of envy, doubt, vulgarity, and slander, and all those hidden campaigns, which the forces of darkness so cunningly manipulate. The forces of evil and the forces of ignorance—these shameful synonyms—are closely united. Of all feelings, love and hatred are the most unifying and powerful.

True, in spite of all the avid attempts of ignorance, enlightened knowledge progresses in the whole world. Let us remember the recent achievements which gave joy to the world of education. Let us remember the remarkable discoveries of the great biologist Sir Jagadis Bose concerning the life of plants. Professor A. H. Compton states that human thought is the most important factor in the world. Prof. S. Metalnikoff of the Pasteur Institute conducts most important research in the field of immunity and the immortality of Protozoa. Dr. Kotick investigates the transfer of sensitiveness. Dr. Walter Stempell of the University of Muenster proves the existence of invisible radiation coming from all living organisms. Dr. Paul Dobler of Heilbronn University asserts the existence of Earth's radiations and their relation to human magnetism, which has up to recently been ridiculed. Prof. Harry M. Johnson of the University of Virginia arrives at instructive conclusions regarding insanity. Dr. Otrian, in charge of a meteorological station in Germany, investigates the influence of atmospheric manifestations. Abbé Moré, the French astronomer, makes most interesting deductions regarding sun-spots. The American biologist Bernard Proctor investigates special conditions of life on heights. The French scientist Dr. Lévi-Valency warns of possible epidemics of insanity. Dr. Riese experiments with the effect of rhythm.

Dr. Bernard Reid, a British scientist, draws a parallel between ancient medicine and modern vitamin research. A young Hungarian scientist discovers rays which cause invisibility. Everyone knows of the experiments of Professors Richet and Geley and the conclusions of Sir Oliver Lodge. Prof. V. van Haas of Leiden University proves the impossibility of absolute zero. Dr. Cannon of Harvard makes deductions regarding the reasons for the element of luck in scientific discoveries. The chemist Midgley gives a bold prognosis of future discoveries. Prof. J. B. Rhine and Prof. William McDougall reach astonishing results at Duke University in the field of extrasensory perceptions and thought-transference. So many wonderful achievements! Thus, in every country there are enlightened seekers who untiringly and fearlessly pioneer in the field of science. And yet those great men remain alone and are compelled, each in his own field, to overcome undeserved obstacles, and at times public opinion.

One can quote pages of research conducted recently which widen the frame of conventional thinking. Actually, nature itself comes to the aid of every thinker. Sunspots with all the deductions about them, of which the greatest authorities of our time, Sir James Jeans of Cambridge and Dr. C. G. Abbot of the Smithsonian Institution, remind us that the time is not far off when astrology, which is so greatly ridiculed, will turn out to be nothing else but a formula of astrochemistry and thus another great branch of science will be freed from calumnies. People will understand that they live surrounded by powerful chemisms and that they themselves represent the most refined and powerful chemical laboratory. Everyone has read of the recently conducted experiments with the chemism of human secretions and with radiations from the finger tips and that some radiations of certain people were so powerful that they could kill harmful bacteria. Let us also remember the experiments of Prof. Yourevitch which prove that the energy radiated by man is a conductor and a unifier for certain elements which otherwise could not be combined. And did not the experiments of Keeley, who was so unjustly persecuted, prove the same? Thus the investigation of human radiations and of psychic energy imperatively calls humanity to the forthcoming remarkable accomplishments.

Ignoramuses like to scoff at the yogis of India. For them, walking on fire, sitting upon water, swallowing the strongest poisons, the stopping or acceleration of the pulse at will, burial alive and return to life after several weeks—all these are but skillful tricks and charlatanism. Yet in the very positive and well known magazine "Modern Review" there is an article, supported by photographs, about fire-walking in Mysore. The journal quotes this in connection with the demonstrations in London of the Kashmiri, Khuda Buks, widely announced through the press of the whole world. Sitting upon the water of the Ganges was regarded as charlatanism, and even cautious people who had witnessed it whispered, "Who knows? Perhaps there was some support under the water." And quite recently the British press reported the case of a woman who changed her weight to such an extent that such a manifestation upon the water was quite easy for her, due to the change of polarity. The whole world was amazed to read about the striking phenomena, from the point of view of conventional science, of Therese Neumann of Bavaria, and at present the newspapers are filled with astounding accounts of Shanti Devi in Delhi, a nine-year-old girl. That remarkable case has been verified by many reliable people.

From Latvia comes news of the extraordinary ability of a girl of eight to read thoughts, which was described in a whole brochure. Recently there also have been recorded indisputable cases of the reception of radio waves without a receiver, and the astonishing faculty of two Italian boys to see through walls and other opaque objects. No doubt, during the time of the Inquisition all these unfortunate people would have been burnt at the stake owing to their unusual abilities. But even nowadays the man who could catch radio waves directly had a taste of being in a lunatic asylum!

Let us also not forget the remarkable clairvoyance and clairaudience of Joan of Arc, who saved France, but who for her abilities was burnt at the stake by her ignorant contemporaries. And even at present not only the persons who are in possession of these extraordinary faculties but those who have conducted research in this field have been subjected by ignoramuses to all kinds of persecutions. Let us also remember the unjust derision to which the Society for Psychical Research was so often subjected. Every nucleus of a new unprejudiced scientific conquest is persecuted. This creates an unusually ugly spectacle. On one side new educational institutions are being opened, which by their very aspect seem to invite new research; yet on the other side every unusual fact which did not as yet enter into the elementary textbooks is not only ridiculed but even becomes an object for all kinds of attacks. It means that the hydra of ignorance is to be found not only in illiteracy but also in fossilized perception and in hatred of man.

"Every denial of Truth is ignorant and harmful not only for the denier himself but also spatially. Antagonism to Truth infects space, but there is a still more loathsome action when people after having once realized Truth later shrink from it. Such a retreat into darkness is madness! It is possible to find periods in the history of humanity when, after particles of the Truth had been already grasped, certain pseudo-teachers, because of extreme ignorance, tried to again conceal from people the immutable position of things; this resulted in what will some time be regarded as shameful pages of history. The usurpers offered no proofs, but commanded that the obvious be denied. It is as if denial of the sun's existence were prescribed, because someone weak of eyesight could not look at the sun! . . . Some, ignorant of them, through egotism forbade others to know the reality. Let people remember how many recessions into darkness have taken place in different ages. Perhaps such recollections will move humanity toward justice and honesty."

Thus, everyone, for whom education and culture are not empty words, should, in his own field, fight ignorance as far as his strength allows. Let no one say that he has no possibility of doing so—this would be untrue. Alas! Open and hidden ignorance in all its deception and cunning exists everywhere. In every household a clear mind can discern where dust and filth have to be removed. And at present when in the world guns thunder and poisonous gases compete with each other, precisely now, the combating of ignorance is especially needed. A defense of the best, of the most beautiful, and of the most enlightened will be needed.

If someone does not succeed in his beneficent efforts, still this will be efforts and not abstract intentions. Besides, in every effort there is already an element of action. Therefore every effort is already creativeness for good. No doubt some agents of ignorance will whisper that precisely now words about culture and enlightenment are out of place. This is their typical trick, they try to find at every moment in life a reason why exactly at that hour striving to culture and enlightenment are untimely. By this formula the servitors of ignorance betray themselves. Precisely good, culture, and enlightenment are always timely.

There cannot be a state of consciousness in which it is unfitting and untimely to be humane. And only misanthropy could whisper about such untimeliness; misanthropy which, in the darkness of its lair, always dreams of turning mankind into monsters devouring each other.

Verily, from small to great, everyone can, and is, duty bound to bring his mite to the cause of combating ignorance. Uniting in groups and singlehandedly everyone can somewhere put an end to the deriding monster of ignorance. Every labor already contains an effort for perfectment and enlightenment. Only ignorance can belittle labor as such and can shamelessly scoff at the quests for knowledge. In rightful indignation against every act of ignorance, against every ignorant negation, the worker for culture will find a vital thought and a powerful word, and will mark by beautiful deeds the victorious path of enlightenment.

Glory to the defenders of culture! Glory to the heroes of labor! Glory to the fearless!

Urusvati, Himalayas, June 10, 1936.

GORKI

THE great Russian writer Maxim Gorki passed away in Gorki, near Moscow, on June 18.

During the last months three great Russians have left this world: the great physiologist Pavlov, the composer Glazunov, and now Gorki. All three were known to the entire world. Who has not heard of the famous experiments in the field of reflexes conducted by Pavlov? Who, next to Tchaikovsky and Rimski-Korsakov, did not also admire Glazunov? And who has not read among other great Russian classics the works of Gorki, who has recorded unfading images of Russian life?

Over half a million people went to pay homage to the remains of the great writer, and seven hundred thousand of his admirers accompanied the funeral procession. The state representatives of the Soviet Union stood as a guard of honor and after the cremation carried the urn to the Kremlin Wall, where it was immured. The entire diplomatic corps was present. A salute of guns resounded in honor of the great writer. Some French papers were amazed at the way a whole nation paid tribute to its national hero. There were wreaths from the French and Czechoslovakian governments. The foreign press unanimously hailed the achievements of Gorki.

The state resolved to erect monuments in honor of Gorki in Moscow, Leningrad, and in Nizhni Novgorod; the latter now bears his name.

The Municipal Council of Prague decided to name a street in the Czechoslovakian capital in his honor.

Beneš, the President of Czechoslovakia, sent the following telegram to Moscow: "The death of Maxim Gorki will compel the entire world and Czechoslovakia in particular to ponder the progress of the Russian people during the last fifty years and of the Soviet Union since the revolution. The participation of Gorki in this process was, in its spiritual aspect, extremely great and convincing. For me personally, Gorki as well as all other Russian classics were my teachers in many respects; and I remember him with gratitude."

H. G. Wells sent a hearty message from England, and Romain Rolland telephoned the following message from Switzerland to Moscow: "At this painful hour of parting, I remember Gorki not so much as a great writer, or even his colorful path of life and mighty creativeness. I remember his full, saturated life which, like his mother Volga, flowed richly in his creations, in streams of thoughts and images. Gorki was the first among the world artists of the word who cleared the path for the people's revolution, who gave it his strength, the prestige of his glory, and his rich life experience. . . . Like Dante, Gorki emerged from hell. But he emerged from there not alone, he brought out with him, and saved, his comrades in suffering."

The Paris papers that have reached the Himalayas record many signs of a world-wide esteem for the late writer. He was honored not only by friends but by all countries and by all sections of cultural life. Even the most restrained obituaries comment highly upon such of Gorki's works as *The Lower Depths, Song of the Stormy Petrel, The Town of Okurov, The Smug Citizens, Mother,* and his last works, *The Artomonov Business* and *Klim Samgin* and conclude with "a man and an artist whom we all loved has passed away." Thus art has united both friends and foes.

From the very beginning of his vivid literary career, Aleksei Maksimovich Peshkov, whom the whole world knows better by his pen name, Maxim Gorki, achieved an exclusive position among Russian classics. Just as about every great man and great talent, there abound many legends about Gorki together with much fiction. Some tried to represent him as a soulless materialist, others based themselves on isolated expressions, by which it is impossible to judge a man and his work. But incorruptible history will depict this great image to full extent, and people will find in him many quite unexpected traits.

About his last minutes, Dr. L. Levin writes in "Izvestia" of June 20: "Aleksei Maksimovich died as he lived, a great man. In these painful hours of illness he never once spoke about himself. All his thoughts were in the Kremlin, in Moscow. Even in the interval between two oxygen masks, he asked me to show him the newspaper with the plan of Stalin's new constitution. During the short periods of relief from his illness he spoke about his beloved subjects—literature and the possibility of a future war, which worried him very much. The last day and night he was delirious. Remaining constantly at his bedside, I discerned the following short phrases: 'There will be war... One should be ready. . . . Fasten up all buttons!'"

N. Berberova, who worked with Gorki, writes in the Paris press of a characteristic episode in Gorki's life:

"This was on the day when the current issue of 'Sovremennye Zapiski' ('Contemporary Review') was received with the concluding chapter of Bunin's novel *Mitya's Love*. Everything was put aside—work, correspondence, newspapers. Gorki locked himself up in his study and was late for lunch and absent-minded. . . . Only at tea it became clear: 'Do you understand ... a remarkable work . . . truly remarkable!' In these words he characterized *Mitya's Love*. ... It is difficult to believe that Gorki could cry with real tears when reading the poems of Lermontov, Blok, and many others..." Further, N. Berberova quotes from a letter she received from Gorki, in which his attitude to poets and poetry was clearly expressed: "I am greatly attracted by the broadness and multifacetedness of themes and subjects in poetry. I consider this quality as a good sign. It shows the broad outlook of the author, his inner freedom, the absence of being chained by any conventional moods, by any preconceived ideas. It seems to me that the definition, 'the poet is the echo of universal life' is most correct.

Of course, there are and should be ears which sense only the bass tones of life, and souls who hear only the lyricism of it. But Pushkin heard everything, felt everything, and therefore has no equal. Can there be anything higher than literature—the art of words? Certainly not. It is the most astounding, mysterious, and beautiful thing in this world!" Gorki's praise of Bunin's novel is characteristic of his sweep of judgment, for Bunin belongs to another literary camp, and therefore his praise is especially valuable.

Many of Gorki's valuable traits will reveal themselves in the course of time. I happened to meet him on many occasions, in private talks and at all kinds of committee meetings, gatherings, etc. On all occasions I could trace some new remarkable details of his character, which very often did not correspond to the outwardly stern appearance of the writer. I remember how once during the organizing meeting of a big literary enterprise, when an urgent decision was required, I asked Gorki for his opinion. He smiled and said, "There is nothing to argue. You as an artist will feel what is needed. Yes, yes, precisely you will feel—you are an intuitivist. Often one should grasp the very essence—above reason!"

I also recollect how once at a friendly gathering Gorki revealed, quite unexpectedly for many, another interesting side of his character. We spoke about yogis and various unusual phenomena which exist in India. Some of the guests looked at Gorki, who kept silent, and they apparently awaited a severe resume. But his resume amazed many. He said, filled with an inner light, "The Hindus are a remarkable people. I will tell you of my personal experience. Once in the Caucasus I met a Hindu, about whom many mysterious stories were circulating. At that time I was rather inclined to shrug my shoulders about many things. At last we met and I will tell you what I saw with my own eyes. He unwound a long thread from a spool and threw it up into the air. To my surprise it remained hanging in the air without falling down. Then he asked me whether I would like to look at his album and precisely what I would like to see in it. I said I would like to see pictures of Indian cities. He took out his album and looking at me said, 'Please, look at these pictures of Indian cities.' The album contained polished brass sheets, on which were beautifully reproduced views of different cities, temples, and other views of India. I looked over the entire album attentively studying the pictures. Then I closed the album and returned it to the Hindu. He smiled and said, 'Well, you have seen views of India.' Then he blew at the album and returned it into my hands inviting me to look at it again. I opened the album and to my surprise found only polished plates without any pictures whatsoever. These Hindus are indeed remarkable people."

Does not this characteristic trait of Gorki prove his all-embracingness and broad consciousness?

He wanted very much to have one of my paintings. He selected from those which I had at the time, not a realistic landscape, but one of the so-called prewar series, "The Doomed City"; precisely such a painting as would correspond to the mood of a poet. Indeed, the author of *Song of the Stormy Petrel* could be only a great poet. Through all the ups and downs of life, by all the paths of his many-sided talent, Gorki walked the path of the Russian people, encompassing the entire multifacetedness and richness of the Russian soul.

"Izvestia" of June 21 carried the following article from the Paris newspapers under the title "Gorki in the Role of Harun-al-Rashid." The story is accompanied by a photo of Gorki dressed as a tramp: "This happened in 1928. Gorki wanted to see what goes on in new public bars, what kinds of people visit them, whether he would find there any types similar to his old ones from *The Lower Depths*, what became of them, what the new visitors are like, etc. But how to arrange such an expedition? Gorki decided to recall his youth and to disguise himself as a tramp. Wearing a beard and with hair overgrown like a bear, skillfully disguised, he entered into intimate talks with the people there, and as a result wrote an article which forms part of his book *Across the Soviet Union.*

"Those who know Gorki will understand that this episode is indeed typical of him. Being a true realist in the broadest sense, he considered it necessary to convince himself practically, not so much for the sake of entering sketches of new types into his notebook, but in order to affirm a synthesis for an actual expansion of his consciousness.

"He was trustful, he trusted, he loved to trust, and he was often deceived. . . . Once he came out of his study singing, and his face expressed such glowing enthusiasm that everybody was amazed. It turned out that he had read a newspaper report that somewhere, somebody has discovered a new microbe."

Once I encountered Gorki at a meeting when the two publishing houses—Sytin in Moscow and the publishers of "Niva"—were merged into one big concern. Vast popular programs in the literary and educational fields were projected. It was interesting to witness how every conventionality and formality annoyed Gorki, who wanted to overcome all formal obstacles without delay. He knew how to build on a broad scale. Take, for example, the plan offered by him for three mighty cultural institutions: "The House of World Literature," "The House of Scientists," and "The House of Art." These three ideas show the creative scope of Gorki's thought, who was striving to find, in spite of all difficulties, the eternal words—words of enlightenment and culture. Throughout life he carried his chalice of service to humanity unspilt.

In the name of the "League of Culture" let us offer our sincere, heartiest thoughts to the memory of Gorki, which will remain forever steadfastly and vividly affirmed in the Pantheon of World Culture.

Urusvati, Himalayas, June 12, 1936.

MIR

NOT by accident in Russian does *mir* mean Universe and also peace. Not without reason are these two great concepts united in one sound. If one imagines the Universe, one also thinks about peaceful labor. Beginning work, one also becomes conscious of the Universe.

People talk about peace especially when they are afraid of war. Yet there are different kinds of wars—internal and external, visible and invisible. Which of them is more horrible remains to be seen.

"Indeed, the worst calamity for both ancient and present humanity is that the greatest poet and wisest teacher, blind Homer, appeared to be a bard of war and not of peace. Together with his faith in the gods, he also lost faith in peace.

'As between men and lions there is no pledge of faith, nor wolves and sheep can be of one mind, but imagine evil continually against each other, so is it impossible for thee and me to be friends, neither shall be any pledge between us until one or other shall have fallen and glutted with blood Ares, the stubborn god of war.'[25] "

This means that "all will kill each other." "There will be no end of war in the world."

"In the *Iliad*—the Trojan war begins endless war which, throughout ages of universal history lasts until our days"— exclaims Merezhkovski in his *Atlantis*. There are not a few soul-stirring lamentations, and Dante has found infernally burning abodes for murderers and all malefactors.

In examining all the symbols and ancient testimonies

---

[25] The *Iliad*, Book XXII.

one finds everywhere in images and hieroglyphics the very same longing, the heartily felt sacred prayer for peace.

And there are also other testimonies.

"Do not do evil to animals" is the ordainment of Triptolemus, the messenger sent by Demeter to savage people after the great flood; Triptolemus was to teach people agriculture and uplift them from the bestial to human life. "Do not do evil to animals" in Biblical language means: Blessed are those who have pity for everything living, for "the whole creation groaneth and travaileth in pain until now." They suffer together with man, they perish with man, they are saved with him.

Should man kill animals in order to feed on meat? "No. By no means." ordains Demeter, the goddess of the fruitful earth. With bloody food there enters into man the spirit of killing, the spirit of war; but the spirit of peace enters only with bloodless food.

And Hesiod, the shepherd on Mount Helicon sings:

"For the son of Cronos has ordained . . . That fishes and beasts and winged fowls Should devour one another, for right is not in them. But to mankind he gave right which proves for the best. . . ."[26] The Truth: Do not kill! For everybody the first step is always possible—not to kill, not to make war. "If you kill you will die; give life and you will live. A child understands this, and yet this is the mystery of mysteries!"

Should one defend culture? Yes, one should, always and in everything.

Should one help the workers of culture, the depressed and burdened? Yes, one should, always and in everything.

Should one unite around the sign of culture to overcome the onset of destruction and decay? Yes, one should, always and in everything.

Perhaps culture, knowledge, beauty are sufficiently guarded and affirmed everywhere? Perhaps the bases of culture are fully strengthened everywhere?

---

[26] Hesiod *Works and Days.*

Perhaps the workers for culture are especially safeguarded by laws and in the consciousness of the people?

As before, the League of Culture, as the voice of public opinion, is indeferrably needed!

We have to talk about peace and non-killing. What does this mean? Is it possible that millenniums have not taught people that which has been ordained by all Commandments? But what do we see? The further we go, the more one has to reiterate the necessity of peace. Then where is evolution when a threatening cannon is already aimed and death-bringing poison is madly sown? People have become so skillful that poison and death already fall from the sky, from the same sky from whence pours prana, the panacea.

What has happened? Under the ground there are explosive mines and tunnels! From the blue sky comes poison and death! The barrels of gigantic guns are raised high. Probably there will soon be a "festival of projectiles" when they accomplish a flight around the world, when they shall reach everything that can be destroyed.

"Nations do not perceive what terrible danger humanity faces in case of a new war," writes Prof. André Meier in his report to the League of Nations. "The poison gases of the last war are child's play in comparison with what we shall see if a new war breaks out" adds another expert, Prof. V. Cannon of Columbia University. According to Dr. Hilton Jones of New York, a newly invented gas can destroy a whole army as easily as "blowing out a candle."

Truth! The inventor of poison believes that he creates truth. The caster of a cannon is proud that his implement will annihilate a man even beyond the horizon. The forger of the sword anticipates that steel will pierce all shields. Such are the thoughts of man!

Alas, such truth is not needed. "Mankind needs another truth," says Gorki, a truth which would heighten creative energy. A truth is needed which would stimulate man's trust in his will, striving toward wisdom, and creativity for good.

Others make impenetrable armor and shields. Perhaps

they hope to create a defense against all evil intrusions? Let it be so.

The defense of culture, the defense of the Motherland, the defense of human dignity does not think of violent invasion. The armor of defense is not the poison of destruction. *Defense is justified and assault is condemned.*

It has some special meaning that in Russian the word mir is synonymous with peace and the Universe. These synonyms are not due to the poverty of the language—indeed the language is rich. They are mutually significant. They are synonymous in their essence. The Universe and peaceful creativeness are indivisible. The ancient ones wanted to make this salutary healing unanimity understandable through all kinds of hieroglyphics.

Mir, the Universe, and *mir,* peaceful universal labor; the creative sowing, and the beauty of the world—the conqueress.

Urusvati, Himalayas, July 24, 1936

SIGNS OF THE ERA

"We love that life which is manifested on Earth,
for we know nothing about any other."

EURIPIDES

THE Institute of Psychosynthesis in Rome under the directorship of Dr. Roberto Assagioli; several institutes of parapsychology in Germany; metapsychical institutes in France; courses in psychology at Duke University in North Carolina conducted by Prof. Rhine; the Neurologial Institute in Russia, and the Physiological Institute in the name of Pavlov; courses in psychology held by Professor Jung in Zurich; The Eranos conferences in Ascona, Switzerland; The Institute for Research in Evolutionary Biology in London; the interesting researches of the Lister Institute in London; the experiments of the Icelandic Professor Kohlman in thought-photography; a special chair of Psychical Research at the University in Stockholm, and the innumerable societies for psychical research spread throughout the world. One can enumerate endlessly such hearths of living thought, which strive toward expansion of new limits in science. Even if these wonderful achievements are as yet not united and are often under the pressure of all kinds of conventional limitations, still every unprejudiced observer can prove to himself that lately the paths of liberated science, as true signs of our epoch, are widened.

In the ocean of printed matter it is difficult to summarize qualitatively and quantitatively the entire scope of what takes place. Besides, not all ways of communication are accessible to the self-sacrificing workers who, in most cases, do not possess means. For usually the means are subsidized only in case of obviously utilitarian experiments. Similarly, in the Middle Ages it was easier to find the means for experiments in transmutation of baser metals into gold; and now also, the great guiding power of thought is hardly ever appreciated by the narrow utilitarian and mechanical consciousness.

Of course, all sorts of congresses, intercourse, and correspondence serve the purpose, but in all these much remains unsaid and misunderstood, and thus the contemplated results are again delayed. Yet one thing is clear—the so-called spiritualization of science is gradually reinforced everywhere. The hysterical outcries of ignorant critics and all those who harbor evil intentions against knowledge remain isolated in their malicious destructiveness. It is true, these thundering attacks of ignorance are still deafening, however there is awakening in public opinion a persistent desire to combat ignorance. In encyclopaedias one can find instructive examples of how recent stern condemnations of the labors of daring pioneers are already replaced by more cautious judgments. Thus, all defenders of knowledge, being ready to battle with ignorance in all its manifestations, can compile instructive and encouraging records of what is being attained at present.

Yet to fight ignorance is imperative and indeferrable. No one should lull himself in the thought that there is already sufficient knowledge. In infinity there is never sufficient knowledge. The more efforts that are used toward realization of knowledge, the stronger and uglier will be the convulsions of ignorance. Was not Paracelsus, so highly venerated today, killed by enviers who could not tolerate his attainments? Even in our times we witnessed how the great Mendeleyev was not elected to the Academy of Science. There are further numerous examples proving that true achievements are appreciated far away from their birthplace. I recall the significant words of Rabindranath Tagore after he received the Nobel Prize. The great poet and thinker said to a delegation which had come to congratulate him, "Why do you congratulate me now and not before?"

In the savings bank of life can be found a number of examples which in the field of culture are quite unfitting and should not be repeated in the forthcoming evolution. The organized battle with ignorance, the self-sacrificing crusades for culture, the defense of knowledge against all destructive attempts should become the significant emblem of our age. The might of thought! The realization of psychic energy!

"Let us meet each movement toward perception amicably. Let us find the strength to renounce personal habits and superstitions. Let us not think that it is easy to overcome atavism; for physical stratifications bear within themselves the prejudices of many ages. But if we firmly realize the weight of such precipitations, then one of the most difficult locks will be opened. The next one also is unlocked when we apprehend why we must apply every action in earthly life. Only by such a path do we approach the third entrance, where we apprehend the treasure of the basic energy entrusted to mankind. Whoever shall teach the recognition of it will be a true teacher.

"Man does not arrive at an understanding of his power without a Guide. Many different traps are hidden on man's path. Each sheltered manifested viper hopes to conceal from man that which is most precious. Like a traveler who has lost his way, he does not know in what element to seek success ; yet the treasure is within himself.

"The wisdom of all the ages enjoins—'Know thyself!' In this counsel attention is turned to the most secret, which has been ordained to become revealed. The fiery might, called for the time being psychic energy, will give to man the path to future happiness. But let us not hope that people will easily recognize their heritage. They will invent all kinds of arguments in order to bring disrepute upon each discovery of the energy. They will pass over in silence the decreed quality of their advance, but, nonetheless, the path is one!"

We shall never deny that we watch with the greatest enthusiasm the attainments of science. Be this in the Society for Psychical Research, or in the case of thought transmission at Duke University, or in the case of a remarkable little girl in Delhi, or in the matter of photographing the invisible world—absolutely in all enlightened experiments every cultured person should have an open, benevolent mind. In *Diary Leaves*, in "Combating Ignorance" is given, as it were, a reply to uncultured, evil machinations. The aims of the Society for Psychical Research, spiritualism in its high manifestations, and also all experiments concerning psychic energy should be met with magnanimity and should call forth thorough scientific research.

Only ignoramuses are not aware of the many most useful institutions and university courses for the investigation of psychic phenomena which have been started in many countries lately. Only ignoramuses do not want to know how many scientific books have been published by such eminent scientists, as, for example, Dr. Alexis Carrel who worked with Lindbergh during recent years. Thus let every uncultured attack on knowledge meet a clear, well-founded resistance, so that the mad, militant ignoramuses may remain in their own puddle as they deserve. Ignoramuses must be revealed by the strongest means.

We shall aways remain well-wishers toward all sincere seekers of knowledge. The Theosophists, psychic researchers, spiritualists, and physiologists, to whatever camp they may belong, are pioneers of the science of the future. Subtle manifestations and the power of thought, as the basis of human creativeness and progress, will find their merited place among the achievements of evolution. "Study all surroundings." "Learn untiringly." "The Heart is infinite." "Winged is thought."

From the depths of the ages are borne many encouraging calls. The human co-operative receives support from all the strongholds of ancient and new knowledge.

"Study of the progression of collective energy can demonstrate that unity is not only a moral concept but also a powerful psychic motive force. When We reiterate about unity, We wish to inculcate consciousness of the great force which is found at the disposal of each man. It is impossible to demonstrate to an inexperienced investigator the extent to which collective energy multiplies. For such a manifestation it is necessary to prepare the consciousness. The success of an experiment depends upon the striving of all participants; if even one does not desire to participate whole-heartedly it will be best not to begin the experiment. "In antiquity people already knew about the power of united force. Sometimes single observations were united in general investigations; and thus an entire chain was formed, and each observer placed his hand on the shoulder of the one in front of him. It was possible to see unusual oscillations of energy; intensified force resulted from the concordant striving. Thus, when I speak about unity, I have in mind a real force.

"Let all remember who need to remember. "In antiquity psychic energy was sometimes called the heart's air. By this, people wished to say that the heart lives by psychic energy. Actually, as man cannot continue to live long without air, so does the heart deprived of psychic energy cease to live.

"Many ancient definitions should be re-examined with good will. Long ago people observed the above manifestation which nowadays remains in neglect.

"The magnetization of water placed near a sleeping man will indicate the secretion of his radiations, and will demonstrate the precipitation of his force upon objects. Such precipitations should be observed most attentively; they can remind about the obligation of man to fill his surroundings with beautiful deposits. Each sleep is not only a lesson for the subtle body but is also a nursery of psychic precipitations.

"Also indicative are experiments upon diffusion of the force of precipitations. It can be observed that energy evaporates in varying degrees. Certain strong radiations can act incomparably longer, but they will have been sent by pure thinking. Thus, pure thinking is not only a moral concept but also a real multiplication of force. Ability to perceive the significance of moral concepts pertains to the domain of science.

"It is inadmissible to light-mindedly divide science into the material and the spiritual, the boundary line is non-existent.

"Observations should be carried out not only on concordant factors but also upon disjunctive manifestations. Many-sided experimentation is valuable. It is impossible to predetermine at the beginning of an investigation precisely what ingredients will be required for augmenting the effect.

"It is possible to invoke the cooperation of the most unexpected objects, for the properties of the subtlest energies cannot be limited. Such an infinitude of possibilities does not at all lessen the scientific value of the experiment. One may apply individual methods and accept such new manifestations courageously.

"No one can indicate where the power of man terminates. Besides, not a superman but just a most healthy man can be winged with successful attainment. In each everyday life psychic energy can be studied. No especially costly laboratories are needed in order to cultivate the consciousness.

"Each age bears its own tidings to humanity. Psychic energy has a destiny to help mankind amidst problems which it finds otherwise insoluble.

"Learn to observe patiently what conditions are most favorable for experimentation. There may be cosmic conditions which will favor experiments either with color radiations, or with minerals, or animals. ... It can be observed how the presence of a person in the next room can react upon the current of energy. . . . But people do not pay attention to their mood at a given time.

"It can be observed that a man may affirm his mood to be the very best, when an apparatus will show irritation or other bad feelings. Not from falsehood will the man be concealing his inner feelings, but usually from failure to know how to distinguish his sensations.

"Besides investigating psychic energy by the use of color, make tests of it with sound and aroma. It is possible to obtain indicative reactions to music; furthermore, observe both the effect of distance and of the most consonant harmonies. Much is said about the influence of music upon people, but almost no illustrative experiments are carried out. One may observe the influence of music upon people's moods, but that will be commonplace. Indeed, it is assumed that gay music communicates joy, and sorrowful—sadness, but such deductions are insufficient. It may be ascertained what harmony most closely adjoins the psychic energy of man, what symphony can have the strongest quieting or inspiring influence upon people. Different musical compositions need to be used in tests. The very quality of harmonization will give the best indications about the paths of sound and the life of man.

"Likewise, it is indispensable to investigate the influence of aromas. It is necessary to approach both fragrant flowers and different compounds, which must stimulate or diminish psychic energy.

"Finally, one can combine color, sound, and aroma, and observe the cooperation of all three motive forces.

"People will finally apprehend what powerful influences surround them. They will realize that all their routine of life manifests a great reaction upon their destiny; they will learn to consider attentively each object; they will surround themselves with true friends, and guard themselves against destructive influences.

"Thus the salutary energy helps in the reconstruction of life.

"Usually the most important matter is allotted the least attention. But We shall not weary of repeating that which is urgently needed by humanity. Among these apparent repetitions, We affirm the desire for knowledge. People have become too accustomed to the idea that someone will do their thinking for them and that the world is obligated to take care of them. But each one must bring in his own cooperation. Learning how to apply one's own psychic energy means the gradual cultivation of the consciousness."

In the family, in schools, in public life there will be affirmed the cognizance of subtle energies. The art of thinking, in all its beauty, will again became the beloved sport—the true wings of humanity.

Urusvati, June 14, 1936.